KARL MARX

TEXTS ON METHOD

KARL MARX
TEXTS ON METHOD

Translated and edited by

TERRELL CARVER

OXFORD
BASIL BLACKWELL
1975

ISBN 0 631 15730 1

Printed in Great Britain by
Western Printing Services Ltd, Bristol
and bound at the Kemp Hall Bindery

For my
Mother and Father

Foreword

The two texts presented here in new English translations provide important material for resolving a persistent difficulty about Marx's 'scientific' work and his 'scientific' method: how did he reconcile his debt to Hegel, as declared in the *Afterword* to the second German edition of *Capital*, i, with his assiduous 'scientific' research into political economy and the facts of capitalist economic life?

Both the *Introduction* (1857) to the *Grundrisse* and the *Notes* (1879–80) *on Adolph Wagner* demonstrate that Marx brought his studies in philosophy, logic, and history to bear on political economy, and that, rightly or wrongly, his own scientific work was based on (among other things) a considerable amount of hard philosophical thought about human social life, about concepts and categories in general, and about the particular concepts and categories used by political economists. In the prefatory and interpretive material below I discuss the place of each text in the development of his critical work on political economy, and of his methods of dealing with the subject.

I am grateful for the assistance of Bernard Dod, and I should like to thank Leszek Kolakowski, David McLellan, and John Torrance for their criticisms, advice, and encouragement. Errors and deficiencies remain my own responsibility.

Oxford   TERRELL CARVER

Contents

List of Works Cited in
Abbreviated Form

Bastiat (1851)   Bastiat, Frédéric. *Harmonies of Political Economy*. Trans. from 3rd edn. P. J. Stirling. 2nd edn. Edinburgh, n.d. [1881?].

BZLM   Lassalle, Ferdinand. *Nachgelassene Briefe und Schriften*. Ed. Gustav Mayer. iii. *Der Briefwechsel zwischen Lassalle und Marx*. Berlin, 1922.

CAP i   Marx, Karl. *Capital*. i. Trans. S. Moore and E. Aveling. Ed. D. Torr. London, 1946, repr. 1957.

CAP ii   —. ii. Ed. F. Engels. Moscow, 1957.

CAP iii   —. iii. Ed. F. Engels. Moscow, 1959.

Carey (1837)   Carey, H. C. *Principles of Political Economy*. 3 vols. Philadelphia, 1837–1840.

CCPE   Marx, Karl. *A Contribution to the Critique of Political Economy*. Trans. S. W. Ryazanskaya. Ed. M. Dobb. London, 1971.

CHR   *Karl Marx. Chronik seines Lebens in Einzeldaten*. Moscow, 1934.

CHRR   —. Repr. Frankfurt, 1971.

ET   Marx, Karl. *Early Texts*. Trans. and ed. David McLellan. Oxford, 1971.

FBME   *Freiligraths Briefwechsel mit Marx und Engels*. Ed. Manfred Häckel. 2 vols. [East] Berlin, 1968.

GDW   *Deutsches Wörterbuch*. Edd. J. and W. Grimm, *et al*. Leipzig, 1854 etc.

GEL   *Greek-English Lexicon*. Edd. H. G. Liddell

and R. Scott, *et al.* Oxford, 1883, repr. 1968.

GI   Marx, Karl, and Engels, Frederick. *German Ideology.* Ed. S. Ryazanskaya. London, 1965.

GR   Marx, Karl. *Grundrisse der Kritik der politischen Ökonomie.* [East] Berlin, 1953.

Hegel (1807)   Hegel, G. W. F. *Sämtliche Werke.* Ed. H. Glockner. ii. *Phänomenologie des Geistes.* Stuttgart-Bad Canstatt, 1964.

Hegel (1812)   —. *Science of Logic.* Trans. A. V. Miller. London, 1969.

Hegel (1821)   —. *Sämtliche Werke.* Ed. H. Glockner. vii. *Grundlinien der Philosophie des Rechts.* Stuttgart-Bad Canstatt, 1964.

Hegel (1837)   —. xi. *Vorlesungen über die Philosophie der Geschichte.* Stuttgart, 1961.

HF   Marx, Karl, and Engels, Frederick. *Holy Family.* Trans. R. Dixon. Moscow, 1956.

James Mill (1826)   Mill, James. *Elements of Political Economy.* 3rd edn. London, 1826.

Jevons (1888)   Jevons, W. Stanley. *Theory of Political Economy.* 3rd edn. London, 1888.

J. S. Mill (1848)   Mill, John Stuart. *Principles of Political Economy.* 2 vols. London, 1848.

KAP i   Marx, Karl. *Das Kapital.* i. 3rd edn. Hamburg, 1883.

KAP ii   —. ii. Ed. F. Engels. Hamburg, 1885.

KAP iii   —. iii. Ed. F. Engels. 2 parts. Hamburg, 1894.

Kautsky (1903)   Marx, Karl. *Einleitung.* Ed. Karl Kautsky. In *Die Neue Zeit.* 21 Jahrgang, 1 Band. (Stuttgart, 1903). Nr. 23, pp. 710–18; nr. 24, pp. 741–5; nr. 25, pp. 772–81.

McLellan (1971a)	Marx, Karl. *Marx's Grundrisse*. Ed. David McLellan. London, 1971.
McLellan (1971b)	McLellan, David. *Thought of Karl Marx*. London, 1971.
MEA I. v.	*Arkhiv Marksa i Engel'sa*. Ed. D. Ryazanov. Ser. I, vol. v. Moscow/Leningrad, 1930, repr. Nendeln/Liechtenstein, 1969.
MEGA	Marx, Karl, and Engels, Friedrich. *Historisch-kritische Gesamtausgabe*. Edd. D. Ryazanov, *et al*. Frankfurt and Berlin, 1927 etc.
Mészáros (1970)	Mészáros, István. *Marx's Theory of Alienation*. London, 1970.
MEW	Marx, Karl, and Engels, Friedrich. *Werke*. [East] Berlin, 1956 etc.
MO	Marx, Karl. *Oeuvres: Économie*. Ed. M. Rubel. Paris, 1965 etc.
NYT	New-York *Tribune*. (Also known as New-York *Daily Tribune* from 22 April 1842 to 9 April 1866.)
OED	*New English Dictionary*. Edd. J. A. H. Murray, *et al*. Oxford, 1884 etc.
OLD	*Latin Dictionary*. Edd. C. T. Lewis and C. Short, *et al*. Oxford, 1880.
Ollman (1971)	Ollman, Bertell. *Alienation*. Cambridge, 1971.
PCEF	Marx, Karl. *Pre-capitalist Economic Formations*. Trans. J. Cohen. Ed. E. J. Hobsbawm. London, 1964, repr. 1969.
PH	Hegel, G. W. F. *Philosophy of History*. Trans. J. Sibree. New York, 1956.
PM	—. *Phenomenology of Mind*. Trans. J. B. Baillie, 2nd edn. London, 1949, repr. 1966.

PP
Marx, Karl. *Poverty of Philosophy*. Moscow/London, n.d. [1955?].

PR
Hegel, G. W. F. *Philosophy of Right*. Trans. T. M. Knox. Oxford, 1952, repr. 1965.

Proudhon (1846)
Proudhon, P.-J. *Système des contradictions économiques, ou philosophie de la misère*. 2 vols. Paris, 1846.

Ricardo (1821)
Ricardo, David. *On the Principles of Political Economy and Taxation*. 3rd edn. London, 1821.

Rosdolsky (1968)
Rosdolsky, Roman. *Zur Entstehungsgeschichte des Marxschen 'Kapital'*. 2 vols. Frankfurt, 1968.

Rubel (1956)
Rubel, Maximilien. *Bibliographie des oeuvres de Karl Marx*. Paris, 1956. *Supplément*. Paris, 1960.

Rubel (1957)
—. 'Les cahiers de lecture de Karl Marx', *International Review of Social History*, ii (Amsterdam, 1957), 392–420.

Rubel (1968)
—. Intro. Marx, Karl. *Oeuvres: Économie*. Paris, 1968.

Ryazanov (1930)
Ryazanov, David. 'Siebzig Jahre "Zur Kritik der politischen Ökonomie" ', *Archiv für die Geschichte des Sozialismus und der Arbeiterbewegung*, xv (Leipzig, 1930), 1–32.

Say (1821)
Say, J.-B. *Treatise on Political Economy*. Trans. from 4th edn. C. R. Prinsep. 2 vols. London, 1821.

Smith (1776)
Smith, Adam. *Inquiry into the Nature and Causes of the Wealth of Nations*. 2 vols. London, 1776.

Steuart (1767)
Steuart, Sir James. *Inquiry into the*

	Principles of Political Oeconomy. 2 vols. London, 1767.
Storch (1823)	Storch, H. *Cours d'économie politique . . . avec des notes par* J.-B. Say. 4 vols. Paris, 1823.
Storch (1824)	—. *Considérations sur la nature du revenu national*. Paris, 1824.
SW	Marx, Karl, and Engels, Frederick. *Selected Works*. 3 vols. Moscow, 1969–1970.
TP no. 5	*Theoretical Practice*. No. 5 (London, 1972).
TSV	Marx, Karl. *Theories of Surplus Value*. Edd. S. Ryazanskaya, *et al.* 3 vols. Moscow, 1963–72.
Wagner (1879)	Wagner, Adolph. *Allgemeine oder theoretische Volkswirthschaftslehre*. Erster Theil. *Grundlegung*. 2nd edn. Leipzig and Heidelberg, 1879. Issued as vol. i of Rau, Karl Heinrich. *Lehrbuch der politischen Ökonomie*. New edn. Edd. Adolph Wagner and Erwin Nasse.
Walton (1972)	Walton, Paul, and Gamble, Andrew. *From Alienation to Surplus Value*. London, 1972.

Note to the Reader

All translations are my own, unless another acknowledgement is given.

In translating Marx's manuscripts I have tried to keep as close to the original as possible, while still providing the reader with an intelligible and helpful English text. Neither of the manuscripts presented here was revised by Marx for the press; nonetheless, my intention has been to reproduce rather than rewrite these works, even though the author's language is sometimes strange or unidiomatic, e.g. *Konkretum* ('concretum'), *ist nicht erfindbar* ('cannot be made out').

I have tried to assist the reader by inserting editorial elucidation and notes; moreover in the case of the *Introduction* (1857) to the *Grundrisse*, my detailed Commentary follows the text, since Marx's draft is extraordinarily rich in ideas, and the arguments are lengthy and complex. I treat the less elaborate comments of Marx's *Notes* (1879–80) *on Adolph Wagner* in an Editor's Preface, and I insert, in the translation, cross-references to the first volume of Marx's *Capital*.

Marx's use of terms and phrases from Hegel's works and the Hegelian philosophical tradition can never be reproduced in modern idiomatic English, since there are no precisely corresponding terms or phrases; such equivalents as exist are not familiar usage at present. I have found the Oxford dictionary helpful in selecting and defining English equivalents for terms and phrases current in nineteenth-century German philosophy and logic (such as determination, universal, moment, mediate, immediately, ideal), and I thought it only just to acknowledge this assistance, and similar help from other works of reference.

Both of the texts presented here are technical works of investigation or comment, rather than polished examples of the author's prose. Marx does not, in these works, employ a large vocabulary, so I have tried to preserve such distinctions as he might have intended when he chose one term rather than another, and stuck to it, e.g. *herrschend* ('dominating'), *übergreifend* ('transcending'), *Gliederung* ('arangement'), *Bau* ('structure'). There seems to be little variation of terms for purely stylistic reasons, and I think Marx's writing more precise than some critics and commentators have suggested.

Dates in parentheses after the titles of books are the dates of first publication, unless otherwise noted.

My own insertions are enclosed in square brackets. I have made certain simple insertions (e.g. the verb 'to be', repetition of subjects or verbs within a sentence) without note. Similarly, I have incorporated minor emendations by the editors of GR and MEW xix into my translations without comment, e.g. for W[agner] I read Wagner.

I have followed the italicization of the original texts, except as follows:

> Book-titles and words in neither English nor German, which appeared in the original texts in roman type, have been italicized to conform with the usual treatment in English of titles and foreign words, e.g. for

'dignitas, wertvolle Beschaffenheit'. (*Ziemann*, 'Mittelh[och]d[eutsches] Wörterbuch'.)

> I read

'*dignitas*, valuable quality'. (*Ziemann, Middle High German Dictionary.*)

> Inversely, words in neither English nor German, which were italicized in the original texts for emphasis, appear in my translation as foreign words in roman type for emphasis, e.g. for '*aestimatio*' I read 'aestimatio', and for 'ein *wahres jus gentium*' I read 'a *true international law* [jus gentium]'.

PART I

Marx's *Introduction* (1857) to the *Grundrisse*

Editor's Preface

Voyons les choses d'un peu plus près

Marx (1847)

Marx's *Introduction* (1857) to the *Grundrisse der Kritik der politischen Ökonomie*

The first work presented here in translation is the unfinished *Introduction* (*Einleitung*) to a critique of political economy by Karl Marx. The manuscript, written while he lived in London, was first published in a version edited by Karl Kautsky in *Die Neue Zeit* (Stuttgart) for 1903. A more accurate text appeared in the collection of manuscripts published as Karl Marx, *Grundrisse der Kritik der politischen Ökonomie* (Moscow, 1939–41; reprinted East Berlin, 1953). The present translation was taken from the reprinted text.[1]

According to the editors of the *Grundrisse*, the *Introduction* was begun on 23 August 1857 and laid aside about the middle of September. Marx's correspondence with Engels seems to have stopped between 27 August and 14 September 1857; on the 15th Marx commented, 'much work'. (MEW xxix. 168–9, 174–5.)

The 1857 text is manifestly unfinished, since numerous points are made only in an abbreviated, even fragmentary way, and the work itself tails off to a series of notes and reminders in the final section. Marx's manuscript seems to be the draft of a work intended for publication, since he gave it the title *Introduction*, but a revised introduction along similar lines never materialized. A great deal of his work in this text consists in an effort to

---

[1] For further information on the manuscript, the published text, and other translations into English, see pp. 220–1 below.

3

investigate a number of fundamental questions—particularly
questions about the logical relations that obtain among the
concepts and 'categories'[2] of political economy—by putting his
thoughts down on paper. In the *Introduction* (1857) he came
eventually to views and conclusions which were presupposed
and used in various later works, even though the arguments
were not always explicitly repeated.

Hence this text is unique with respect to the type of material
it provides for the study of Marx's methods, and his views on
what they should be. In his manuscript he recorded certain
methodological innovations[3] which immediately preceded the
writing (during late 1857 and 1858) of the bulk of the *Grundrisse*,
the vast rough draft towards the *magnum opus* that was to have
included his critique of political economy, of which *Capital* was
only the beginning. The innovations of August/September
1857 help us to explain why his work took such a sudden leap
forward.

The *Introduction* (1857) is one of the most deeply investigative
of Marx's writings. In it he broke off from his criticisms of
specific political economists, and of political economy in
general, to work out the logic of the subject for himself. Those
sections, and others which are less abstract, provide examples
of various aspects of his 'mode of investigation' (*Forschungsweise*).
'Investigation', as he noted in an *Afterword* (dated 1873) to
Capital, i, 'has to appropriate the material in detail, analyse its
different forms of development, and trace their inner link'.
Other passages in the text, which are also couched in the

---

[2] Marx sometimes uses 'category' (*Kategorie*) to cover both the sense of
'concept' as the idea of a thing in general and the sense of the more
specific term 'category' as a class or division formed for a particular
discussion or inquiry.

[3] See pp. 27–8 below. I take an 'innovation' to be the alteration of
given material by the introduction of new forms or elements. (Cf. OED
s.v. Innovation 1.) An innovation, in my view, does not necessarily
entail a rejection of previous views or practices. In this work I use the
term to refer to methods not previously employed on a large scale and
to summary statements not explicitly recorded in earlier writings.

language of philosophy and logic, bear directly on his 'mode of presentation' (*Darstellungsweise*), in which 'the life of the material' was to be 'mirrored in ideas'. (KAP i. pp. xviii–xix; cf. CAP i. pp. xxix–xxx.)[4]

Because of its investigative and innovatory content, the *Introduction* (1857) represents an important link in the development of Marx's thought from the early to the late writings. It contains proof that part of the preliminary investigations for *Capital* (which was subtitled 'Critique of Political Economy') consisted in a critical analysis of the concepts of political economy and the procedures of various political economists, using ideas, distinctions, and methods derived from his earlier writings and from his studies in philosophy and logic. The results were presupposed (and reproduced in part) in his later works, especially *Capital*, both in the views expressed there and in the structure of his presentation. The 1857 text reveals that Marx did not merely dabble in philosophy, but undertook philosophical investigations that were complex, and fundamental to his critical study of political economy.

The remainder of my Editor's Preface provides the interpretive and factual background for a commentary on the text. I consider first the nineteenth-century science[5] of political economy, and Marx's studies and plans for a critical work on the subject, in order to establish the precise position of the *Introduction* (1857) in the development of his critique; then I discuss my own conclusions about the 1857 text and what it contributes towards a reappraisal of his later writings.

[4] *Spiegelt . . . ideell wieder* ('mirrored in ideas') is translated in CAP as 'ideally reflected as in a mirror'—a reading which tends, incorrectly, to link Marx with a simple, reflectionist epistemology.

[5] The English political economists referred to their subject as a science and their work as scientific, since they sought to deal with observed facts. Marx used the terms *Wissenschaft* (which applies to many more disciplines than the modern English 'science') and *wissenschaftlich* (which may mean abstract, factual, logical, rigorous etc.). (GDW *s.v.* Wissenschaft *passim*.) I discuss Marx's conception of science on pp. 40–1 below.

In the Commentary, which follows an annotated translation of the text, my aim will be to explicate Marx's criticisms, investigations, and conclusions, in order to present the different ways in which he utilized (in the later works) views developed in the earlier writings, and the various ideas and methods (used by other writers) which struck him as relevant to his own researches, or even useful for the substance or organization of his critical study.

Nineteenth-century political economy (*Nationalökonomie* or *politische Ökonomie* in German) was the 'science of the production, distribution, and consumption of wealth'.[6] It was different from much of modern economics, whether neo-classical, Keynesian, or post-Keynesian, since it posed different questions, developed different sorts of answers, and had a somewhat different methodological bias. The political economists attempted to give an account of production, distribution, consumption, and exchange, and their mutual interrelations. They also tried to explain how a commodity acquires its 'value in exchange' (i.e. the worth of one commodity in terms of another or in monetary terms), and how that value was determined and regulated. In his pioneering work, published in 1776, Adam Smith set the terms for a lengthy debate on 'exchangeable value':

What are the rules which men naturally observe in exchanging them [goods] either for money or for one another, I shall now proceed to examine. These rules determine what may be called the relative or exchangeable value of goods. . . . In order to investigate the principles which regulate the exchangeable value of commodities, I shall endeavour to shew,

[6] *Encyclopaedia Britannica*, xix (Edinburgh, 1885), 346–7. The definition is taken from the work of Jean-Baptiste Say, the French political economist of the early nineteenth century. For a discussion which distinguishes between political economy and various sorts of modern economics (though it does not cover Marxist economics or 'revisionist' economics influenced by Marx and Marxist writing), see R. D. Collison Black, intro. W. Stanley Jevons, *Theory of Political Economy* (Harmondsworth, 1970), 7–11.

First, what is the real measure of this exchangeable value; or, wherein consists the real price of all commodities.

Secondly, what are the different parts of which this real price is composed or made up.

And, lastly, what are the different circumstances which some-times raise some or all of these different parts of price above, and sometimes sink them below their natural or ordinary rate; or, what are the causes which sometimes hinder the market price, that is, the actual price, of commodities, from coinciding exactly with what may be called their natural price. (Smith (1776), i. 33–4.)

Much of the effort of the political economists went into what appears today to be a very general inquiry, with statements and defences of their views on definitional questions, and some of the moral and political issues entailed. But with the rise of the neo-classical economists of the late nineteenth and early twen-tieth centuries, many of the problems which had previously seemed important (such as the theory of value) were pushed aside or redefined in favour of new problems and a more immediately mathematical approach.

For convenience, the dividing line between political economy and neo-classical economics may be drawn in England at W. S. Jevons's *Theory of Political Economy*, first published in 1871, since his work presaged neo-classical economics in certain ways that Marx's did not. Jevons wrote that 'Economics, if it is to be a science at all, must be a mathematical science'. (Jevons (1888), 3.) Not surprisingly, he reformulated the problems charac-teristically set by political economists to suit his own conception of the new science of economics. The problems would now, according to Jevons, be 'purely mathematical in character', even though this might pose difficulties at first:

Many will object, no doubt, that the notions which we treat in this science are incapable of any measurement. . . . It might thus seem as if a mathematical theory of Economics would be necessarily deprived for ever of numerical data.

I answer, in the first place, that nothing is less warranted in science than an uninquiring and unhoping spirit. . . . If we trace the history of other sciences, we gather no lessons of discouragement. (Jevons (1888), 7–8.)

Since the 1870s, most economists have, like Jevons, rejected many of the questions which the political economists had tried to answer; most modern economists would dismiss a theory of value (i.e. a theory of natural or real prices) as a metaphysical adventure. For example, this problem, as put by Ricardo, would probably be regarded today as confused and senseless:

Two commodities vary in relative value, and we wish to know in which the variation has really taken place. (Ricardo (1821), 9.)

And his theory of natural prices would be dismissed as unnecessary and unwarranted:

In speaking then of the exchangeable value of commodities, or the power of purchasing possessed by any one commodity, I mean always that power which it would possess, if not disturbed by any temporary or accidental cause, and which is its natural price. (Ricardo (1821), 85.)

Hence the problems and concepts presented in modern textbooks are not in many cases the concepts of political economy, or political economy as re-presented in a critical way by Marx. It does not follow, however, that Marx's work has been completely superseded, or that neo-classical economics and later schools were an unqualified improvement on political economy. But his work does make better sense if we see it as a critical study of political economy (*not* economics) from his own point of view. From that point of view, much of Jevons's work, and most of modern economics, would not seem an advance over political economy at all—rather the opposite.

Marx does not seem to have set out to write a work *of* political economy; his method in the first instance was not, so far as we can tell, one of observation, data gathering, and then the writing of an explanatory and predictive system. Rather he aimed to study social production (since he assigned to the 'mode of production' a determining role in social development) by looking critically at the contemporary *science* of social production, because it provided, in easily accessible form, much material of social and technical significance. This, I think, is the force of his remark that by 1843–4 he had decided to seek *in* political economy the anatomy of bourgeois society, and later, in the commodity, its *microscopic* anatomy. (MEW xiii. 8; cf. SW i. 503. KAP i. p. vi; cf. CAP i. p. xvi.)

Marx was too well educated in philosophy to have imagined that he could just observe the world, gather 'facts', and write an explanation, without some work on previously developed concepts and theories. There were two advantages for him in starting his study of capitalist production by investigating, in a critical way, the concepts and theories of political economy: they attempted, with a certain amount of success, to describe and explain economic activity in capitalist society; at the same time, they were *marked*, in his view, as products of that society. In his critique of political economy he aimed to clarify the situation on both counts, by improving the accuracy and scope of economic studies (this cost him a great deal of time and effort) and by unravelling the 'mysteries' contained in economic concepts and categories, mysteries which he explained in *Capital*, i, as manifestations of alienated life in bourgeois society. An important part of his preliminary work on the latter project—the critical investigation of the 'mysterious' categories of political economy—was recorded in the *Introduction* (1857).

Marx's interest in political economy began early in his career and continued up to its very end. Although his projects and preoccupations were numerous, and, after about 1842 or 1843, closely related to his philosophical and political commitments, nonetheless his critical work on political economy occupied a special place in his plans for research and publication. The critique seems to have represented, for Marx, the definitive exposure of various influential political economists, and presumably, commonplace theories and prejudices which drew on their works, or from which they had drawn their ideas; but it was also the medium for the rigorous exposition of his own views and discoveries.

The critique of political economy was intended by Marx to be one of his contributions to the working-class movement, or as he put it, 'a scientific victory for our party'. (Marx to Weydemeyer, 1 February 1859, MEW xxix. 572.) His background and education, and his dedication to criticism (even highly technical criticism) as a *practical* activity, specially suited him to make an intellectual contribution of a very high standard to the proletarian cause, and, in addition, to write polemics and tracts based on his researches; he was also, of course, involved in ventures into organized political activity.

The account given by Marx in 1859 of how he came to be concerned with 'so-called material interests' and with 'economic questions' provides a concise summary of his interests and activities from 1842 to mid-1844—the beginning of his career:

It was in the years 1842–3, as editor of the *Rheinische Zeitung* [a newspaper published in Cologne], that I first got into the embarrassing situation of having to put in a word on so-called material interests. The proceedings of the Rhenish Assembly on the theft of wood and the parcelling out of landed property, the official polemic which Herr von Schaper, then *Oberpräsident* of Rhenish Prussia, opened with the *Rheinische Zeitung* on the conditions of the Moselle peasantry, and finally, the debates on free trade and protection, were the first occasions for my pursuit of economic questions. (MEW xiii. 7–8; cf. SW i. 502.)

Descriptions of Marx's excerpt-notebooks (*Exzerpthefte*) for the years 1840–1, 1842, 1843, and 1844 have been published, and it is easy to trace the drift in the subject-matter of his studies from works of philosophy to aesthetics, religion, politics, and history—and then to political economy. However, it does not follow that his interests in philosophy, politics, history, or even aesthetics were dropped after 1844, or late in life. Indeed the very opposite is true, since at various times he wrote or planned to write articles, reviews, and contributions on those subjects.

Marx's researches will be presented here in some detail, because it is interesting to see exactly what he read; a general sketch of the range of his interests would not be nearly so informative. A number of the writers which appeared in his early studies turn up again in the *Introduction* (1857) and later works, by name or by allusion; indeed, the complex, eclectic character of his methods in criticizing political economy is directly linked with this early reading.

His studies in Berlin during 1840–1 were philosophical: Aristotle, Spinoza, and Leibniz (in Latin editions); Hume's *Treatise of Human Nature* (translated into German); and Karl Rosenkranz's *History of Kantian Philosophy* (in German). (MEGA I, i(2). 107–13.)

The Bonn notebooks for 1842, which dealt with religion and aesthetics, contained excerpts from C. Meiners's *General Critical History of Religions* (in German), Charles de Brosses's *Cult of the Fetish-Gods* (translated into German), C. A. Böttiger's *Mythological Art* (in German), and Johann Grund's *Greek Painting* (in German). The extracts from de Brosses and Böttiger, which dealt with religious fetishism, are of particular interest because of their connection with Marx's later work, especially the chapter on the 'fetishism of commodities' in *Capital*, i.[7] (MEGA I, i(2). 114–18.)

In the Kreuznach notebooks for 1843, which covered political theory and history, Marx took excerpts from C. F. E. Ludwig's *History of the French Revolution* (in German), P. Daru's *History of the Venetian Republic* (in French), Rousseau's *Social*

---

[7] In de Brosses's work (first published in 1760) a fetish was 'an inanimate object worshipped by savages on account of its supposed inherent magical powers'. (OED *s.v.* Fetish 1b.) Marx used the term 'fetishism' with reference to that sense of 'fetish'.

Contract (in French), Montesquieu's *Spirit of the Laws* (in French), John (1st earl) Russell's *History of the English Government and Constitution* (translated into German), Leopold Ranke's *History of the Reformation in Germany* (in German), Thomas Hamilton's *Men and Manners in America* (translated into German), and Machiavelli's *Discourses* (translated into German). (MEGA I, i(2). 118–36.)

Marx's Paris notebooks date from the beginning of 1844, about the same time as he received Engels's *Outlines of a Critique of Political Economy* (*Umrisse zu einer Kritik der National-ökonomie*).[8] These notebooks, which continued to the beginning of 1845, dealt mainly with works on political economy: Bois-guillebert's *Dissertation on the Nature of Wealth* (in French), Eugène Buret's *On the Poverty of the Working Classes in England and France* (in French),[9] Destutt de Tracy's *Elements of Ideology* (in French), Lauderdale's *Inquiry into the Nature and Origin of Public Wealth* (translated into French), J. R. MacCulloch's *Discourse on . . . Political Economy* (translated into French), James Mill's *Elements of Political Economy* (translated into French), Ricardo's *Principles of Political Economy* (translated into French), J.-B. Say's *Treatise on Political Economy* (in French), and Adam Smith's *Wealth of Nations* (translated into French). (MEGA I, iii. 411–583.)

The so-called *Economic and Philosophical Manuscripts* were written in Paris between April and August 1844, and it was probably to that material (and to the Paris excerpt-notebooks) that Engels referred in his letter to Marx of the beginning of October 1844 (the first surviving letter of their long correspon-dence), when he wrote 'Take care that the material which you have collected shall soon be flung out to the world. It is damned high time'. (MEW xxvii. 8.)

Marx's *Preface*, one of the last of the 1844 *Manuscripts* to be

---

[8] For an English translation of Engels's 'sketch' see the Appendix to Karl Marx, *Economic and Philosophic Manuscripts of 1844*, ed. Dirk J. Struik (London, 1970), 197–226.

[9] For a discussion of Buret and Marx, see Rubel (1968), pp. lvii–lviii.

written, contained an account of how he came to write them and a plan for the publication of numerous critical works, the first of which was to be a critical study of political economy and the last, a 'special work', demonstrating the 'connection of the whole' —this was to be his 'final' refutation of Hegelian theories of such a connection.[10] Marx's 'long obsession' with the criticism of political economy seems to have begun with an expansion of his unfinished *Critique* (written in 1843) of Hegel's *Philosophy of Right* (1821). (Rubel (1968), p. xvii.) In Marx's plan of 1844, as outlined below, the critique of political economy was to have been the first of a series of 'self-contained brochures':

I have announced—in the *Deutsch-Französische Jahrbücher* [the sole number of which appeared in February 1844]—the critique of legal and political science [*Rechts- und Staatswissenschaft*] in the form of a critique of Hegel's *Philosophy of Right* [*Rechtsphilosophie*]. Preparations for the press revealed that the mingling of the critique directed only against the work of Hegel and Hegelians [*Spekulation*] with the critique of the different materials themselves was completely unsuitable . . . I will therefore produce in succession the critique of law, morals, politics etc. in diverse, self-contained brochures, and in conclusion I shall attempt in a special work to render the connection of the whole, the relation of the individual parts, by way of the final critique of the Hegelian [*spekulativen*] treatment of that material. For this reason in the present work [on political economy] the connection of political economy with the state,[11] law, morals, bourgeois life etc. is touched on only so far as political economy itself touches *ex professo* on those subjects.

I need hardly assure the reader familiar with political economy that my results have been attained through a wholly empirical

---

[10] The 'general result' which Marx summarized in his *Preface* to *A Contribution to the Critique of Political Economy* (1859) represents a 'connection of the whole' which also functioned as a critique of the Hegelian presentation of philosophy, history, law etc. (MEW xiii. 8–9; cf. SW i. 503–4.)

[11] Rubel speculates that the 'major theme' of Marx's proposed work on the state would have been 'bureaucracy'. (Rubel (1968), p. xxv.)

analysis based on the scrupulously critical study of political economy. (MEW Ergänzungsband i. 467; cf. ET 131.)

Engels wrote to Marx on 20 January 1845 exhorting him to get on with his 'book':

Make sure that you get finished with your book on political economy, even if you yourself remain unhappy with much of it; it makes no difference, the climate is ripe, and we must strike while the iron is hot. (MEW xxvii. 16.)

And on 1 February 1845 Marx signed a contract with the publisher Leske, of Darmstadt:

Dr. Marx entrusts to the bookseller and publisher C. W. Leske his work entitled 'Critique of Politics and Political Economy' [*Kritik der Politik und Nationalökonomie*], which will be two volumes in 8° format, each over twenty printer's sheets [*Druckbogen*] in size. (MEW xxvii. 669.)

But the proposed book ran into difficulties with its prospective publisher. In a letter to P. V. Annenkov[12] written on 28 December 1846 Marx commented:

With this letter I would gladly have sent you my book on political economy, but it has not been possible for this work and the critique of German philosophers and socialists [the *German Ideology*, written during 1845–6], of which I told you in Brussels, to be published. (MEW xxvii. 462.)

This letter to Annenkov is well known as the precursor of Marx's attack on P.-J. Proudhon, published in Paris and Brussels as the *Poverty of Philosophy* (*Misère de la philosophie*) in 1847. But because the letter dealt with Proudhon's presentation of the 'economic categories', it was also a precursor of the

[12] P. V. Annenkov (1812–87) was a liberal Russian landowner who met Marx during a tour of Western Europe. (MEW xxvii. 704.)

Introduction (1857); Marx developed his view that economic categories are abstractions which express different aspects of real, but changing social relations:

Thus M. Proudhon, mainly from want of historical knowledge, has not noticed that men, since they develop their productive powers, i.e. since they live, develop determinate relations with one another, and that the sort of relations [they develop] necessarily changes with the transformation and growth of those powers of production. He has not seen that the *economic categories* are only *abstractions* of those real relations, that the economic categories are true only so long as those relations persist. (MEW xxvii. 457.)

Marx's excerpt-notebooks for 1845–6 (Brussels, Manchester, and then Brussels again) represented a continuation of the Paris studies of 1844–5, but at the later date he was able to read and take notes in English, as well as French. These notebooks contained extracts from a great many works on political economy and economic conditions, e.g. J. A. Blanqui's *History of Political Economy* (in French), Thomas Cooper's *Lectures of the Elements of Political Economy* (in English), J. S. Mill's *Essays on some unsettled Questions of Political Economy* (in English), Richard Parkinson's *On the present Conditions of the Labouring Poor in Manchester* (in English), works of Quesnay and Sismondi on political economy (in French), H. Storch's *Political Economy* (in French), and Thomas Tooke's *History of Prices* (in English). (MEGA I, vi. 597–618.) Since 1844 Marx's interests and abilities had broadened to include works on contemporary English political and economic questions, e.g. Chartism, free trade, and the population question; he also undertook a detailed study of the works of Robert Owen.

Although the contract with Leske was cancelled in February 1847, Marx continued his work on political economy, but in direct connection with the German-speaking workers' movement in Brussels. Some of the material which he developed for lectures and classes appeared in April 1849 as *Wage-labour and*

C

Capital (*Lohnarbeit und Kapital*) in the *Neue Rheinische Zeitung—Organ der Demokratie*, edited by Marx (with Engels) and published in Cologne. Some of the rest of Marx's work from this period has survived in manuscript.[13] On 1 August 1849 he wrote to his friend Weydemeyer[14] about having this material published in 'brochures':

Dear Weydemeyer! . . . I would like to know in what way you think it possible to publish brochures?

I would like to begin with the brochure on wages, of which only the beginning was published in the *Neue Rheinische Zeitung*. I would write a short political preface on the present *status quo* [*sic*]. Do you believe that e.g. Leske would agree to it? However, as soon as he received the manuscript, he would have to pay straight away, and to be sure, pay well, since I know that this brochure will be a success and find a mass of ready subscribers. (MEW xxvii. 506.)

The London continuation of the *Neue Rheinische Zeitung*, edited again by Marx (with Engels), appeared during 1850 and carried the words *Politisch-ökonomische Revue*, with the explanation that a review, as opposed to a newspaper, 'permits detailed and scientific inquiry into the *economic* relations which form the basis of the whole political movement'. (MEW vii. 5.)

Marx's researches at the British Museum began in the summer of 1850, and his twenty-four notebooks for the period September 1850 to August 1853 contain more material on specific topics in political economy: commodity, money, capital, wage-

---

[13] For the cancellation of the contract by Leske, see MEW xxvii. 618. *Wage Labour and Capital*, as published in SW i. 150–74, is a translation of the 1891 edition, with 'corrections' by Engels. Marx's own German text is reproduced in MEW vi. 397–423, with Engels's 'corrections' given in footnotes. Marx's manuscript *Wages* (*Arbeitslohn*) appears in MEW vi. 535–56; see also the note in MEW vi. 658.

[14] Joseph Weydemeyer (1818–66) was a German socialist, a member of the League of Communists (which Marx and Engels joined in 1847), and a participant in the revolution of 1848. He emigrated to the USA in 1851. (MEW xxvii. 739.)

labour, landed property, international trade, history of technology and inventions, credit, the population question, economic history, world market, and colonization. Nearly all of those terms appeared again in his later plans for publication, e.g. the plan in the *Introduction* (1857).

His sources for these investigations included *The Economist* for 1843–50 and numerous writers on political economy and economic history, including Ricardo, Adam Smith, Nassau Senior, Hume, Locke, Torrens, Malthus, Owen, Proudhon, Ure, Carey, and others less well known. During this period Marx re-read in English a number of the classics of political economy which he had previously read in French translations; some of his comments on Ricardo for 1850–1 have been published in the Appendix to the *Grundrisse*. He also produced a manuscript entitled the *Money System Perfected* (*Das vollendete Geldsystem*) in 1851, but according to the editors of the *Grundrisse*, only part of the text has survived, and it remains unpublished. (GR 766, 769–839, 986–7; see also Rubel (1957), 405, where the title is given as *Das unvollendete Geldwesen*.)

During 1851 Marx worked very hard on political economy, but the course of his studies was not always smooth. The German socialist Ferdinand Lassalle wrote to him on 12 May with words of praise, but took the opportunity to outline his own views on Ricardo. Marx could hardly have agreed with Lassalle's claim for Ricardo's definition of rent, since he was working on a critique of just that aspect of the Ricardian theory. But Rodbertus's book, to which Lassalle also referred, proved to be important:

I hear that your *Political Economy* will at last see the light of day. Three fat volumes at once! . . . But I wish to see the three-volume wonder of the Ricardo turned socialist, the Hegel turned economist, on my desk—for you will and must unite them both. Don't misunderstand me if I say Ricardo turned socialist. In fact, I take Ricardo for our direct ancestor. I consider his definition of ground rent an important communistic fact . . . Anyway, [political] economy appears to have come into favour with aristocratic

Germans. Rodbertus[15] has written 'socialist [*sic*] letters' in which he, so I hear, will have every interest-bearing power of capital banned etc. Have you read them? (BZLM 28–9.)

Engels, who knew more about Marx's work on Ricardo, had also read the latest *Social Letter* by Rodbertus, and on 19 May he attempted to explode some of Marx's more extravagant hopes:

Dear Marx . . . The latest is that you are completely sunk. You think that you have discovered the correct theory of ground rent. You think that you are the first to overthrow Ricardo's theory. Poor unfortunate that you are. You are surpassed, nullified, struck down, and overwhelmed. The whole basis of your 'monument more lasting than bronze'[16] has collapsed. Listen to this: Rodbertus has just published the third volume of his *Social Letters to v. Kirchmann*— eighteen printer's sheets. This volume contains a 'complete refutation of Ricardo's doctrine of ground rent and the exposition of a new theory of rent'. Leipzig *Illustrated News* of last week. Now there's a treat for you![17] (MEW xxvii. 259.)

The reply (if there was one) did not survive.

Marx worked at the British Museum from May through August 1851, and in his letters for those months he commented on some of his intellectual pursuits and domestic setbacks, and reported some progress in finding a publisher for his *Economy*:

[21 May 1851] Dear Engels! . . . Now I am always at the library from 10 in the morning until 7 in the evening, and am putting off the [Great] Industrial Exhibition until your arrival. (MEW xxvii. 262–4.)

[15] Lassalle refers to Johann Karl Rodbertus (Jagetzow), *Sociale Briefe an von Kirchmann, Dritter Brief* (Berlin, 1851), *passim*. Rodbertus was a landowner who advocated 'state socialism'. (MEW xxvii. 732.)

[16] Horace, *Carmina*, iii. 30.

[17] Engels was mistaken when he wrote in his *Preface* to *Capital*, ii (1885), and in his *Preface* to the first German edition of Marx's *Poverty of Philosophy* (1885), that Marx did not know of Rodbertus's *Third Social Letter* until 1858 or 1859. (KAP ii. pp. ix–x; cf. CAP ii. 7–8. PP 8.)

[27 June 1851] Dear Hans [Weydemeyer]! . . . Generally I am at the British Museum from 9 in the morning until 7 in the evening. The stuff that I am working on has ramified so damned much that even with every effort I shan't succeed in finishing before 6–8 weeks. There are always the everyday interruptions, unavoidable in the poverty in which one vegetates here. In spite of everything, the project is hurrying to its conclusion. One must break off forcibly. (MEW xxvii. 557–9.)

[31 July 1851] Dear Engels!
I have just received your letter which gives very agreeable views on the trade crisis.

I have not written for about fourteen days because I was hounded during the time I did not spend at the library, and so in spite of the best will, could not ever get down to writing . . . As far as the proceedings with Ebner[18] in Frankfurt are going, he writes that Cotta will probably take my *Economy*—a plan of which I sent—and that, if not, he will run down another publisher. I would have finished at the library a long time ago. But the interruptions and disruptions are too great, and at home, where everything is always in a state of siege, and floods of tears the whole night through make me weary and angry, I can naturally not do very much. (MEW xxvii. 291–3.)

[14 August 1851] Dear Engels! . . . As far as the New York *Tribune* is concerned, you must help me now when I have my hands full with the *Economy*. Write a series of articles on Germany, from 1848.[19] (MEW xxvii. 312–14.)

On 13 October Marx reported more negotiations, summarizing the information he had received from Freiligrath,[20] and

---

[18] The editors of MEW identify Hermann Ebner as a 'journalist' and 'secret agent of the Austrian police' during the 1840s and 50s. (MEW xxvii. 714.)

[19] Engels wrote the articles, which were published in the New-York *Tribune* in 1851–2 under Marx's name and later titled *Revolution and Counter-revolution in Germany*. (MEW xxvii. 657.)

[20] Ferdinand Freiligrath (1810–76) worked with Marx on the *Neue Rheinische Zeitung* (Cologne) and was a member of the League of Communists. He emigrated to London in 1851. (MEW xxvii. 716.)

telling Engels more about his work on political economy:

Dear Engels! . . . After my offer for the brochure against Proudhon [a German translation of Marx's *Poverty of Philosophy*] was declined by Campe, [then] Cotta and later Löwenthal (with Ebner handling the negotiations) refused the offer of my *Economy*; finally a prospect for the latter appears to be opened. In a week I will know whether it will be realized. There is a bookseller in Dessau, also arranged through Ebner. This Ebner is a friend of Freiligrath. . . . The last time I was at the library, which I continue to visit, I was grinding away mainly on technology, the history of same, and agronomy, so that at least I can come to some sort of view on that rubbish.
How goes the commercial crisis? (MEW xxvii. 356–9.)

Marx's plan from this period for his *Economy* has not survived, nor has his manuscript (if there was one). (Ryazanov (1930), 4–5, 8–9.) But since Marx and his prospective publishers had quite different views about how the material should be arranged for publication, we have some hints on what he intended:

[24 November 1851] Dear Frederic [Engels]! . . . Ebner has written to me that Löwenthal wants to experiment with one volume, but I never said that I was to begin with the '*History* of Economy.' This would upset my whole plan. Furthermore, Ebner wrote that Löwenthal could only pay 'poorly'. That would be all right, if he published what I want first. But if he forces me to destroy my whole plan, then he must pay me as much as if I wrote directly on his commission. However, for the present I shall mention it to Ebner. He has informed me that he will not conclude anything without my approval. What do you think? (MEW xxvii. 370.)

Engels's reply gives further information on Marx's plans, and an insight into the nature of their collaboration. Marx had apparently expected to give a critical account of socialist theory, as well as the 'history of economy', but the critique of political economy seems to have been the most crucial part of the project. Engels, as usual, urged Marx to work with immediate political and commercial considerations in mind:

[27 November 1851] Dear Marx . . . I believe, as far as beginning with the history of economy . . . that if Löwenthal really intends to do this, Ebner can at best make difficulties for him, [e.g.] it would not do to upset your whole plan, you have already begun to work out the critique etc. However, should it not work out, Löwenthal must engage himself for two volumes and you would also require this space, partly to anticipate the critique, partly to make the history profitable to some extent for you, with the honorarium calculated in any case on the London cost price. Then the socialists would come as volume 3 and as volume 4 the critique—what is left of it—and the famous 'positive', what you 'really' want. In that form the thing has its difficulties, but it has the advantage that the long-awaited secret is expressed in full only at the end, and only after the curious bourgeois has held his breath through three volumes is it revealed to him that we are not making palliatives. For people of some intelligence the indications of the first volumes, [and] the 'Anti-Proudhon' [*Poverty of Philosophy*], and the [*Communist*] *Manifesto* will suffice to get them on the right track; the buying and reading mob will not be interested in the history any more if the great mystery has been revealed in volume 1; the mob has, as Hegel says in the *Phenomenology*, read 'the preface', and there's where you get the general idea. . . . The main thing is that you will make your debut before the public with a fat book, and best of all with the least risky, the history. . . . There is the additional consideration that you can write the *History* only in London, while you can write the *Socialists* and the *Critique* wherever you go. Hence it would be good for you to make use of the opportunity now, before the philistines do something silly and put us back onto the international stage. . . . You should write to Ebner that he has full power of attorney and can conclude things right away. . . . The more I think the matter over, the more practical it appears to me to begin with the historical. Show a little commercial sense! (MEW xxvii. 373–5.)

Political events on the continent (as Engels feared) and Marx's subsequent work on the *Eighteenth Brumaire of Louis Bonaparte* (published in New York in 1852 by Weydemeyer) gave the *Economy* a setback, and a scheme concocted by Freiligrath and Lassalle for a company to finance the publication of Marx's book never got under way. (CHR 115; FBME i. 29–30; BZLM 48 n.)

The plan for Marx's *Economy*, as it emerged from the correspondence of 1851, called for an initial volume (the critique of political economy), a second volume on the socialists (this appears to be a development of the earlier plans of 1844 and 1845–6 for a critical work on politics, and of volume ii of the *German Ideology*, and of section III of the *Communist Manifesto*, published in London in 1848), and a third volume (on the history of political economy) not mentioned in either of the earlier plans. The concluding volume of the plan of 1844, showing the 'connection of the whole' as the critique of the 'speculative presentation' of various subjects, was missing from both the plans of 1845–6 (the two-volume critique of politics and political economy) and of 1850–1 (the three-volume work described above). Marx evidently reckoned that he had settled (in book form) with Hegelian or 'speculative' philosophy after the publication (in Frankfurt a.M.) of the *Holy Family* (1845), the *Poverty of Philosophy*, and the *Communist Manifesto*, and the writing of the *German Ideology*, since he and Engels mentioned the last three of those works as prefatory to the critique of political economy. The idea of writing a *history* of political economy (apparently a history both of the theory of political economy and of economic development) separate from the *critique* of political economy, dates from 1847–51, but it is not clear precisely whose idea it was—Marx's, or one of his correspondents or prospective publishers.

The wide scope of Marx's plan was in keeping with the tradition of political economy. In particular, it resembled Adam Smith's plan for the *Wealth of Nations* (1776), since each opened with the author's presentation of (or views on) political economy, each considered the history of economic development and various theories of political economy, and each developed a 'political' section which was both critical and prescriptive: Smith on revenue and taxation, and Marx on the socialists and socialism. The tendency of political economists, especially

Adam Smith, to connect their studies with 'larger considerations' was noted with approval by J. S. Mill in the *Preface* to his own survey of the subject, the *Principles of Political Economy* (1848). But Marx's conception of a *critique* of political economy was even larger in scope than any of the works written or planned by political economists.

During 1852 he continued his attempts to find a publisher for his *Economy*, and soldiered on with various studies at the British Museum, e.g. history of civilization, feudalism, literature. (Rubel (1956), 226.) On 30 January he wrote to Weydemeyer: 'What is the state of the German book trade in America? Could I find a publisher there for my *Economy*, since the thing has fallen through in Germany?' (MEW xxviii. 486.)

An approach by Marx to the Leipzig publisher Wigand in March 1852 met with rejection because of the risk of 'running up against the state'. (CHR 121.) But Marx seems to have pressed on; Engels wrote to him on 18 March, saying

. . . you must . . . if you are finished with the preliminary work on your *Economy*, come over here with your whole family for six months—we would live in New Brighton on the sea [near Liverpool], and you would still save money on it. (MEW xxviii. 42.)

But by the end of 1852 negotiations for a publisher had petered out, and on 7 December Marx wrote to Adolf Cluss[21] in Washington, D.C., that the Cologne communist trial, and his *Revelations* on the subject (published in Basle, and Boston, Massachusetts, in 1853), had taken him away from his *Economy*. (MEW xxviii. 560; Rubel (1956), 96.)

Until August 1853 he continued to make occasional additions to the economic notebooks begun in 1850. From September 1853 to May 1854 he worked on the 'Eastern Question' and events leading to the Crimean War; during 1853–4 he also

[21] Adolf Cluss (c. 1820—after 1889) was a member of the League of Communists. He emigrated to the USA in 1849 and was an associate of Weydemeyer. (MEW xxviii. 778.)

worked on the histories of India and Spain in connection with his articles for the New-York *Tribune*. There are allusions to some of this material in the *Introduction* (1857).

Between November 1854 and January 1855 he began a work entitled *Money, Credit, Crises* (*Geldwesen, Kreditwesen, Krisen*—still unpublished), but did not finish the manuscript. Most of his energies during this period were spent on the journalistic activities required to support his family, but the subject-matter of the articles was not unrelated to his studies in political economy, and he did not lose interest in writing a critique, especially during the 'crises' of capitalist production, which he connected with the eventual victory of the revolutionary working-class movement. (GR 766, 1044; Rubel (1956), 226.)

Marx had written to Weydemeyer on 19 December 1849 linking the possibility of a new revolutionary outbreak with a 'terrible industrial, agricultural, and commercial crisis'. The article 'May to October' by Marx and Engels, which appeared in the *Neue Rheinische Zeitung* (London) in 1850, gave a history of 'commercial depression' from 1837 to 1850 in connection with the European revolutionary movement, and in November 1852 Marx published articles in the New-York *Tribune* titled 'Pauperism and Free Trade—the impending Trade Crisis' and 'The political Consequences of the Commercial Paroxysm'. (MEW xxvii. 516; vii. 421–63; viii. 367–78.)

On 11 March 1853 Engels wrote to Marx, urging him once again to hurry his book along because a favourable political situation was developing:

As far as recruiting goes, I think that as soon as we are back in Germany we will find enough young men of talent who have, in the interim [since 1848–9], enjoyed the forbidden fruits [and] not without success. If we had the means for making sober and scientific propaganda for two to three years with books on no matter what, we would be so much the better for it. But that is not to be; the storm clouds are already on the horizon. You should get finished with your *Economy*; we could publish it in weekly numbers as soon as we have a newspaper, and what the populace does not understand, [our] disciples would expound, correctly and badly, but not without effect. (MEW xxviii. 226.)

Marx's articles for the autumn of 1853 included 'Rise in the Price of Corn—Cholera—Strikes—Sailors' Movement', 'Panic on the London Exchange—Strikes', and 'War—Strikes—Scarcity'. (MEW ix. 297–9, 341–6, 447–55.) On 15 September 1853 he wrote to the emigré Cluss, connecting the expected 'commercial collapse' with his desire to work on the *Economy*:

In any case the movement might come down on my head before I would wish it (I think that a commercial collapse will begin in the spring, as in 1847). I always hope before things go too far to take a couple of months in solitude and to be able to work out my *Economy*. It appears that I am not to do it. The continual scribbling for newspapers bores me. It takes up much of my time, fritters it away, and finally comes to nothing. (MEW xxviii. 592.)

In January 1855 he published a series of articles in the *Neue Oder-Zeitung* (Breslau) on the current industrial and trade crisis. (MEW x. 602–9.) And in a letter to Lassalle of 23 January 1855 he traced the history of the 'present crisis' back to 1847, and drew his usual conclusion:

I have tossed out the above history in order to answer your question in a completely general way. What I can dig up in the way of definite figures in my notebooks, I shall see. Books, as is said, will make a good appearance *just now*. . . . (MEW xxviii. 615.)

And on 13 February 1855 he wrote to Engels:

I have contracted an eye ailment from reading through my notebooks on economy, if not to work the thing out, in any case to master the material and to have it ready for work. (MEW xxviii. 434.)

Much of Marx's time during 1855–6 was taken up with illness and journalism, but he greeted reports of a financial crisis in

September 1856 with hopes of getting back to his 'books', and with a series of articles for the New York *Tribune* on the economic and monetary crisis in Europe. (MEW xii. 49–70.)

[26 September 1856] Dear Frederick [Engels] . . . This time the thing has a general European dimension as never before, and I do not believe that we can look on from here for very long. The very fact that I am so far along with setting up house again[22] and getting down to my books, proves to me that the 'mobilization' of our people is at hand. (MEW xxix. 74–6.)

Marx worked on various notebooks from September 1856 to July 1857, covering such items as silver, banking, money, and the latest volumes of Tooke's *History of Prices*. (CHR 160–5; Rubel (1957), 405 n.) Then in July he set to work on some of the material published posthumously as the *Grundrisse* (the 'sketches' on the political economists Bastiat and Carey) and on numerous articles for the New-York *Tribune* concerning the European financial and trade crisis. (GR 842–53; MEW xii. 234–7, and *passim.*) The unfinished *Introduction* (1857) followed in late August and early September.

Another commercial crisis (or in Marx's view, the same general crisis) erupted in October; the remainder of the notes and drafts which appear in the *Grundrisse* were written between October 1857 and June 1858 (except for certain fragments published in the Appendix). At the same time he wrote a series of articles on the economic crisis for the New-York *Tribune*, and his correspondence with Engels contained numerous exchanges on the subject. The American crash, Marx commented (in English) on 20 October 1857, was 'beautiful'. (MEW xxix. 198.)

The material which he wrote between October 1857 and June 1858, i.e. the bulk of the *Grundrisse*, has been called the

---

[22] Marx was in the process of moving from 28 Dean Street, Soho, to 9 Grafton Terrace, Maitland Park, Haverstock Hill, Hampstead, in London.

'centrepiece of Marx's thought', and in some ways, the best and 'completest' of all his works. (McLellan (1971a), 3, 15.)

Why, when Marx set to work in October 1857, did he work so hard and so well?

Without testimony from Marx himself it is impossible to discover exactly why his work improved and expanded so suddenly. The trade crisis of October 1857 is usually cited in connection with the increased pace of his work, since he mentioned in a letter to Lassalle of 21 December 1857 that it had 'spurred me to work seriously on my *Principles of [Political] Economy*, also to prepare something on the present crisis'. (MEW xxix. 548.)

But Marx had predicted or experienced trade crises in 1850, 1851, 1852, 1853, 1855, 1856, and the spring and summer of 1857, and he had managed to do *some* work on political economy during those years (at least twenty-four notebooks and two unfinished manuscripts) in spite of his appalling circumstances. Poverty, ill-health, and journalism continued unabated through 1857 and 1858, and yet he wrote the *Grundrisse*. Any number of things may have facilitated the dramatic change in the quantity and quality of his work, but the methodological innovations of the *Introduction* of August/September 1857, written just before the great burst of activity which began in October, probably play a large part in the explanation.

In the *Introduction* (1857) Marx stated that he was considering 'material production', and went on to confirm the view, already formulated in the 1844 *Manuscripts*, that productive activity was crucial to the nature of man and his social life and to the development of the modern individual and modern bourgeois society. Marx then restricted himself to 'modern bourgeois production'; the 1844 *Manuscripts*, the *Communist Manifesto*, and *Wage-labour and Capital* had dealt with various aspects of that subject, as had the *Poverty of Philosophy*, in which he criticized the views of Proudhon in particular. But the *Introduction* (1857) did not merely repeat Marx's earlier views and criticisms.

Three important innovations in his methods and plans were

recorded in the 1857 text. The first was that he dealt analytically with the meanings and logical interrelations of economic concepts and categories, and he put these thoughts down on paper at length—an innovation in his 'mode of investigation'. Working as a logician, he set out the connections which those concepts have with one another and with the things and processes of the real world, in order to understand them fully and to avoid confusing 'ideas and things'. (See Marx to Annenkov, 28 December 1846, MEW xxvii. 453.)

In his earlier efforts at a critique of political economy he had begun with wages or wage-labour and the treatment of the labourer as a commodity. The second innovation of 1857 was that Marx decided to begin the substantial part of his critique with *capital*, since it represented the 'power ruling over everything' in bourgeois society. His train of thought led him from an analysis of the category labour, the starting point of previous discussions, to the society in which its abstract form was 'truly practical'. In that society, he claimed, capital was the dominant relation of production; hence it formed the starting point and terminal point of his analysis and presentation—an innovation in his plans for a critique of political economy.

The third innovation was Marx's endorsement of a version of the method of logical synthesis—proceeding from abstract, simple forms, to concrete, complex entities. This proved to be an important stage in the development of a 'mode of presentation' for his critique of political economy.[23]

In the *Introduction* (1857) Marx decided where to begin his critique, developed some ideas on his mode of presentation, and investigated the logical distinctions needed to re-present the categories of political economy in a *critical* way. The link between the 1857 text and his famous letter to Lassalle of 22 February 1858 is clear:

The first work in question is the *Critique of the Economic Categories* [*Kritik der ökonomischen Kategorien*], or, if you like, the system of

[23] See pp. 134–5 below.

bourgeois [political] economy critically presented. It is the presentation [*Darstellung*] of the system and, at the same time, through the presentation, its critique.[24] (MEW xxix. 550.)

A plan for Marx's critique appeared in the *Introduction* (1857), just after the section in which he had decided to begin with capital.[25] Book 1, 'the general abstract determinations which more or less belong to all forms of society', represents a clarificatory introduction (presumably a tidied-up version of certain sections of the *Introduction* of 1857) which did not appear as the opening to Marx's *A Contribution to the Critique of Political Economy* (published in Berlin in 1859) or *Capital*, i (published in Hamburg in 1867),[26] though some of his material on that theme appeared in those volumes *passim*. He opened both published works with book 2 on bourgeois society (viz. capital, wage-labour, landed property), his 'proper subject', as he put it in the *Introduction* (1857).

However, he had by no means solved all his organizational problems in September 1857. Having decided to begin with capital, he was left with the question: where do I begin in *that* presentation?

Marx's plans of October and November 1857 (see GR 138–9, 175) corresponded in general to the plan of August/September 1857 given in the *Introduction* of that year, though the introductory book on the 'general abstract determinations' had disappeared.[27] Instead, he said that 'in the first section,

---

[24] This letter is dated a year too early in McLellan (1971a), 10.

[25] See p. 82 below.

[26] I disagree with David McLellan on this point; cf. McLellan (1971b), 85. Roman Rosdolsky suggests that Marx was still intending to write an introduction concerning the 'general abstract determinations' as late as January 1863, since Marx's plan of that date for his work on capital opened with 'Introduction. The Commodity. Money.' However, Marx did not specify in any further detail what that introduction was to cover. (Rosdolsky (1968), i. 24–5 n; MEW xxvi(1). 389.)

[27] However, there are references to such an introduction in Karl Marx, *Grundrisse*, trans. Martin Nicolaus (Harmondsworth, 1973), 298, 320.

where exchange-value, money, and price are considered, commodities always appear at hand'. (GR 138.) This was probably the substance of the 'introductory chapters' to which he referred in his letter to Lassalle of 22 February 1858, where he recorded some rearrangements in his plan of August/ September 1857: 'capital, wage-labour, landed property' (the former book 2) became books 1–3, and the former books 3–5 became books 4–6. Marx now envisaged the critique of political economy falling into six books, rather than five, and he suggested that those six books would be the 'abstract' or 'logical' or 'scientific' (*wissenschaftlich*) section of his work, and that the critique (presumably specific criticisms) and history of political economy and socialism 'should on the whole form the subject of another work'. In other words, he still had in mind something like the three-volume plan of 1850–1 (critique of political economy, critique of the socialists, and history of political economy) but with these differences: the critique of political economy was now to be an abstract presentation of the economic categories, and his material on particular economists and on political economy in general (apart from his abstract re-presentation of the subject) was lumped together with the history of the subject and with socialism; the third volume (a 'brief *historical sketch* of the development of the economic categories and relations') was a work along lines suggested in the *Introduction* (1857), where he had carefully distinguished between the logical ordering of the economic categories, their historical order of development, and their order of importance in modern bourgeois society.

[22 February 1858] Dear Lassalle. . . . The first work in question is the *Critique of the Economic Categories*. . . . The presentation, I mean the style, is completely scientific [*wissenschaftlich*], and therefore not police-prone in the usual sense. The whole is divided into six books. 1. On capital (contains a few introductory chapters). 2. On landed property. 3. On wage-labour. 4. On the state. 5. International trade. 6. The world market. Naturally I cannot resist taking a critical look at other economists now and then, especially a polemic against Ricardo, so far as he himself, *qua* bourgeois, is forced to commit blunders *from a strictly economic point of view*. On the whole, however, the critique and history of political economy and of socialism should form the subject of another work. Finally, the brief *historical sketch* of the development of the economic categories and relations [should form] a third [work]. (MEW xxix. 550–1; see also GR 1012.)

In his next letter to Lassalle, Marx drew a distinction between the sort of work he intended to do on the first three books (capital, landed property, and wage-labour) and the less detailed work necessary for the books on the state, international trade, and the world market:

[11 March 1858] . . . It is in no way my intention to work equally on all six books into which I divide the whole, but to give the last three in bold strokes, while in the first three, which contain the basic economic development proper, detailed discussions are not on the whole to be avoided. (MEW xxix. 554.)

Lassalle once again undertook to find Marx a publisher for his *Economy*, and reported success this time in a letter of 26 March 1858. Franz Duncker of Berlin had agreed to publish the work in short instalments (*Lieferungshefte*), retaining the right to break off the arrangement with the third. (BZLM 118–21.) Marx wrote to Engels from the British Museum on 29 March and predicted that the first instalment would be ready by the end of May. (MEW xxix. 309.)

His letter to Engels of 2 April 1858 repeated the same general plan that he had recorded in the letter to Lassalle of 22 February, but gave more information on the organization of the first three chapters of the first book (of the six-book critique of political economy), as well as further details on the nature and content of his critical presentation:

I. Capital. First section. Capital in general . . . . 1. Value . . . 2. Money . . . (a) Money as standard . . . (b) Money as the means of exchange or simple circulation . . . (c) Money as money . . . (d)

D

Simple circulation considered for itself . . . 3. Capital. This is really the [most] important [chapter] of the first instalment, on which I must have your general views. (MEW xxix. 312–18.)

The index to his seven notebooks (i.e. the notebooks which formed the bulk of the *Grundrisse*) was written in June 1858 in the same notebook (*Heft* M) as the *Introduction* of August/September 1857. In the index he gave the same plan for the opening instalment on capital as the one he had given to Engels in April: (I) Value . . . (II) Money . . . (III) Capital in general. (GR 855–9.)

Ill-health and other interruptions during the summer of 1858 kept Marx from his work until September. But in November he wrote to Engels, indicating a change in his plan: the first instalment on capital now begins with 'the commodity', rather than 'value':[28]

[29 November 1858] Dear Frederick . . . the first part has grown bigger, since the first two chapters, of which the *first: The Commodity*, has not been written in rough draft, and the *second: Money or Simple Circulation*, is only in quite a short outline; the first part has been argued more elaborately than I had originally intended. (MEW xxix. 371–2.)

In January 1859 Marx was ready to send his first instalment to Duncker's, but he had only his two expanded sections on the commodity and money ready for the press. He was somewhat put out at having to go back on the plan for a 'self-contained brochure' which he had outlined in an earlier letter to Lassalle:

[11 March 1858] . . . Under all circumstances the first instalment would have to be a relative whole, and since the basis for the whole development is contained in it, it would be difficult to do in under five or six printer's sheets . . . It consists of 1. Value [in November Marx altered this to The Commodity], 2. Money, 3. Capital in general. . . . This forms a self-contained brochure. (MEW xxix. 554.)

[28] See pp. 134–5 below.

Since chapter 3 was not completed, Marx was in the embarass-ing position of beginning his critique with capital (as he had decided in the *Introduction* of 1857), but in a way not obvious to the reader, who would see only chapters 1 and 2. Nevertheless, Marx found some advantages in the situation:

[13–15 January 1859] Dear Engels . . . The manuscript is about twelve printer's sheets (three notebooks), and . . . although [it has] the title 'Capital in general', these notebooks still contain *nothing* on capital, except only the two chapters: 1. *The Commodity*, 2. *Money or Simple Circulation*. You see that the part worked over in detail (in May, when I came to see you) has still not appeared at all. This is a good thing in a couple of ways. If the thing comes off, then the third chapter on capital can quickly follow. Secondly, in the published part, according to the nature of the thing, the dogs cannot limit their criticism to mere bitching about [political] tendencies, and the whole looks exceedingly serious and scientific; [thus] I force the scoundrels to take my later views on capital rather seriously. Moreover, I think that apart from all practical purposes the chapter on money will be interesting for specialists. (MEW xxix. 383.)

He told Weydemeyer much the same story on 1 February 1859, but added, 'You understand the *political* reasons which oblige me to withhold the third chapter concerning "Capital" until I have a firm footing again'. (MEW xxix. 572–3.)

The plan for Marx's book of 1859 called for two chapters, one on the commodity and the other on money; but super-imposed on that scheme were three sections in which he summarized and criticized the work of various political economists on the commodity, money, and the circulation of money. He had evidently changed his mind about a general separation of his historical and critical material from his abstract, critical presentation, or perhaps he simply could not resist including polemics against the political economists which he had been polishing up for years. Engels objected (in letters of 1858 and 1867) to an excessively abstract presentation of Marx's critique, both in connection with *A Contribution to the*

Critique of Political Economy and the first edition of *Capital*, i.
Ryazanov suggests that the reinstatement of the historical
sections in the *Contribution* was a case of Marx following Engels's
advice. (MEW xxix. 319; xxxi. 303–4. Ryazanov (1930), 22.)

After the publication in June 1859 of his two chapters on the
commodity and money, Marx planned for a time to write the
third chapter, 'Capital' or 'Capital in general' (he used both
designations). A draft plan of February/March 1859 for part of
the third chapter appears in the Appendix to the *Grundrisse*.
(GR 969–80.)

In a letter to Kugelmann[29] of 28 December 1862 Marx
indicated that he was still working on the third chapter, and
confirmed that he had not abandoned the six-book critique of
political economy. But he suggested that he was beginning to
give up hope of ever completing the job himself. Separate
critical works on 'law, morality, politics etc.', 'the socialists',
and the 'history of the economic categories and relations' seem
to have dropped out of the picture altogether:

I was very pleased to see from your letter that you and your friends
take such a warm interest in my [*A Contribution to the*] *Critique of
Political Economy*. The second part is finally finished, i.e. up to making
a clean copy and the final polishing for the press. It will be approxi-
mately thirty printer's sheets. It is the continuation of the first
instalment, but it will appear self-contained under the title *Capital*
with 'A Contribution to the Critique of Political Economy' merely
as a subtitle. In fact it only comprises what was to form the third
chapter of the first part, namely 'Capital in general'. Therefore it
does not include the competition of capitals and the credit system.
This volume contains what the English call 'the principles of
political economy'. It is the quintessence (together with the first
part [already published as *A Contribution* etc.]); and the development
of the following parts (with the exception perhaps of the relations
of the different forms of the state to the different economic structures

[29] Ludwig Kugelmann (1829–1902) was a doctor, a participant in the
revolution of 1848, and a member of the International. (MEW xxxii.
875.)

of society) would be easily worked out by others on the basis which I have provided. (MEW xxx. 639.)

In January 1863, a month after his letter to Kugelmann, Marx drafted a plan for *Capital* which indicated that he had scrapped the idea of publishing a third chapter on its own, in favour of a revised presentation of the chapters on the commodity and money, together with his new material on capital in general (though he did not get round to explaining this to Kugelmann until 1866). (MEW xxvi(1). 389.)[30]

The critical and historical material on political economy (part of the middle volume, according to the plan of 22 February 1858) turned up again in the 'final' arrangement of Marx's critical work into four books, but if he had lived to prepare the materials designated for books 2–4 of this plan beyond the rough manuscript stage, he might have rearranged things yet again. In a letter of 31 July 1865 he indicated that there were to be three theoretical books and one 'historico-literary' effort:

Dear Engels . . as far as my work is concerned, I'll give it to you straight. There are still three chapters to be written in order to get finished with the theoretical part (the first three books). Then there is still book 4 to be written, which is historico-literary, which is for me relatively the easiest part, since all questions in the first three books have been resolved, and the last book is therefore more repetition [*sic*] in historical form. But I cannot decide to put anything aside before the whole lies before me. Whatever shortcomings they may have, the virtue of my writings is that they are an artistic whole, and that is only possible with my way of never publishing them until they lie *complete* before me. (MEW xxxi. 131–2.)

In a letter to Kugelmann of 13 October 1866 Marx spelled out the four-book plan for his critical work, and explained the

[30] A manuscript chapter intended for *Capital*, i, but not included in the work as published, survives from this period; see 'Results of the immediate Production Process' (*Resultate des unmittelbaren Produktionsprozesses*), *Arkhiv Marksa i Engel'sa*, ed. V. Adoratskii (Moscow, 1933), ii(vii). 1–267. Cf. McLellan (1971b), 84, 118–20.

relation of *Capital*, i, to his *Contribution*, as published in 1859; he had revised the two chapters of the *Contribution* to improve (but not reject) his earlier work:

My circumstances (incessant physical and everyday, bourgeois interruptions) have led to the result that the *first volume* must appear before the others, not both at once, as I had at first intended. Also, there will now probably be three volumes.

The whole work divides into the following parts:

Book I. Production Process of Capital.
Book II. Circulation Process of Capital.
Book III. Form of the Process as a Whole.[31]
Book IV. Contribution to the History of the Theory.

The first volume contains the first two books. [Marx later had to alter this: book I appeared as the first volume in 1867.]

The third book, I think, will fill the second volume, and the fourth book, the third volume.

I deemed it necessary to begin the first book again *ab ovo*, i.e. to summarize the work published by Duncker into *one* chapter on the commodity and money. I consider it necessary, not only for completeness, but because even good brains did not comprehend the thing completely correctly; therefore there must be something defective in the first presentation, particularly the *analysis of the commodity*. (MEW xxxi. 534.)

After the publication of *Capital*, i, in 1867, Marx prepared a second German edition, which is dated 1872 (though his *Afterword* is dated 24 January 1873); a French translation (with substantial alterations by Marx) appeared in Paris in 1872–5; a Russian translation (for which he gave advice) was published in St. Petersburg in 1872; and a third German edition (based on the French edition) appeared in 1883, the year of his death.

Capital, ii, *Circulation Process of Capital* (book II of Marx's

[31] As early as 11 March 1858 Marx indicated that his discussion of 'Capital in general' was to include 'Production Process of Capital', 'Circulation Process of Capital', 'Unity of the Two or Capital and Profit, Interest', i.e. what later became books 1–3 of *Capital* as published. (Marx to Lassalle, MEW xxix. 554.)

plan of 1866) was edited by Engels from manuscripts which Marx had written between 1867 and 1879, and was published in Hamburg in 1885. *Capital*, iii, *Process of Capitalist Production as a Whole* (book III of the plan of 1866) appeared in Hamburg in 1894, and was also edited by Engels, but from manuscripts written (for the most part) between 1864 and 1865 (i.e. before the manuscript of *Capital*, i.)

Book IV of Marx's plan appeared as *Theories of Surplus Value*, i–iii, edited by Karl Kautsky from manuscripts of the years 1861–3 (i.e. before the manuscript of *Capital*, i). Volumes i and ii were published in Stuttgart in 1905; volume iii, in 1910. (Rubel (1956), 169–73; see also Engels's prefaces to *Capital*, ii, and iii.)

Even if we consider *Capital*, i–iii, and *Theories of Surplus Value*, i–iii, as Marx's finished work, he still completed only a tiny fraction of what he had intended to write at any stage of his plans after 1844 (discounting proposals for scaled-down works to interest publishers). The published material represents very roughly, and not in the proposed order,[32] only part of the content of the six-book critique of the economic categories ('the system of bourgeois economy critically presented') and part of the historical and critical material which was to follow the six-book critique, according to his most ambitious scheme, which was developed directly from the principles and plans of the *Introduction* (1857).

CONCLUSIONS

Far from being a tentative effort, the *Introduction* (1857) was investigative and analytical in tone. In it Marx explored the science of political economy and, in particular, its basic categories, using methods derived from his studies in philosophy

[32] For attempts to relate the various sections of Marx's plans of 1857–8 to *Capital*, i–iii, as published, see Rosdolsky (1968), i. 75, and David McLellan, *Karl Marx* (London, 1973), 467.

and logic. His conclusions about the organization of his critical presentation of political economy survived, with slight modification, in the overall structure of *Capital*, i, as published, and the rest of the work, as planned. His philosophical standpoint and views on bourgeois society and its development (both historical and future) were much the same in the *Introduction* (1857) as in his earlier works back to 1844; there was some repetition in the 1857 text of his earlier premises and arguments, but in compressed form.

The most striking difference between the *Introduction* (1857) and Marx's earlier and later writings was his overt interest in the investigation of the logical interrelations of the concepts and categories of political economy. He pursued that sort of investigation at length (using what he called, in the *Preface* (1867) to *Capital*, i, the 'force of abstraction'), confident that he was not falling into any idealist traps, since there were frequent references to his own anti-idealist views. Having settled his accounts with philosophical idealism in the early works (and put down, to his own satisfaction, various socialists with idealist leanings) he applied what he had learned from his criticisms of them, and from Hegel in particular, to his critical inquiry into political economy, a subject in which he had been educating himself slowly and painfully since 1844.

At first glance the late works seem to have sacrificed the philosophical themes of the early writings for economic studies, but a continuity in Marx's views from the early to the late works can be established from the texts.[33] The early manuscripts were, after all, *economic*, as well as philosophical. For various reasons (e.g. his education and immediate political objectives) Marx's critique of philosophy (and of philosophically oriented writers on social and economic affairs) preceded his full-blown critique of political economy, for which a great deal of research was required.

However, the late works not only presupposed and in some cases reproduced the views of the early writings, but in *Capital*

[33] See the examples cited in Mészáros (1970), 328–31.

(and other studies) those views were utilized and presented in a more polished and focussed way—a way which was also, of necessity, more complex.

Marx's critical work on political economy did not show a simple continuity, but a process of detailed refinement; that was why Lukács was able to offer something like a reconstruction of the 'early Marx' before the 1844 *Manuscripts* and other works were published. The views and conclusions of the early manuscripts were there in the *Introduction* (1857) and *Capital*, along with new material which presupposed or developed what the early writings had only hinted at. The early views were not toned down, disguised, or put into a less philosophical form as part of the mature critique of political economy, but refined, elaborated, and stated in a more precise, highly philosophical way in, for example, his presentation of 'the commodity'.

In his later works (as in the earlier writings) Marx wished to avoid sounding like the philosophers whom he had criticized, and he would certainly have objected to being labeled a philosopher, since he had gone to great lengths to dissociate himself from various writers who styled themselves as such or philosophized (badly and impotently, in his view) in print. He had no pressing reason to discourse on alienation as such when his topic was the critique of political economy and the presentation of his 'discoveries', e.g. the theory of surplus value.[34] Yet he made ample use of the concept of alienation (and other philosophical concepts and distinctions), and even phrases and arguments from the early manuscripts, while writing *Capital*. His final riposte to the philosophers (and pseudo-philosophers) was not to drop philosophy, but to make use of his own philosophical views about human activities (especially production) in preparing and presenting his critical study of political economy.

---

[34] The connection between Marx's early works and some of his later critical contributions to political economy is discussed in Walton (1972), *passim*.

The advantage of seeing Marx's critical work on political economy in those terms is that they not only emphasize the links between the early and late works, but also indicate the ways in which they differ, and why this is the case. Between 1844 and the publication of *Capital*, i, in 1867, his study and research had advanced on the philosophical, technical, and documentary-historical fronts, in ways that suggest that the views of the early works were still well in mind. He seems to have felt free to apply his early ideas and views to the critique of political economy as he came to conceive it, without necessarily spelling them out all over again.

That Marx was a philosopher (among other things) is not, these days, an unusual conclusion; nevertheless the philosophical complexity and subtlety of the late works is often underestimated or overlooked, because some of the terms (and certain aspects of the whole enterprise) are unfamiliar. Although his presentation of the commodity laid the foundation for his economic theories and views, it also represented a philosophical advance, not a 'break'. In the opening chapter of *Capital*, i, he attempted to spell out the nature of the 'alien world of objects' (mentioned in the 1844 *Manuscripts*), and to explain what was involved in the particular sort of alien object produced in bourgeois society: the commodity. What emerged was a very complex argument (which presupposed and developed some of his earlier views) concerning the social perception of some objects as commodities in capitalist society—how this happens, and why.

Marx's conception of science was broad enough to include what appear to be philosophical analyses, assertions, and conclusions. Science for him seems to have represented the active search for, and presentation of, truths and evidence for them, using arguments and data which related not simply to what could be touched or counted, but to what could be stated, in more general terms (including moral terms), to be the case with man and his world. The searching process for Marx was essentially active, investigative, critical, and practical; a scientific presentation, in his view, seems to have been one which solved conceptual mysteries and presented the human world accurately, intelligibly, and politically. To say that he aimed at presenting an accurate 'reflection' of the facts discounts the intellectual, philosophical effort he threw into solving the puzzles and dissipating the 'mysteries' presented by capitalist society and one of its products—political economy.

It is clear from the *Introduction* (1857) and many other works that Marx's scientific research did not aim at the discovery of universal, or, as he put it, 'eternal' laws of political economy or of human behaviour, though he did not seem to regard as mutable his presuppositions about the nature of man. In his work he emphasized what has changed and developed in the human world by human agency, not what has remained the same and is 'eternally' true. He seems to have taken the view that such truths are of little significance; in any case, the opposition of man to what is necessary and cannot be changed is quite unlike the view of man (who works on many aspects of the material world and thereby changes it *and* the human social world) which was presented in the early writings, and presupposed in the later ones. Marx did compare his methods to those of the physicist, and he would never have denied the existence of physical laws (which might be 'eternal') and a minimum number of necessary truths, yet he was careful to limit the analogy between his work and that of the natural scientist. (See, for example, CAP i. pp. xvi–xvii, and 43.) As to the inevitable working out of 'iron laws', that, in his view, was a feature of the capitalist system of production, not a general truth about the human situation. Those iron laws, he believed, would give way to the conscious control by man of the social, as well as the physical environment. In this he displayed a streak of optimism (more common in the nineteenth century than today) concerning the prospects for the establishment of a humane and rational social world.

In the *Introduction* (1857) Marx set out a number of distinctions concerning the economic categories (the basic categories,

such as production, distribution, exchange, and consumption)
and other fundamental concepts, such as labour and money.
After he had sorted out what those concepts were and were not,
and how it was that they applied to all epochs generally and to
certain epochs in certain ways, his plans for the presentation of
his critical work crystallized around the priority of production
over the other categories and the dominance of capital over
other aspects of bourgeois society. In *Capital*, i, entitled 'The
Process of Capitalist Production', he dealt primarily with some
of the 'categories which constitute the inner arrangement of
bourgeois society', as he put it in the *Introduction* (1857); some
of his material on the more general aspects of economic concepts
and categories and their historical development, as discussed
in the 1857 text, was also presented in *Capital*, i, *passim* (e.g. the
remarks on the labour-process and co-operation in CAP i.
156–64, 315–26.)

Moreover, Marx planned to re-present (critically) the
categories of political economy in the particular order dictated,
in his view, by the structure of bourgeois society, as he had
decided in principle in the *Introduction* (1857). And in *Capital*
(the first category) he proceeded from the 'individual' to the
'general' (a development of the views on logical synthesis
recorded in the *Introduction* of 1857), from the commodity, to
money and simple circulation, capital, absolute and relative
surplus value, accumulation of capital, circulation of capital,
and the process as a whole. But he also interspersed comments,
digressions, contributions on various topics, and discussions of
the history of political economy throughout the work.

By opting for an abstract opening to *Capital* (i.e. the re-presentation of the basic concepts of the science, beginning with the
commodity), he set himself a task of enormous size and complexity. His job was to investigate and understand an entire
body of theory (the theory of political economy as found in the
works of selected political economists) and to re-present it
critically, a process which necessarily involved knowing the
subject thoroughly, breaking it down into basic concepts and

propositions, and putting it back together again to make particular points about life in capitalist society.

One of the difficulties in reading this critique today is in recognizing that much of it is a re-presentation of the theories and concepts of other writers, with Marx's own criticisms (of different kinds) built into the presentation. He assumed that his readers would be familiar with the science of political economy and able to distinguish its concepts (for which he sometimes gave a source) from his own critical contributions: a theory of the relationship between political economy and bourgeois society (i.e. a specific instance of his 'general result' of 1859);[35] a critique, using philosophical methods, of the basic concepts and presuppositions of political economy; additions and corrections to political economy (though on the basis of the philosophical critique); and some unusual conclusions about economic trends in capitalist society.

The *Introduction* (1857) reveals some of the philosophical thought which formed the foundation of Marx's critique of political economy. His familiarity with Hegel's *Logic*, for example, is amply displayed in the 1857 text.[36] In his letter to Engels of 16 January 1858 (when Marx was writing the *Grundrisse*) he stated that he had found the *Logic* helpful in dealing with a particular economic problem (profit); Freiligrath had offered him Bakunin's old copy in October 1857. (MEW xxix. 260; FBME i. 96.) But the text of the *Introduction* suggests, in any case, that Hegel's work was very much in Marx's mind in August/September of that year.

However, in the *Logic* Hegel presupposed a familiarity with the development of logical science up to his own time; Marx had that background as well. In his *Afterword* to *Capital*, i, he proclaimed himself a 'disciple' of Hegel, but he was also a competent student of logic and able to see Hegel's work in context.

The commentary on the text of the *Introduction* (1857)

[35] See p. 151 below.   [36] See pp. 130–3 below.

investigates in detail the notion that Marx's work in the *Grundrisse* was in some way 'Hegelian'. Marx admired and remembered specific passages from Hegel's works, and he was clearly impressed with Hegel's method of 'grasping' contradictions and working out the logical relations between concepts, and the ways in which concepts have changed and developed through history—though he was concerned to reject the metaphysical aspects of Hegel's views. In the 1857 text the ideas of Hegel and other philosophers were well digested; Marx did not borrow from them in any simple way, but used their ideas in the development of his own.[37] Other aspects of his work were, however, Hegelian in the sense that he set out to consider and refute Hegel and his admirers. Some of Marx's views and arguments in the *Introduction* (1857), as elsewhere, seem distinctly peculiar until they are seen as replies and ripostes.

In the works which followed the 1857 text his philosophical views and methods took on more sophisticated forms, but a more obvious development was his grasp of some of the technical aspects of his critical attack on political economy. There were few examples of that sort of criticism in the *Introduction* (1857), where he was primarily concerned with the language of political economy and of its critique.

The Marx of the 1857 text was apparently less dogmatic than the Marx of later works, since he seemed to test his thesis about the determination of various kinds of social phenomena by the mode of production, or at least to talk about testing it. The confidence displayed in the published works themselves could be explained, moreover, by many considerations apart from narrow-mindedness and dogmatism. It cannot be said, on the other hand, that the published and posthumously published works suggest that Marx was a man torn with doubts concerning the validity of his discoveries. His criticisms of others were relentless and seldom appreciative, and some of his attacks in

[37] See for example pp. 136–40 below.

the *Introduction* (1857) were certainly hasty and ungenerous, yet his objections were nearly always on matters of importance.

The 1857 text must be taken into account in developing a view of Marx and his work, because it reveals his interest in and grasp of traditional logic and its Hegelian critique, and demonstrates that this interest was directly and fundamentally connected with his economic studies. Though the concepts and categories which Marx analysed and re-presented in the first chapters of *Capital* do not correspond exactly to the economic concepts in use today, not all senses of the terms on which he left his views (e.g. commodity, money, capital) are completely out of use in modern economics, or ordinary language. His work is at least a reminder that a critique of an economic study need not be restricted to 'facts and figures' but can begin (and perhaps ought to begin, if it is to be effective) with a close examination of basic concepts and presuppositions.

Introduction (1857) to the Grundrisse

CONTENTS

A. INTRODUCTION

The Introduction *is found in a notebook marked* M.
*It was begun on 23 August 1857 and laid aside
about the middle of September.*

[This table of contents appears in GR 4. Marx's
Introduction follows in GR 5–31.]

A. Introduction

I. PRODUCTION, CONSUMPTION, DISTRIBUTION, EXCHANGE (CIRCULATION)

(I) PRODUCTION

Autonomous Individuals. Eighteenth-Century Ideas.[1]

[Commentary, pp. 88–101.]
(a) The subject at hand is, to begin with, *material production.*

Individuals producing in society—hence the starting point is naturally the socially determined[2] production [carried on] by individuals. The individual—and individuated—hunter and fisher,[3] with which [Adam] Smith and Ricardo begin, belongs to the unimaginative conceits of eighteenth-century stories *à la Robinson Crusoe*, which in no way express, as cultural historians[4] imagine, a simple reaction against over-refinement

---

[1] According to the editors of the *Grundrisse*, the headings printed here in SMALL CAPITALS appear in Marx's manuscript. Sub-headings printed in *italic type* have been adapted by the Moscow editors from Marx's 'References to my own Notebooks' (written about February 1859), which are published in the Appendix in GR 951–67. One sub-heading, on p. 58 below, is entirely the product of the Moscow editors, as they explain in GR p. xv; all insertions by the Moscow editors appear, translated into English, in double square brackets.

[2] Marx makes frequent use of the verb *bestimmen* (to determine or define) and its derivatives. I have translated *bestimmten* as 'definite', 'determinate' or 'determined', meaning 'limited' or 'conditioned'.

[3] 'The individual—and individuated—hunter and fisher' seems a better reading of Marx's *Der einzelne und vereinzelte Jäger und Fischer* than the more usual rendering of *vereinzelte* as 'isolated'; see pp. 89–90 below.

[4] There is a suggestion in Engels's review (published on 6 August 1859) that Marx might have been thinking of (among others) W. H. Riehl (1823–97), author of the *Natural History of the People as the Basis for a*

and a regression to a misconstrued natural life. [Those stories] no more rest on such naturalism than does Rousseau's social contract, which brings naturally independent subjects [*Subjekte*][5] into relation and association by means of a contract. This is the pretence, and merely the aesthetic pretence, of small- and large-scale stories *à la Robinson Crusoe*. It is rather the anticipation of 'bourgeois society', which had been in preparation since the sixteenth century and had made giant strides towards its maturity in the eighteenth. In that society of free competition the individual appears detached from the natural bonds etc., which in earlier historical epochs make him into an appendage of a determined, delimited, human conglomerate. The prophets of the eighteenth century, on whose shoulders Smith and Ricardo are standing, conceived of that eighteenth-century individual—the product, on the one hand, of the dissolution of feudal forms of society, and on the other, of the powers of production newly developed since the sixteenth century—as an ideal [conception],[6] which may have had an existence in the past. [They did not conceive of that individual] as an historical result, but rather as the starting-point of history. Because [they conceived of that individual] as the individual in conformity with nature, in keeping with their conception of nature, [they conceived of him] not as originating historically, but as posited by nature. That fallacy has been characteristic of each new epoch up to

    German Social Policy, Stuttgart, 1851 etc., and the later *Cultural Studies*, Stuttgart, 1859. (See MEW xiii. 469, 755; cf. CCPE 219.)

[5] Here and elsewhere by *Subjekt* ('subject') Marx means a thinking, acting agent, rather than a subject of study. *Objekt* ('object') in this text is usually that on which the subject acts or of which it takes cognizance; *Gegenstand* (in one of its senses) is a natural object, i.e. something concrete; see n. 11 on p. 50, and n. 46 on p. 86 below.

[6] 'as an ideal [conception]' (*als Ideal*). I take Marx to mean an 'ideal' in the sense of 'something existing only as a mental conception'. That usage agrees better with his well-known hostility to philosophical idealism than the more usual English sense of an 'ideal' as 'a perfect type'; similarly, I use 'ideal' as an adjective ('existing only in idea'), and the adverb 'ideally' ('in idea, mental conception, or imagination'). (OED *s.v.* Ideal B2.B1.A4; Ideally 2.)

now. [Sir James] Steuart, who in some ways is in opposition to the eighteenth century and as an aristocrat takes a more historical point of view, has escaped that gullibility.

The further back we go into history the more the individual, hence also the producing individual, appears as dependent, [and] belonging to a larger whole: at first in a still wholly natural way in the family and in the family extended into the tribe; later in the different forms of the community,[7] which arose from the antagonisms and mergers of tribes. In the eighteenth century, in 'bourgeois society', the different forms of the social connection first confront the individual as a mere means for his private purposes, as external necessity. However, the epoch which produces that point of view, that of the individuated individual, is precisely the epoch of the most developed social relations up to now ([the most developed social relations] are general relations from that point of view). Man is in the most literal sense a *zoon politikon*,[8] not only a sociable animal, but an animal which can individuate itself only in society. Production by an individuated individual outside society—a rarity which can indeed happen to a civilized man (who already possesses dynamically within himself the powers of social life), driven into the wilderness by accident—is just as absurd as the development of language without individuals living *together* and talking together. This need not detain us any longer. The point would not have been touched on at all had not that inanity, which had rhyme and reason for the people of the eighteenth century, been seriously reintroduced into the very middle of the most modern [political] economy[9] by [Frederic]

---

[7] I have translated *Gemeinschaft* as 'community', as opposed to *Gesellschaft* ('society') and *bürgerliche Gesellschaft* ('bourgeois society'); similarly, *Gemeineigentum* ('common property') and *Gemeindeeigentum* ('communal property').

[8] ζῷον πολιτικόν. Aristotle, *Politics*, 1253a3ff. Aristotle's phrase has been variously translated as 'man is by nature a political animal' (Jowett) and 'man is by nature an animal intended to live in a polis' (Barker).

[9] Marx uses both 'economy' (*Ökonomie*) and 'political economy' (*politische Ökonomie*). I take the former to be a shortened form of the latter,

Bastiat, [H. C.] Carey, Proudhon etc. For Proudhon (and others) it is naturally agreeable to develop historico-philosophically the source of an economic relation when he is ignorant of its historical origin, [so] that he mythologizes that Adam or Prometheus fell on a ready-made idea, [and] then the idea was instituted etc. Nothing is more tediously arid than the fantasizing common place.[10]

*Eternalization of the historical relations of production.
—Production and distribution in general.—Property.*

[Commentary, pp. 101–14.]

Thus if we are talking about production, we are always talking about production at a definite stage of social development— we are talking about production by social individuals. Hence it might seem that in order to speak generally about production we must either trace the historical process of development in its various phases, or declare at the outset that we are dealing with a definite historical epoch, e.g. modern bourgeois production, which is, in fact, our proper subject.[11] However, all epochs of production have certain features in common, common determinations.[12] *Production in general* is an abstraction, but a

since he never seems to draw a distinction. A translation of *ökonomie* as 'economics' begs the question whether there are distinctions to be made between political economy, Marx's works which deal with it, and the modern studies known as economics; see pp. 6–8 above.

[10] 'the fantasizing common place' (*der phantasierende locus communis*). Marx uses the Latin philosophical term meaning 'a general theme or argument applicable to many particular cases'. (OED *s.v.* Commonplace.) The reference is to the use of 'Adam or Prometheus' to explain the origin of something.

[11] Marx uses both *Gegenstand* and *Thema* in this text; I have translated both as 'subject', where he means a subject or object of study.

[12] 'determinations' (*Bestimmungen*). 'A determining attribute', essential constituent, or limiting factor. Also in this text, 'determination' (*Bestimmung*) as 'the rendering of a notion more determinate or definite by the

sensible abstraction, in so far as it actually picks out what is common, fixes it, and consequently spares us repetition. Nevertheless this *universal*,[13] or that which is common, separated out by [a process of] comparison, is [something which is] itself many times divided, [something which] splits into different determinations. A few [of those determinations] belong to all epochs; others are common to a few epochs. The most modern epoch will have [[a few]] determinations in common with the oldest. One cannot conceive of production without them; however, if the most developed languages have laws and determinations in common with the least developed, then that which constitutes their development must have the difference[14] from that which is universal and common, [hence] the determinations which are applicable to production generally must be precisely separated [from that which constitutes its development], so that beyond the unity [of those determinations]—a unity which arises from the fact that the subject [*Subjekt*], mankind, and the object [*Objekt*], nature, are the same [in all epochs]—the essential divergence [of those determinations] is not forgotten. For example, the whole wisdom of the modern economists who prove the eternity and harmony of the existing social relations lies in forgetting that [divergence]. For example. No production is possible without an instrument of production, even if that

addition of characters or determining attributes'; the opposite of generalization. (OED *s.v.* Determination 5b(b).5b(a).)

[13] 'This *universal*' (*dies* Allgemeine). I have translated *allgemein* as 'general', *im Allgemeinen* as 'in general', *Allgemeinheit* as 'generality', *überhaupt* as 'generally', except in passages, such as this one, in which Marx uses the technical vocabulary of logic. A 'universal' is 'that which is predicated or asserted of all the individuals or species of a class or genus', i.e. a common factor. (OED *s.v.* Universal B1.)

[14] 'the difference' (*den Unterschied*). Marx uses a sense of 'difference' related to the philosophical term *differentia*, meaning 'a quality, mark, or characteristic, that distinguishes a thing from all others in the same class'. (OED *s.v.* Difference 4c.) He argues that determinations relating to development (in production) are different from those common to all forms of production.

instrument is only the hand. No [production] is possible without past, accumulated labour, even if that labour is only the skill which is gathered and concentrated in the hand of a savage through repeated practice. Capital is, among other things, both an instrument of production and past, objectified labour. Therefore capital is a general, eternal, natural relation; that is, if I omit precisely the specifics which make 'instrument of production', [and] 'accumulated labour' into capital in the first place. Hence the whole history of the relations of production appears with Carey, for example, as a falsification maliciously perpetrated by the government.

If there is no production in general, then there is also no general production. Production is always a *particular* branch of production—e.g. agriculture, husbandry, manufacture etc. —or it is the *totality* of production. However, political economy is not technology. The relation of the general determinations of production at a given stage of society to the particular forms of production is to be developed elsewhere (later). Finally, production is not merely a particular [form of production]. Rather it is always a certain social body, a social subject [*Subjekt*], which is active in a greater or lesser totality of branches of production. Likewise the relation of scientific[15] presentation to real movement does not belong here yet. Production in general. Particular branches of production. Totality of production. [Three meaningful senses of 'production'.]

It is the fashion to preface the [typical work of political] economy with a general section in which the *general conditions* of all production are discussed—and it is precisely that section which figures under the title 'production' (see, for example, J. S. Mill). That general section consists or supposedly consists in: (1) the conditions without which production is not possible.

---

[15] 'scientific' (*wissenschaftlich*). The German *Wissenschaft* has a broader reference than the modern English 'science' and is much less related in the first instance to the natural and physical sciences. (GDW *s.v.* Wissenschaft C.) See n. 5 on p. 5 above.

This is in fact nothing but stating the essential moments[16] of all production. However, this reduces itself in fact, as we shall see, to a few very simple determinations which are drawn out into superficial tautologies; (2) the conditions which more or less advance production, as for example Adam Smith's progressive and stagnant state[s] of society. In order to raise that [conception], which had its value in his work as an *aperçu*, to a more scientific meaning, inquiries would be necessary into the durations of the [different] *degrees of productivity* in the development of a single people—an inquiry which lies outside the proper limits of the subject [modern bourgeois production]; however, so far as it belongs in the subject, it is to be placed with the development of competition, accumulation etc. In the general understanding [of the subject] the answer [which is given to that inquiry] amounts to the generality that an industrial people enjoys the height of its production at the moment at which it occupies its general historical height. In fact, a people is at its industrial height so long as gain is not yet the main thing, but [the process of] gaining. So the Yankees are ahead of the English. Or else [another answer]: that, for example, certain races, dispositions, climates, natural relations, like the position of the sea, the fertility of the earth etc., are more favourable to production than others. [That answer] also amounts to the tautology that wealth is created more easily to the degree that its elements are subjectively and objectively [*subjektiv und objektiv*] present to a higher degree.

However, this is not all that is actually discussed by economists in that general section. Rather, production is supposedly represented—see, for example, J. S. Mill—in distinction from distribution etc., as framed in eternal natural laws independent of history; this is the occasion for passing off, in an underhand way, *bourgeois* relations as irrevocable natural laws of society

---

[16] 'moments' (*Momente*). A 'moment' in this context is 'one of the elements of a complex conceptual entity'; a standard term in mid-nineteenth-century logic. (OED *s.v.* Moment 9.)

in the abstract. This is the more or less conscious purpose of the whole proceeding. With distribution, on the other hand, men are said to have been allowed, in fact, all kinds of arbitrary action. Apart from the crude sundering of production and distribution and their actual relation, it must be made clear at the outset that, however heterogeneous distribution may be at different stages of society, it must be just as possible [with distribution] as well as with production to pick out common determinations and just as possible to confound or extinguish all historical differences in *general human* laws. For example, the slave, the serf, the wage-labourer all retain a ration of food which makes it possible for them to exist as slave, as serf, as wage-labourer. The conqueror who lives by tribute, or the official who lives by taxes, or the landowner who lives by rents, or the monk who lives by alms, or the Levite who lives by tithes, all retain a share of social production, which is determined according to laws other than that [law which determines the ration] of the slaves etc. The two main points which all economists place under that rubric [*Rubrik*] are: (1) property; (2) safeguarding of property by the judiciary, the police etc. Those points can be answered very briefly:

On 1. All production is the appropriation of nature on the part of the individual within and by means of a determinate form of society. In that sense it is a tautology to say that property (appropriation) is a condition of production. However, it is ludicrous to leap from that [tautology] to a determinate form of property, e.g. private property. (What is more, [private property] is an antithetical form which implies as a condition *non-property* as well as [property].) Rather history shows that common property is the original form [of property] (e.g. in India, among the Slavs and ancient Celts etc.), a form which still plays a significant role under the shape of communal property. We have not yet come to the question whether wealth develops better under this or that form of property. However, that there can be no talk of production, hence no talk of society, where no form of property exists, is a tautology.

An appropriation which does not appropriate anything is a contradiction in the thing spoken of.[17]

On 2. Safe-keeping of acquisitions etc. If those trivialities are reduced to their real content, they express more than their preachers realize. Namely, that each form of production produces its own legal relations, form of government etc. The [economists'] crudeness and the mechanical character of their thought lie in haphazardly relating to one another things which belong together organically, [and] in bringing [them] into a simple connection based on reflection.[18] The bourgeois economists have in mind that a modern police force lets us produce better than, for example, the law of the jungle. They simply forget that the law of the jungle is also a law, and that the law of the stronger persists under another form even in their 'Rechtsstaat'.[19]

If the social conditions corresponding to a determinate level of production are just originating, or if they are already disappearing, breakdowns of production naturally occur, although in different degrees and with different effects.

To summarize: there are determinations, common to all stages of production, which are fixed by thinking[20] as universal;

[17] 'a contradiction in the thing spoken of' (contradictio in subjecto). (OLD s.v. subicio, subjectus C.) Another term from Marx's training in logic.

[18] 'A simple connection based on reflection' (ein blosser Reflexionszusammenhang). Marx uses a similar expression (Reflexionsverhältnis) in his unfinished Critique of Hegel's Philosophy of Right (written in 1843): 'A relation of reflection is the highest identity between things which are essentially different'. (MEW i. 277.) He alludes to the discussion of 'reflection' in Hegel (1812), 394–431. The English sense of 'reflection' or 'reflex' here is that of an image which reproduces certain features of something else.

[19] 'A state whose aim is the protection of the rights of all its citizens: the modern Rechtsstaat as opposed to the feudal state of the middle ages and to the police state'. (GDW s.v. Rechtsstaat.) Elsewhere I have translated rechtlichen as 'legal' or 'to do with rights', depending on the context.

[20] 'by thinking' (vom Denken). The context suggests 'thinking' in a philosophical sense as reasoning which establishes connections or relations in logic.

however, the so-called *general conditions* of all production are nothing [other] than those abstract moments, with which no actual historical stage of production is grasped.

(2) THE GENERAL RELATION OF PRODUCTION TO DISTRIBUTION, EXCHANGE, CONSUMPTION

[Commentary, pp. 114–16.]
Before entering into a further analysis of production, it is necessary to consider the different rubrics which the economists set alongside it.

The [economists'] conception is as plain as can be: in production, the members of society appropriate (bring forth, form) natural products to human needs; distribution determines the proportion in which the individual shares in those products; exchange supplies him with the particular products into which he wants to translate the quota coming to him through distribution; finally, in consumption the products[21] become objects [*Gegenstände*] of enjoyment, of individual appropriation. Production brings forth the objects corresponding to needs; distribution divides them according to social laws; exchange again divides, according to the individual need, that which has already been divided; finally, in consumption the product emerges from that social movement, becomes directly the object and servant of the individual need, and satisfies it in enjoyment. Thus production appears as the starting point, consumption as the end-point, distribution and exchange as the middle term, a term which is itself twofold, since distribution is determined as the moment deriving from society, exchange as the moment deriving from individuals. In production, the person is objectified [*objektiviert sich*], [and] in consumption[22]

---

[21] The editors of GR have substituted 'products' for 'production' in the manuscript. (GR 10.)

[22] The editors of MEW xiii suggest emending 'the person' (in the GR text) to read 'consumption'. (MEW xiii. 621.) The argument seems to

the thing is subjectified [*subjektiviert sich*]; in distribution, society in the form of general, dominating determinations takes over the mediation[23] between production and consumption; in exchange, production and consumption are mediated through the contingent determinateness[24] of individuals.

Distribution determines the proportion (the ration) in which products fall to individuals; exchange determines the production[25] in which the individual commands the share assigned to him by distribution.

Production, distribution, exchange, [and] consumption thus form a regular syllogism; production, the universality; distribution and exchange the particularity; consumption, the individuality in which the whole is contained. This is indeed a connection, but a superficial one. Production is [in that view] determined by general natural laws; distribution, by social chance, and distribution can therefore promote production more or less effectively; exchange lies between the two as a formal social movement, and the concluding act of consumption, which is understood not only as ultimate goal, but also as ultimate purpose, lies properly outside [political] economy, except in so far as it reacts back on the starting point and begins the whole operation anew.

be that in economic life, as the political economists conceive it, the person engaged in production becomes an 'object' and in his consumption the product becomes a 'subject', i.e. the production and consumption processes themselves rule economic life.

[23] I have translated *vermitteln* as 'to mediate' in this sense: 'To be the intermediary or medium concerned in bringing about (a result) [e.g.] . . . 1861 Goschen . . . A country which, like England, mediates the transactions of many others'; similarly, *Vermittlung* as 'mediation', *vermittelt* as 'mediated', and *vermittelnd* as 'mediating'. (OED *s.v.* Mediate 5.) See n. 26 on pp. 58–9 below for a related sense of 'immediate'.

[24] That is, through the activities of particular individuals, rather than through a more general social framework of rules and distinctions independent (to some extent) of individual choice or action.

[25] The editors of MEW xiii read 'products' for 'production' in the GR text. (MEW xiii. 621.)

The opponents of the political economists—whether they are opponents inside or outside their circle—who reproach the political economists with the barbarous sundering of something which belongs together, either take the same point of view as the political economists, or an inferior one. Nothing is more familiar than the objection that the political economists consider production too exclusively as an end in itself. They might just as well [according to their opponents] depend on distribution. At the basis of that objection lies the economic conception that distribution dwells next to production as an autonomous, independent sphere. Or [another objection, that] the moments were not understood in their unity [by the political economists]. As if that sundering [e.g. of production and distribution] had not sprung from real life into the textbooks, but on the contrary had sprung from the textbooks into real life, and as if it were a matter of a dialectical equation of concepts and not the apprehension of real relations!

[[*Consumption and Production*]]

[**Commentary, pp. 117–23.**]

(a_1) Production is immediately[26] also consumption. Consumption is twofold, subjective and objective: [Firstly:] the individual, who develops his capabilities in producing, expends them as well; he consumes them in the act of production just as natural reproduction is a consumption of life-forces. Secondly: consumption of the means of production, which are used and worn out and decomposed into the common elements again (as for example in fuel). It is the same with the consumption of raw material, which does not remain in its natural form and condition, rather the natural form and condition is consumed. Hence the act of production is itself in all its moments also an

---

[26] 'immediately' (*unmittelbar*). Since Marx uses *direkt* elsewhere, I use this non-temporal sense of 'immediately': 'Without intermediary, intervening agency, or medium . . . directly'; similarly, *unmittelbar* as an

act of consumption. But the [political] economists admit this. Production as directly identical with consumption, [and] consumption as directly coincident with production, they call *productive consumption*. That identity of production and consumption is tantamount to Spinoza's proposition: determination is negation.

But this determination of productive consumption is only set up in order to segregate the consumption which is identical with production from consumption proper, which is understood rather as the nullifying antithesis of production. Let us consider consumption proper.

Consumption is immediately also production, as in nature the consumption of elements and chemical materials is the production of the plant. For example, it is clear that in nourishment, a form of consumption, man produces his own body. But this is the case with any other type of consumption which in one way or another produces man in some aspect. Consumptive production. However, says [political] economy, that production which is identical with consumption is a second [form of production] arising out of the nullification of the first product. In the first [form of production] the producer materializes himself; in the second [form of production] the thing created by the producer personifies itself [i.e. becomes part of a person]. Therefore this consumptive production—although it is an immediate unity between production and consumption—differs essentially from production proper. The immediate unity, in which production coincides with consumption and consumption with production, lets their immediate duality persist.

Therefore production is immediately consumption, [and] consumption is immediately production. Each is immediately its opposite. At the same time, however, a mediating movement takes place between the two. Production mediates consumption, whose material it creates; without production, consumption

adjective is translated as 'immediate', and *Unmittelbarkeit* as 'immediacy'. (OED *s.v.* Immediately 1.)

lacks an object. However, consumption also mediates production, since it creates first the subject for the products, the subject
for which they are products. The product only receives its last
finish[27] in consumption. A railway on which no one rides,
which is therefore not worn out, which is not consumed, is only
a railway virtually,[28] not a railway in actuality. Without
production there is no consumption; however, without consumption there is no production, since production [without
consumption] would be purposeless. Consumption produces
production in two ways, (1) since only in consumption does the
product become a real product. For example, a dress actually
becomes a dress only in the act of wearing [it]; a house which
is not lived in, is in fact not a real house; therefore [a product],
in distinction from a mere natural object, only proves itself
as a product, only *becomes* a product, in consumption. Consumption, by decomposing the product, only gives it the finishing
stroke, for the product[29] is a product not as a materialized
activity, but only as an object for the active subject; (2) since
consumption creates the need for *new* production, [and] therefore the ideal, inner, impelling reason for production, a reason
which is a presupposition of production. Consumption creates
the impetus to produce; it also creates the object which is
active in production as a purpose-defining object. If it is clear
that production presents the object of consumption externally,
then it is just as clear that consumption *posits* the object of
production *ideally*, as an inner image, as a need, as an impetus,
and as a purpose. It creates the objects of production in a form

[27] Marx uses the English phrase 'last finish'; possibly a reference to tailoring
or cloth manufacture.

[28] 'virtually' (δυνάμει). (GEL *s.v.* δύναμις IV.) In this case 'virtually' is
understood as 'in respect of essence or effect . . . as far as essential
qualities or facts are concerned'. (OED *s.v.* Virtually 1.) The German
dynamisch ('dynamically'), which Marx uses on p. 49 above, is etymo-
logically related to δυνάμει, but quite different in meaning.

[29] Marx uses the English phrase 'finishing stroke'. The editors of MEW
xiii have emended 'production' (in the GR text) to read 'product'.
(MEW xiii. 623.)

which is still subjective. Without need there is no production. But consumption reproduces the need.

There are corresponding points on the side of production: (1) it supplies the material, the object for consumption.[30] Consumption without an object is not consumption; therefore production creates in this respect, [or] produces, consumption. (2) But it is not only the object which production creates for consumption. Production also gives to consumption its determinateness, its character, its finish.[31] Just as consumption gave the product its finish as a product, production gives consumption its finish. *For one thing*, the object is not an object generally but a definite object which must be consumed in a definite way, a way [[to be]] mediated again by production itself. Hunger is hunger, but hunger which is satisfied with cooked meat eaten with knife and fork is a hunger different from that which devours raw meat with the help of hand, nail, and tooth. Hence not only the object of consumption but also the mode of consumption is produced by production, not only objectively but also subjectively. Therefore production creates the consumer. (3) Production not only supplies the need with a material, but also supplies the material with a need. If consumption has emerged from its first natural crudeness and immediacy—and lingering in that [state] would itself be the result of a [mode of] production stuck in [a state of] crudeness—then production as an impetus is itself mediated by the object. The need which consumption feels according to the object is created through the perception of the object. An *objet d'art*—just like any other product—creates a public sensitive to art and capable of enjoying beauty. Hence production produces not only an object for the subject but also a subject for the object. Hence production produces consumption, (1) since production creates the material for consumption, (2) since production determines the mode of consumption, (3) since production produces the products which

---

[30] The editors of GR have substituted 'consumption' for 'production' in the manuscript. (GR 13.)

[31] Marx uses the English word 'finish' here and in the following sentence.

are posited by it first as an object, [then] as a need in the consumer. Hence production produces the object of consumption, the mode of consumption, [and] the impetus of consumption. In the same way consumption produces the *disposition* of the producer, since consumption requires him to determine a need purposefully.

Therefore the identities between consumption and production appear threefold:

(1) *Immediate identity*: production is consumption; consumption is production. Consumptive production. Productive consumption. The political economists call both productive consumption. But they still make a distinction. The first figures as reproduction; the second as productive consumption. All inquiries into the first are inquiries into productive or unproductive labour; inquiries into the second are inquiries into productive or non-productive consumption.

(2) That each appears as a means to the other; each is mediated by the other; [a mediation] which is expressed as their mutual dependence; a [mediating] movement through which they are related to one another and appear mutually indispensable, but still remain external [to each other]. Production creates the material as an external object for consumption; consumption creates the need as an inner object, as the purpose of production. Without production there is no consumption; without consumption there is no production. This figures in [political] economy in many forms.

(3) Production is not only immediately consumption and consumption immediately production; yet production is only a means for consumption and consumption a purpose for production, i.e. that each supplies the object for the other, production externally for consumption, consumption conceptually for production; but each of them is not only immediately the other, each is still only mediating the other—but each of the two creates the other as it is carried out; each is carried out as the other. Consumption only carries out the act of production, since consumption completes the product as product, since

consumption decomposes the product, since consumption consumes the autonomous material form of the product, since consumption, by means of the need for repetition, raises to a skill the disposition developed in the first act of production; consumption is therefore not only the concluding act through which the product becomes a product, but also the act through which the producer becomes a producer. On the other hand, production produces consumption, since it creates the determinate mode of consumption, and further, since it creates the stimulus to consume, [and] the capacity itself to consume, as a need. That last identity, determined under (3), is illustrated many times in [political] economy in the relation of supply and demand, of objects and needs, of needs created by society and natural needs.

After this, nothing is easier for a Hegelian than to posit production and consumption [as] identical. And that has been done not only by socialist *belletristes*,[32] but also by prosaic economists, e.g. [Jean-Baptiste] Say; [it has been done] in the form, that if one considers a people, [then] its production is its consumption. Or even humanity in the abstract. [H.F.] Storch has proved that Say is wrong, since a people, for example, does not purely consume its product, but also creates the means of production etc., fixed capital etc. Besides, to consider society as one subject [*Subjekt*] is to consider it falsely, speculatively. With one subject, production and consumption appear as moments of one act. The important [point] to be emphasized here is that if production and consumption are considered as activities of one subject or of many individuals, they appear, in any case, as moments of a process in which production is the real starting point and of which it is also the transcending moment.[33]

[32] Marx may be thinking of Proudhon, or of the 'true socialist' Karl Grün, whom he criticizes in the *German Ideology* (written 1845-6). See pp. 120-1 below.

[33] 'transcending' (*übergreifende*). The German term, meaning to overlap, encroach, glide, shift, or spread, is related to the Latin *excedens* ('to go beyond a certain boundary or a certain measure'). (GDW *s.v.* übergreifen *passim*. OLD *s.v.* Excedo 1B2.) The OED gives a sense of

F

Consumption as a want, as a need, is itself an inner moment of productive activity. But productive activity is the starting point of realization, and hence also its transcending moment, the act in which the whole process is dispersed again [in its moments, as at the starting point]. The individual produces an object, and through the consumption of the object returns again as himself, but as a productive individual and a self-reproducing individual. Thus consumption appears as a moment of production.

In society, however, the relation of the producer to the product, as soon as the product is finished, is an external relation, and the return of the product to the subject depends on his relationships with other individuals. The product is not immediately obtainable [by the producer]. Also, the immediate appropriation of the product is not its purpose, if the product is produced in society. *Distribution*, which determines through social laws the share of the producer in the world of products, steps between the producer and the product, [and] therefore between production and consumption.

Is distribution an autonomous sphere alongside and outside production?

Distribution and Production.

[Commentary, pp. 123–5.]

(b_1) If one considers the usual [works on political] economy, one must be struck above all by the fact that everything in them is posited twice over. For example, ground rent, wages, interest, and profit figure in distribution while land, labour, [and] capital figure in production as agents of production. With capital it is obvious from the beginning that it is posited twice over, (1) as an agent of production; (2) as a source of income,

'to exceed' as 'to transcend the limits of'. (*s.v.* Exceed 1.) The argument seems to be that production and consumption are both moments (elements) of a process which is essentially a process of production, *ergo* production 'transcends' all other aspects. See pp. 123, 127 below.

as determining the determinate forms of distribution. Hence interest and profit also figure as such in production, in so far as they are forms in which capital augments itself, increases, [and] therefore they are moments of the production itself of capital. Interest and profit, as forms of distribution, imply capital as an agent of production. They are modes of distribution which have, for their presupposition, capital as an agent of production. In the same way, they are modes of reproduction of capital.

In the same way, wages are wage-labour considered under another rubric: the determinateness which labour has here as an agent of production appears as a determination of distribution. If labour were not determined as wage-labour, then the way in which it shares in the products would not appear as wages, as, for example, in slavery. Finally—to take the most developed form of distribution in which landed property shares in the products—ground rent implies large-scale landed property (properly, large-scale agriculture) as an agent of production. [Ground rent does] not [imply] simple earth, as little as the salary [implies] simple labour. Hence the relations and modes of distribution appear only as reverse sides of the agents of production. An individual who shares in production in the form of wage-labour shares in the products (the results of production) in the form of wages. The arrangement[34] of distribution is completely determined by the arrangement of production. Distribution is itself a product of production, not only with respect to the object, [i.e.] that only the results of production can be distributed, but also with respect to the

[34] I have chosen 'arrangement', rather than 'structure', as a translation of *Gliederung*, in order to avoid begging any question of how distinct or developed an entity Marx had in mind. On p. 84 below he uses *Knochenbau* ('bone-structure'), in a letter to Lassalle of 31 May 1858 (MEW xxix. 561) he uses the phrase *der . . . innere Bau* ('inner structure') and in the *Preface* (1859) to *A Contribution to the Critique of Political Economy* (MEW xiii. 8) he writes of *die ökonomische Struktur* ('economic structure'), so he may have drawn a distinction between *Gliederung* and *Bau* or *Struktur*.

form, [i.e.] that the determinate way of sharing in production determines the particular forms of distribution, the form in which sharing takes place in distribution. It is an out and out illusion to posit earth in production, ground rent in distribution etc.

Economists like Ricardo, who are mostly reproached with considering only production, have determined distribution as the exclusive subject of [political] economy because they instinctively understand the forms of distribution as the most determinate expression in which the agents of production are fixed in a given society.

Distribution naturally appears opposed to the single individual as a social law which conditions his place within production, the place within which he produces, the place which therefore precedes production. The individual has from the start no capital, no landed property. He is assigned from birth to wage-labour through social distribution. But that assignment itself is the result [of the fact] that capital [and] landed property exist as autonomous agents of production.

If whole societies are considered, distribution appears in still another respect to precede production and to determine it; distribution appears, so to speak, as a pre-economic fact. A conquering people divides the land among the conquerors and thus imposes a determinate division and form of landed property; hence [it appears that] the conquering people determines production. Or the conquerors make the conquered into slaves and thus make slavery into the basis of production. Or a people, by means of revolution, breaks up large-scale landed property into parcels; therefore [a revolutionary people] gives production a new character through that new distribution. Or legislation perpetuates landed property in certain families, or divides labour [[as]] hereditary privilege and thus fixes labour into a caste-system. In all those cases, and they are all historical, distribution appears to be arranged and determined not by production, but, on the contrary, production appears to be arranged and determined by distribution.

Distribution, in the most superficial view, appears as the distribution of products, and thus further removed from production and quasi-autonomous against it. But before distribution is the distribution of products it is: (1) the distribution of instruments of production, and (2) (which is a further determination of the same relation) the distribution of members of society among the different types of production. (Subsumption of individuals under determinate relations of production.) The distribution of products is obviously only the result of that distribution which is comprised within the production process itself, and which determines the arrangement of production. To consider production apart from the distribution included in it is obviously empty abstraction, while on the contrary the distribution of the product is [already] given, [in and] of itself, with that distribution which originally forms a moment of production. Ricardo, whose object was to apprehend modern production in its determinate social arrangement, and who is the economist of production *par excellence*, accordingly does *not* declare production to be the proper subject of modern [political] economy, but distribution. The absurdity of the economists who develop production as an eternal truth, while they banish history to the realm of distribution, is another consequence [of declaring distribution to be the proper subject of modern political economy].

What relation this distribution, which determines production itself, bears to production, is obviously a question which falls within [the sphere of] production itself. If it should be said that at least distribution, in that meaning of distribution, precedes production [and] forms its presupposition, since production must proceed from a certain distribution of the instruments of production—then it can be answered that production in fact has its conditions and presuppositions which form its moments. Those may, in the beginning, appear as spontaneous. Through the process of production itself they are transformed from spontaneous into historical [conditions and presuppositions], and if they appear as a natural presupposition of production for one period they are, for another period, the historical result of production. They are continuously altered within production itself. For example, the employment of machinery altered the distribution of instruments of production as well as the distribution of products. Modern large-scale landed property itself is the result of modern trade and modern industry as well as the result of the employment of industry on agriculture.

The questions posed above resolve themselves in the last instance into questions [of] how general historical relations play a part in production and questions [of] the relation of production to historical movement generally. Obviously the question belongs in the discussion and development of production itself.

Nevertheless in the trivial form in which the questions have been posed above, they can likewise be briefly dispatched. With all conquests there are three different possibilities. The conquering people subjects the conquered to its own mode of production (e.g. the English in Ireland in this century, [and] to some extent in India); or the conquering people lets the old mode of production persist and satisfies itself with tribute (e.g. the Turks and Romans); or there arises a reciprocal effect through which something new originates, a synthesis (to some extent [this was the case] in the Germanic conquests). In all cases the mode of production, whether that of the conquering people, whether that of the conquered, whether that proceeding from the merger of the two, is determining for the new distribution which arises. Although that [distribution] appears as a presupposition for the new period of production, it is itself a product of production, not only of historical production in general, but of determinate historical production.

The Mongols, with their ravages in Russia, for example, acted in accordance with their [mode of] production, with pasturage, for which uninhabited stretches [of land] are a main condition. The German barbarians, for whom cultivation of the land with serfs was the traditional [mode of] production and [for whom there was an] isolated life on the land, could subject the Roman provinces more easily to those conditions, since the concentration of landed property which had taken place there had already completely overthrown the older agricultural relations.

It is a well-established conception that in certain periods people lived only by stealing. But in order to be able to steal, there must be something there to be stolen; therefore there was production. And the type of stealing is itself determined by the type of production. A stock-jobbing nation, for example, cannot be robbed [in the same way] as a nation of cowherds.

In the slave the instrument of production is stolen directly. But then production in the country for which the slave is stolen must be so arranged as to permit slave-labour, or (as in South America etc.)[35] a mode of production corresponding to the slave must be created.

Laws can perpetuate an instrument of production, e.g. land, in certain families. Those laws only receive an economic meaning if large-scale landed property is in harmony with social production, as for example in England. In France small-scale agriculture was carried on in spite of large-scale landed property, hence large-scale landed property was broken up by the revolution. But the perpetuation of the parceling out [of land] by laws, for example? In spite of those laws, property again concentrates itself. The influence of laws towards retention of the relations of distribution, and thereby their effect on production, is to be determined in particular cases.

(c₁) EXCHANGE, FINALLY, AND CIRCULATION

Exchange and Production.

[Commentary, pp. 126–9.]
Circulation itself is only a determinate moment of exchange or of exchange considered in its totality.

[35] The editors of GR suggest that Marx has the southern states of the USA in mind, as well as the continent of South America. (GR 984.)

Thus far *exchange* is only a mediating moment between production and the distribution (with consumption) which is determined by production; however, in so far as consumption itself appears as a moment of production, exchange is obviously also comprised in consumption as a moment.

Firstly, it is clear that the exchange of activities and capabilities, which takes place in production itself, belongs directly to production and constitutes it essentially. Secondly, the same applies to the exchange of products as far as exchange is a means for the preparation of the finished product, for the immediate consumption of a determinate product. Thus far exchange itself is an act comprised in production. Thirdly, the so-called exchange between dealers and dealers,[36] both with respect to its organization and as a producing activity itself, is wholly determined by production. Only in its last stage does exchange appear independent alongside, indifferent towards production, the stage where the product is immediately exchanged for consumption. However, (1) there is no exchange without division of labour, whether the division of labour is spontaneous or is itself already an historical result; (2) private exchange presupposes private production; (3) the intensiveness of exchange, like its extension, like its type,[37] is determined by the development and arrangement of production. For example, exchange between town and country, exchange in the country, in the town etc. Thus exchange appears in all its moments either directly comprised in production or determined by it.

The result which we have reached is not that production, distribution, exchange, [and] consumption are identical, but

---

[36] Marx uses an English phrase 'dealers and dealers'. See p. 126 below.

[37] 'intensiveness . . . extension . . . type' (*Intensivität . . . Extension . . . Art*). The OED relates 'intensiveness' to 'intensive' and the latter to 'intension' in its philosophical sense as 'the number of qualities connoted by a term'. (*s.v.* Intensive 3; Intension 5.) 'Extension' is defined as 'of a term or concept: Its range as measured by the number of objects which it denotes or contains under it'. (OED *s.v.* Extension 8b.) Marx argues that exchange, however conceived or practised, is determined by production.

that they all form members of a totality, differences within a unity. Production transcends not only over [sic] itself in the antithetical determination of production [i.e. consumptive production] but also over [sic] the other moments [i.e. distribution, exchange, and consumption]. The process always begins anew from production. It is clear [in and] of itself that exchange and consumption cannot be the transcending [moment]. In the same way [this is true] of distribution as the distribution of products. As distribution of the agents of production, however, distribution is itself a moment of production. Therefore a determinate [form of] production determines a determinate [form of] consumption, distribution, exchange, and the *determinate relations of those different moments to one another*. Of course, production *in its one-sided form*[38] is also determined for its part by the other moments. For example, if the market, i.e. the sphere of exchange, expands, [then] production grows in extent and is more thoroughly compartmentalized. Production varies with variations in distribution; for example, with the concentration of capital, with a different distribution of population in town and country etc. Finally, the needs of consumption determine production. A reciprocal effect takes place between the different moments. This is the case with any organic whole.

(3) THE METHOD OF POLITICAL ECONOMY

[Commentary, pp. 129–53.]
If we consider a given country in the manner of political economy, then we begin with its population, division of the population into classes, town, country, sea, different branches of production, export and import, yearly production and consumption, commodity prices etc.

---

[38] 'one-sided' (*einseitig*). 'Relating to, considering, or dealing with only one side of a question or subject; partial'. (OED *s.v.* One-sided 1.) See pp. 127–8 below.

It appears to be correct to begin with the real and concrete, the actual presupposition, therefore, e.g. in [political] economy, with the population, which is the basis and the subject [*Subjekt*] of the whole social act of production. Nevertheless this is shown, upon closer consideration, to be false. Population is an abstraction, if I omit the classes, for example, of which it consists. Those classes are an empty word if I do not know the elements on which they are based. For example, wage-labour, capital etc. These imply exchange, division of labour, prices etc. Capital, for example, is nothing without wage-labour, without value, money, price etc. Therefore if I begin with population, then that would be a chaotic conception of the whole, and through closer determination I would come analytically to increasingly simpler concepts; from the conceptualized concrete to more and more tenuous abstractions, until I arrived at the simplest determinations. From there the journey would be taken up again in reverse until I finally arrived again at population, this time, however, not [with population] as a chaotic conception of a whole, but as a rich totality of many determinations and relationships. The first way [of proceeding] is one which [political] economy has taken up historically in its formation. The economists of the seventeenth century, for example, always began with the living whole, the population, the nation, the state, more states etc.; they always end, however, in such a way that they discover a few determining, abstract, universal relationships, like division of labour, money, value etc., through analysis. As soon as those individual moments were more or less fixed and abstracted, the economic systems which ascend from the simple [moment], such as labour, division of labour, need, [and] exchange-value, up to the state, exchange among nations and the world market, began [to be formulated]. The latter is obviously the scientifically correct method. The concrete is concrete, because it is the sum of many determinations, [and] therefore a unity of diversity. Hence the concrete appears in thinking as a process of summarization, as a result, not as a starting point, although the concrete is the actual starting point and hence also the starting point of perception and conceptualization. In the first way [of proceeding] the full conception was broken down to the abstract determination; in the second way [of proceeding] the abstract determinations lead to the reproduction of the concrete by means of thinking. Hence Hegel falls into the illusion of understanding the real as the result of self-summarizing, self-engrossing, self-motivating thinking, whereas the method of ascending from the abstract to the concrete is merely the way for thinking to appropriate the concrete, to reproduce it as a mental concrete. However, this is in no way the process of origination of the concrete itself. For example, the simplest economic category, say for example exchange-value, implies population, population producing in determinate relations; also, exchange-value implies certain sorts of familial or communal or political existence etc. Exchange-value can never exist as an abstract, one-sided relationship outside a given, concrete, living whole. On the other hand, exchange-value as a category leads an antediluvian existence. Hence for consciousness—and philosophical consciousness is determined in this [following] way—for philosophical consciousness conceptual thinking is the actual man and hence the conceived world as such is the only actuality—hence the movement of categories appears as the actual act of production (which alas keeps merely an initial impulse from outside), the result of which is the world; and this—however, this is again a tautology—is correct so far as the concrete totality as a thought-totality, as a concrete thought-object, is in fact a product of thinking, of conceiving; however, the concrete totality is in no way a product of the self-delivering [*sich selbst gebärenden*] concept, of the concept thinking outside or above perception and conception, but of the working up of perception and conception into concepts. The whole, as it appears in the head as a thought-whole, is a product of the thinking head which appropriates the world in the only mode possible for it, a mode which is different from the artistic, religious, [and] practical-mental appropriation of that world. The real subject [*Subjekt*], after as before, remains outside the head in autonomous existence; while [on the other hand] the head acts, as we say, only speculatively, only theoretically. Hence with the theoretical method the subject [*Subjekt*], society, must always be borne in mind as the presupposition of [any] conception.

However, do these simple categories not have an independent historical or natural existence before the more concrete categories? That depends. For example, Hegel begins the *Philosophy of Right* correctly with possession as the subject's simplest relationship to do with rights. However, possession does not exist before the family or before relations of domination and servitude, which are much more concrete relations. On the other hand, it would be correct to say that families, [and] whole tribes exist which only just *possess*, [but] do not have *property*. The simpler category [possession] appears, therefore, as a relation of simple familial or tribal association in regard to property. In the higher [forms of] society the simpler category [possession] appears as the simpler relation of a developed organization [e.g. bourgeois society]. The concrete substratum, whose relationship [to man] is possession, is however always presupposed. One can conceive of an individual savage possessing [things]. However, possession is then not a relation of right. It is not correct [to say that] possession is developed historically into the family. Rather possession always implies that more 'concrete category of right' [the family]. Nevertheless it always remains the case that the simple categories [e.g. possession] are expressions of relations in which the less developed concrete [i.e. familial or tribal association] may have been realized, without the many-sided relationship or relation [property rights] which is mentally expressed in the more concrete category [property] having been posited; while the more developed concrete [e.g. bourgeois society] retains that same category [possession] as a subordinate relation. Money can exist, and it has existed historically, before capital existed, before banks existed, before wage-labour existed etc. In that respect it can be said that the simpler category [money] can express the dominating relations of a less developed whole [a pre-bourgeois society] or the subordinate relations of a more developed whole [bourgeois society], relations which already had an historical existence before the whole [i.e. society] was developed according to that side which is expressed in a more concrete category [capital, wage-labour etc.]. Thus far the path of abstract thinking, which ascends from that which is simplest towards that which has been combined, corresponds to the actual historical process.

In another respect it can be said that there are very developed but still historically less mature forms of society in which the highest forms of economy, e.g. co-operation, developed division of labour etc., have a place, without the existence of any kind of money, e.g. Peru. As in the Slavic commune, money (and the exchange conditioning it) does not emerge, or does so [very] little, inside the individual commune, but does emerge at its boundaries in commerce with others, so it is then generally false to posit exchange in the midst of the commune as the original constituting element. Rather exchange, to begin with, emerges earlier in the relationship of different communes to one another than for members within one and the same commune. Further: although money plays a role very early, and plays it all-sidedly [*allseitig*], it is assigned in antiquity only one-sidedly to determinate nations, trading nations. And in the most advanced [period of] antiquity itself, with the Greeks and Romans, the complete development of money, which is pre-supposed in modern bourgeois society, appears only in the period of their dissolution. Therefore that wholly simple category does not appear historically in its intensiveness as it appears in the most developed states of society. By no means [is that simple category] wading [*durchwadend*] through all economic relations. For example, in the Roman empire at its greatest development the [economic] basis stayed taxes and payments in kind. The existence of money [in the] proper [sense of the term] was only completely developed there in the army. Also, money never got a grip on the whole of labour. Thus, although the simpler category [money] may have existed historically before the more concrete category [e.g. capital], it [money] can belong in its complete intensive and extensive development to a combined form of society [e.g. bourgeois society], while [on the other hand] the more concrete category [co-operation] was more completely developed in a less developed form of society [e.g. Peru, the Slavic commune].

Labour appears to be a quite simple category. Also, the conception of it in that universality—as labour generally—is very old. Nevertheless, understood economically in that simple way, 'labour' is a modern category in the same way as the relations which produce that simple abstraction. The monetary system, for example, still posits wealth quite objectively as a thing outside itself in money. It was a great advance against that standpoint [i.e. the doctrines of the monetary system] when the manufacturing or commercial system put the source of wealth out of the object into the subjective activity—commercial and manufacturing labour—but that activity itself was always simply viewed in a limited way as money-making. Opposed to that system is the physiocratic system, which posits a determinate form of labour—agriculture—as that which creates wealth, and posits the object itself no longer in the guise of money, but as the product generally, as the universal result of labour. That product is still [posited], in conformity with the limitation on the activity, as a naturally determined product—an agricultural product, an earth-product *par excellence*.

It was a prodigious advance of Adam Smith to throw away any determinateness in wealth-producing activity—[he conceived of wealth-producing activity as] labour in itself, neither manufacturing, nor commercial, nor agricultural labour, but the one as well as the other. With the abstract generality of wealth-creating activity there is also the generality of the object determined as wealth, as the product generally or, again, labour generally, but as past, objectified labour. How immense and difficult that transition was, emerges from the fact that Adam Smith himself still lapses from time to time into the physiocratic system. It might appear thereby as if only the abstract expression for the simplest and oldest relationship has been discovered, the relationship in which men—in whatever form of society—emerge as producing. This is correct in one way, [but] not in another. The indifference[39] towards a determinate form of labour presupposes a very developed totality of actual types of labour, of which one is no longer dominating [over] the others. Thus the most general abstractions generally develop only with the richest concrete development, where one [moment] appears common to many, common to all. Then one ceases to be able to think only [in terms] of a particular form. On the other hand, this abstraction of labour generally is not merely the mental result of [abstracting from] a concrete totality of labours. The indifference towards the determinate type of labour corresponds to a form of society in which individuals transfer with ease from one type of labour into another and the determinate type of labour is contingent to them, hence indifferent. Here labour has become not only in the category but in actuality a means to the creation of wealth generally and has ceased being attached to individuals as a determination in a particular situation. Such a condition is at its highest development in the most modern form of existence of bourgeois society—the United States. Therefore the abstraction [consisting] of the category 'labour', 'labour generally', labour *sans phrase*, the starting point of modern economy, only here becomes truly practical. Therefore the simplest abstraction, which modern economy puts at its head and which expresses a very old relationship, a relationship

[39] 'indifference' (*Gleichgültigkeit*). The term has a philosophical sense, which might apply here, as 'want of difference in nature or character; substantial equality or equivalence'. (OED *s.v.* Indifference 5.) It also figures in Hegel's *Logic*: 'Being is the abstract equivalence [*Gleichgültigkeit*]—for which . . . the expression indifference [*Indifferenz*] has been employed'. (Hegel (1812), 375.) Thus this passage might be read as 'The abstract equivalence of determinate forms of labour presupposes . . . .'

valid for all forms of society, appears truly practical in that [degree of] abstraction only as a category of the most modern society. One could say [that] that which appears in the United States as an historical product—that indifference towards the determinate [form of] labour—appears, for example, with the Russians, as a spontaneous disposition. However, there is at the same time the enormous difference whether barbarians have the disposition to be assigned to everything, or whether civilized men assign themselves to everything. And then with the Russians the traditional doggedness in a completely determinate [form of] labour—from which they can be shaken only by an outside influence—corresponds practically to that indifference towards the determinateness of labour.

That example of labour shows strikingly how the most abstract categories themselves are, in the determinateness of that abstraction itself—in spite of their validity for all epochs —their validity just on account of being abstractions—just as much the product of historical relations, and how they possess their full validity only for and within those relations.

Bourgeois society is the most developed and most diverse historical organization of production. The categories which express its relations [and] an insight into its arrangement, allow at the same time an insight into the arrangement of production and the relations of production of all extinct forms of society with whose fragments and elements bourgeois society is constructed, whose remains, still not yet entirely obsolete, persist in bourgeois society, [and what were] mere indications [in extinct forms of society] have been developed to a specialized significance. In the anatomy of man there is a key to the anatomy of the ape. The indications of the higher types in the extinct types of animal life, on the other hand, can only be understood if the higher type itself is already well known. Thus bourgeois economy offers the key to [the economy of] antiquity. However, by no means [is this revealed] by the approach of economists who obliterate all historical differences and see in all forms of society the bourgeois forms. One can understand tribute, tithes etc., if one is acquainted with ground rent. However, one must not identify them [with each other]. Furthermore, since bourgeois society itself is only an antithetical form of development, relations of earlier forms will often be found in it only in a completely stunted form, or quite travestied. For example, communal property. Hence, if it is true that the categories of bourgeois economy possess a truth for all other forms of society, then it is to be taken with a grain of salt. They [the categories of bourgeois economy] could contain the same [categories] developed, stunted, caricatured etc., always in [some] essential difference. So-called historical development is generally based on [the fact] that the last form considers the past as stages [in the development] of itself, and, since the last form is seldom capable of criticizing itself, and [then] only under wholly determinate conditions, it always views itself one-sidedly—we are here naturally not discussing those historical periods which present themselves as a time of decay. The Christian religion was only capable of starting on the objective understanding of earlier mythologies as soon as its self-criticism was at a certain stage of completion, [as soon as it was there] virtually, so to speak. Thus bourgeois economy only came to an understanding of feudal, ancient, [and] oriental society as soon as the self-criticism of bourgeois society had begun. So far as bourgeois economy is not purely mythologizing itself, it identifies with the past; its critique resembles earlier critiques, namely the feudal critique with which it had to battle directly, [or] the critique which Christianity practised on paganism, or the critique by Protestantism of Catholicism.

As with any historical social science generally, one must always bear in mind with the progress of economic categories that, as in actuality, so in the head, the subject [*Subjekt*), [which] is here modern bourgeois society, is given, and that the categories express forms of being, determinations of existence, often only single sides of that determinate society, of

G

that subject, and hence that it [social science] does not *really* begin *scientifically* where it is first talked about *as such*. This is to be borne in mind because there is something decisive [*Entscheidendes*] over the disposition [of categories]. For example, nothing appears more in accord with nature than to begin with ground rent, with landed property, since it is bound up with the earth, the source of all production and all existence, and with the first form of production of all societies which are established to some extent—agriculture. However, nothing would be more false. In all forms of society there is a determinate [form of] production which directs all the others, and whose relations therefore direct all the other relations, [and their] position and influence. There is a general illumination in which all other colours are submerged and [[which]] modifies them in their particularity. There is a particular ether which determines the specific gravity of everything in it.[40] For example, with herdsmen (peoples who merely hunt and fish lie outside the point where actual development begins). With them a certain form of cultivation of the earth comes to the fore, a sporadic form. Landed property is thereby determined. It is common [property] and that form is retained more or less as those people more or less cling to their tradition, e.g. the communal property of the Slavs. With peoples [who have reached the stage] of settled cultivation of the land—that settling is already an important step—where that form predominates, as in antiquity and the feudal [epoch], industry itself (and its organization and the forms of property which

[40] During the eighteenth and nineteenth centuries experiments and calculations were undertaken to determine the properties of the 'ether': 'a substance of great elasticity and subtilty, believed to permeate the whole of planetary and stellar space, not only filling the interplanetary spaces, but also the interstices between the particles of air and other matter on earth . . . [e.g.] Perrault represents it as 7200 times more rare than air; and Hook makes it more dense than gold itself'. Specific gravity is the ratio between the density of a substance and the density of some other substance (e.g. air, water, or, in principle, ether) taken as a standard. (OED *s.v.* Ether 5; Gravity 4c.)

correspond to it) has more or less the character of landed property; industry is either wholly dependent on landed property, as with the ancient Romans, or, as in the middle ages, industry, in the town and according to its relations, imitates the country. So far as it is not pure money capital, capital itself in the middle ages, as the traditional tool etc., has that character of landed property. In bourgeois society this is reversed. Agriculture becomes more and more a simple branch of industry and is wholly dominated by capital. It is the same with ground rent. In all forms in which ground rent dominates, the natural relationship is still predominating. In those [forms] where capital dominates, the socially-, historically-created element [predominates]. Ground rent cannot be understood without capital. However, capital [can] indeed [be understood] without ground rent. Capital is the economic power of bourgeois society, the power ruling over everything. It must form the starting point as [well as] the terminal point and must be developed before landed property. After both are considered particularly, their reciprocal relationship must be considered.

Therefore it would be impracticable and false to let the economic categories succeed one another in the sequence in which they were the determining categories historically. Rather, their order of succession is determined by the relationship which they have to one another in modern bourgeois society, and that relationship is exactly the reverse of that which appears as their succession in accordance with nature or that which corresponds to the order of their historical development. We are not dealing with the relation [to each other] which the economic relations take up in the sequence of different forms of society. Still less [are we dealing with] their order of succession 'in the idea' (*Proudhon*), (a hallucinatory conception of historical movement). Rather [we are dealing] with their arrangement within modern bourgeois society.

The purity (abstract determinateness), in which the trading peoples—Phoenicians, Carthaginians—appear in the ancient world, is given through the predominance of the agricultural peoples themselves. Where capital is not yet the ruling element of society, capital as trading or money capital appears in that very abstraction. Lombards [and] Jews take the same place in opposition to the agricultural societies of the middle ages.

As a further example of the different place which the same categories take in different stages of society: one of the last forms of bourgeois society: *joint-stock companies*. However, they also appear in the beginning of bourgeois society in the great privileged trading companies, which were provided with monopolies.

The concept of national wealth itself creeps in with the economists of the seventeenth century—a conception which continues to some extent in the economists of the eighteenth century—that wealth is created merely for the state, but [at the same time] the power of the state stands in proportion to that wealth. It was this still unconsciously hypocritical form in which wealth itself, and the production of it, was proclaimed as the purpose of the modern state, and the modern state is considered [in this view] only as a means to the production of wealth.

Thus the disposition to be made is obviously, (1) the general abstract determinations which more or less belong to all forms of society, but in the sense elucidated above. (2) The categories which constitute the inner arrangement of bourgeois society and on which the fundamental classes are based. Capital, wage-labour, landed property. Their relationship to one another. Town and country. The three great social classes. Exchange between them. Circulation. Credit in general (private). (3) Summary of bourgeois society in the form of the state. [The state] considered in relationship to itself. The 'unproductive' classes. Taxes. National debt. Public credit. Population. Colonies. Emigration. (4) International relation of production. International division of labour. International exchange. Export and import. Rate of exchange. (5) The world market and crises.

(4) PRODUCTION, MEANS OF PRODUCTION AND
RELATIONS OF PRODUCTION. RELATIONS OF
PRODUCTION AND RELATIONS OF COMMERCE.
FORMS OF THE STATE AND FORMS OF
CONSCIOUSNESS IN RELATION TO THE
RELATIONS OF PRODUCTION AND COMMERCE.
LEGAL RELATIONS. FAMILY RELATIONS.

[Commentary, pp. 153–6.]
N.B. in regard to points which are to be mentioned here and
must not be forgotten:

(1) *War* is specialized in the past, like peace; [that is the]
way, as through war and in the army etc., [that] certain
economic relations, like wage-labour, machinery etc., are
developed earlier than in the interior of bourgeois society. Also
the relation of productive force and the relations of commerce
are particularly clear in the army.

(2) *Relation of historiography, hitherto ideal, to real historiography.
Namely* [the relation] *of so-called cultural history,* which [includes]
all history of religion and political history, [to real historio-
graphy]. (On this occasion something can also be said about
the different types of historiography up to now. The so-called
objective [type]. The subjective [type]. (The moral [type],
among others). The philosophical [type].)

(3) *Secondary* [relation] *and tertiary* [relation], generally
derivative, transmitted, relations of production, which are not
original. Here relations play a role internationally.

(4) *Objections concerning the materialism of that view. Relation
to naturalistic materialism.*

(5) *Dialectic of the concept productive force (means of production)
and relations of production,* a dialectic whose limits are to be
determined and which does not abolish[41] the real difference.

---

[41] 'abolish' (*aufhebt*). *Aufheben* may mean to preserve, abolish, or raise, or
a number of those connotations simultaneously. In this case, the context
suggests that only 'abolish' is intended.

(6) *The unequal relation of the development of material production, for example, to artistic production.* Generally the concept of progress is not to be understood in its familiar abstraction. Modern art etc. That disproportion is still not so important and difficult to understand as a disproportion within practical-social relations themselves. For example, education. The relation of the *United States* to Europe. But the really difficult point to be examined here is how the relations of production enter as legal relations into unequal development. Therefore, for example, the relation of Roman civil law (in criminal law and public law it is less the case) to modern production.

(7) *This view appears as* [a view of] *necessary development.* However, justification of the contingent [as opposed to the necessary]. How [to do this?] (Freedom, among other [subjects], also.) (Operation of the means of communication. World history did not always exist; history as world history is a result.)

(8) *The starting point is naturally that of natural determinateness;* subjectively and objectively. Tribes, races etc.

(1) It is known in the case of art that determinate times of artistic flowering by no means stand in a proportional relation to the general development of society, therefore [they do not stand in a proportional relation] to the general development of the material basis, to the general development, as it were, of the bone-structure of its organization. For example, the Greeks compared with the moderns or Shakespeare. It is recognized of certain forms of art, e.g. the epic, that they can never be produced in their epoch-making classical form as soon as there arises the production of art as such; therefore [it is the case] that within the compass of art itself certain meaningful forms of it are only possible at an undeveloped stage of artistic development. If this is the case in the relation of the different types of art within the realm of art itself, [then] it is already less striking that it is the case in the relation of the whole realm of art to the general development of society. The difficulty consists only in the general understanding of those contradictions. As soon as they have been specified, they are already clarified.

Let us take, for example, the relation of Greek art and then Shakespeare's art to the present. It is known that Greek mythology is not only the arsenal of Greek art but [also] its ground. Is the perception of nature and of social relations which lies at the basis of the Greek imagination, and hence of Greek [[mythology]], possible with self-actors[42] and trains and locomotives and electrical telegraphs? What has become of Vulcan against Roberts and Co.,[43] Jupiter against the lightning conductor, and Hermes against the *Crédit mobilier*?[44] All mythology controls and rules and forms the powers of nature in the imagination and through the imagination; therefore mythology disappears with actual domination over natural powers. What has become of Fama beside Printing House Square?[45] Greek art presupposes Greek mythology, that is, nature and social forms themselves are already worked up in an unconsciously artistic mode by the folk imagination. That is its material. Not just any mythology, that is, not just any unconsciously artistic working-up of nature (here under nature everything has the character of a subject [for mythology],

[42] 'A self-acting mule in a spinning-machine'. A 'mule' was 'a kind of spinning machine invented by S. Crompton (*died* 1827)'. (OED *s.v.* Self-actor; Mule 4a.) For an account of Crompton's life and his invention, see Evan Leigh, *Science of modern Cotton Spinning* (2nd edn.; Manchester, 1873), ii. 236–8.

[43] Richard Roberts was the inventor of the self-acting mule with 'quadrant winding motion', patented in 1830. Evan Leigh writes that 'he carried on business at the Globe Works [Manchester] under the title of Richard Roberts and Co.' (Leigh, ii. 242–4.)

[44] *Crédit mobilier*. A finance institution, giving (in theory) loans on movable estate, which had its origin 'in the joint-stock speculation and sanguine promotion of public works which marked many years of the second empire in France . . . the system of business pursued had the result of mixing the credit banks very closely with the various companies and undertakings they were promoting . . . The rates of dividend and the value of the shares consequently fell as rapidly as they had risen.' (*Encyclopaedia Britannica*, vi (Edinburgh, 1877), 557–8.) In May–September 1857 Marx wrote several articles on the *Crédit mobilier* and the French financial crisis. (MEW xii. 202–9, 222–5, 234–7, 289–92.)

[45] London offices of *The Times*; now at New Printing House Square.

hence society is included [among the subjects for mythology]).[46]
Egyptian mythology could never be the seed bed or the womb
of Greek art. However, in any case there must be *a* mythology.
Therefore in no case is there a development of society which
excludes all mythological relation to nature, all mythologizing
relation to nature, all mythologizing relation to social development; therefore in no case is there a development of society
which demands of the artist an imagination independent of
mythology.

From another side: is Achilles possible with powder and
shot? Or, generally, the *Iliad* with the printing press, and,
specifically, with the printing machine? Do not singing and
recitation and the muse cease being necessary with the press-
bar,[47] therefore do not the necessary conditions of epic poetry
disappear?

However, the difficulty does not lie in understanding that
Greek art and epic are tied up with a certain social form of
development. The difficulty is that they still give us artistic
enjoyment and serve in a certain relationship as the norm and
unreachable standard.

A man cannot become a child again, or he becomes childish.
But does not the naïveté of a child delight him, and must he
not himself strive to reproduce its truth again at a higher level?
Does not the character of every epoch revive true to its nature
in the nature of the child? Why should not the historical child-
hood of mankind, where mankind is displayed at its most
beautiful, exercise an eternal charm as a never-recurring stage?
There are naughty children and precocious children. Many of

---

[46] 'has the character of a subject [for mythology]' (*hier darunter alles
Gegenständliche*). This passage might be read as 'everything objective (or
concrete) is under nature, therefore society is included'. However,
elsewhere in this text, Marx uses *Gegenstand* to mean a subject or object
of study, but *subjektiv* and *objektiv* for 'subjective' and 'objective' and
konkret and *abstrakt* for 'concrete' and 'abstract'. See pp. 155–6 below.

[47] Marx may be referring to the Earl of Stanhope's introduction (in 1800)
of a lever-and-screw mechanism to mechanical printing. See Colin
Clair, *History of Printing in Britain* (London, 1965), 210.

the ancient peoples belong in that category. The Greeks were normal children. The charm of their art for us is not in contradiction with the undeveloped stage of society on which it grew. Rather, [the charm] is the result of the art and is inseparably connected with the fact that the immature social conditions under which it originated, and alone could originate, can never recur.

A
COMMENTARY
on Marx's
Introduction (1857) to the *Grundrisse*.

In his *Introduction* (1857) Marx undertakes a critique of various political economists and philosophers, and other writers who were, in his view, their predecessors. His critique is complex and difficult to follow, since he is apt to attack, in quick succession, several different writers and their various critics in order to make quite different points, without quoting the passages to which he objects. Also, he does not limit himself to criticism, but investigates the questions which interest him, and then develops his own point of view—a characteristically Marxian procedure.

A further difficulty with the text is that his critique shows a rapid drift away from simple factual disagreements with the political economists (and their critics and predecessors) towards an attack on their methodologies—their assumptions, presuppositions, purposes, and procedures. Indeed, the *method* of political economy emerges as a subject on its own in part (3) of the *Introduction* (1857), in which Marx is concerned not simply with what the political economists have said that is, in his view, incorrect, incomplete, or misleading, but with how and why they came to write as they did, and how the subject, and its critique, ought to be presented.

(1) PRODUCTION IN GENERAL

Autonomous Individuals. Eighteenth-Century Ideas.

The first long paragraph of Marx's *Introduction* (1857)—the paragraph which follows his declaration that the subject, 'to begin with', is *material production*—is an excellent example of the compressed, critical character of his thought in this text, and it demonstrates his concern to start his own critical discussion in the right place, and in the right way. Like a good post-Hegelian logician he immediately states his starting point; Hegel's *Science of Logic* (*Wissenschaft der Logik*, 1812) opens with an essay, 'With what must the beginning of the science be made?'

Marx then proceeds directly to a statement and critique of the starting points of Adam Smith and David Ricardo. This line of reasoning is not perhaps the obvious way to approach the study of 'material production', but it is comprehensible in the light of his training in philosophy and his long-standing interest in the critical analysis of philosophy, political theory, and political economy.

The announcement of his own starting point, 'the socially determined production [carried on] by individuals', is an abbreviated version of another famous statement of his premisses which appears in the *German Ideology* (written in 1845–6):

The presuppositions, with which we begin, are not arbitrary, nor are they dogmas; they are real presuppositions, from which one can abstract only in the imagination. They are the real individuals, their activity and their material conditions of life, the conditions which they find, as well as those produced through their own activity. (MEW iii. 20; cf. GI 31.)

In the *Introduction* (1857) Marx contrasts his 'real premisses' with the fantasies *à la Robinson Crusoe* which he says are the starting points of Smith and Ricardo, viz. 'the individual—and individuated—hunter and fisher'. Marx has in mind passages such as these, in which Smith and Ricardo give their views on life in primitive societies:

As it is by treaty, by barter, and by purchase, that we obtain from one another the greater part of those mutual good offices which we stand in need of, so it is this same trucking disposition which originally gives occasion to the division of labour. In a tribe of hunters or shepherds a particular person makes bows and arrows, for example, with more readiness and dexterity than any other. (Smith (1776), i. 18.)

Even in that early state to which Adam Smith refers, some capital, though possibly made and accumulated by the hunter himself, would be necessary to enable him to kill his game . . . If we suppose the occupations of the society extended, that some provide canoes and tackle necessary for fishing, others the seed and rude machinery first used in agriculture, still the same principle would hold true, that the exchangeable value of the commodities produced would be in proportion to the labour bestowed on their production. . . . (Ricardo (1821), 16–18.)

By stories *à la Robinson Crusoe* Marx seems to mean the projection of the 'individuated individual' (i.e. a person who sees himself as an independent, self-interested agent) back into some tribal past. Since Smith and Ricardo discuss a *society*, his complaint cannot be that they begin with an 'isolated individual', as the term *vereinzelter Einzelne* is sometimes translated. By 'individuated individual' Marx seems to mean one person made into an individual of the modern bourgeois type, not, in this case, the physical separation or isolation of a single person. Later in this section Marx refers to 'production by an individuated individual outside society', i.e. an isolated individual.

The analogy with *Robinson Crusoe* is not so well taken in the case of Smith and Ricardo, as in Marx's later criticism of the American economist H. C. Carey, since Smith and Ricardo specifically postulate a *society* (albeit of individuals in the modern sense), not a single person, or one person with a companion. Marx's quarrel with the two English economists is that they postulate a *primitive* society of *modern* individuals, or 'Robinsons'.

After identifying the alleged starting point of Smith's and Ricardo's theories and suggesting that it is related to the *Robinson Crusoe* stories, Marx claims that their starting point is absurd and derivative, but nevertheless representative of a particular state of affairs in a particular society—the emerging bourgeois society of the sixteenth and seventeenth centuries. In the *German Ideology* he had discussed the concept bourgeois society, distinguishing modern bourgeois society from his more general conception of the social organization of production which 'is developed directly from production and commerce':

The term bourgeois or civil [*bürgerliche*] society came into use in the eighteenth century, when property relations had already been extricated from ancient and medieval community life. Bourgeois society as such is developed only with the bourgeoisie; the social organization which is developed directly from production and commerce, the organization which at all times forms the basis of the state and the rest of the idealist superstructure [*Superstruktur*], has nevertheless been continually designated by the same name. (MEW iii. 36; cf. GI 48–9, and GR 983.)

At the same time (in the 1857 text) he attacks the 'cultural historians' for missing the point when they ascribe to the stories *à la Robinson Crusoe* (and to Rousseau's social contract) only a literary significance. For Marx the 'individuated individual', as seen in *Robinson Crusoe* and in actual human behaviour, is the product of specific socio-economic changes, viz. 'the dissolution of feudal forms of society' and 'the powers of production newly developed since the sixteenth century'. In one of his early works, *On the Jewish Question* (1844), he outlines his view of the 'individuated individual' in some detail, referring, as he does in the *Introduction* (1857), to Rousseau:

Feudal society was dissolved [e.g. in the French Revolution] into its foundation, into *man*. But into man, as he was actually its foundation, into *egoistic* man.
   That *man*, the member of bourgeois society, is the basis, the presupposition of the *political* state . . . Rousseau depicts correctly the abstraction 'political man'. (MEW i. 369–70; cf. ET 106–7, and GR 983.)

One of the consequences of projecting the modern 'individuated individual' back into a tribal past, according to Marx, is that history is confused with nature. He charges that the 'prophets' of the eighteenth century (presumably Rousseau and others, e.g. Locke), the predecessors of Smith and Ricardo, did not conceive of the individual as originating and developing historically, but as posited once and for all by nature. In Marx's view, the 'prophets' merely projected a modern, unchanging 'individuated individual' into the past, and Smith and Ricardo and others (up to Marx's own time) have repeated that mistake.

Marx writes that Sir James Steuart has not simply taken over fallacious eighteenth-century conceptions, but has developed his own ideas 'in opposition' to the eighteenth century, and that as an aristocrat he 'takes a more historical point of view'.[1] Steuart is quite self-conscious about his method of doing political economy, and rather self-consciously historical. This passage from his *Inquiry into the Principles of Political Oeconomy* (1767) must have impressed Marx, whose later comments on the method of political economy (and the way to present the subject), and on the influence of industry on other branches of production, suggest that he admired certain aspects of Steuart's work:

The next thing to be done, is to fall upon a distinct method of analysing so extensive a subject, by contriving a train of ideas, which may be directed towards every part of the plan, and which, at the same time, may be made to arise methodically from one another.

For this purpose I have taken a hint from what the late revolutions in the politics of Europe have pointed out to be the regular progress of mankind, from great simplicity to complicated refinement.

The first book shall then set out by taking up society in the cradle . . . [Next] we shall find the principles of industry influencing the multiplication of mankind, and the cultivation of the soil. This I have thrown in on purpose to prepare my reader for the subject of the second book . . . From the experience of what has happened these

[1] See also the passages from Steuart and Carey discussed on pp. 103–4 below.

last two hundred years . . . I shall form my third book, in which I intend to treat of credit. . . . The doctrine, then, of debts and taxes will very naturally follow that of credit in this great chain of political consequences.

By this kind of historical clue, I shall conduct myself through the great avenues of this extensive labyrinth. . . . (Steuart (1767), i. 15–16.)

Marx goes on to outline his own view of the actual history of the development of the 'individuated individual' in passages which will be considered below; then he returns for a final riposte against 'Bastiat, Carey, Proudhon etc.', for introducing what he takes to be characteristically eighteenth-century conceptions (conceptions which had 'rhyme and reason for the people of the eighteenth century') into nineteenth-century political economy.

In his *Harmonies économique* (1851) Frédéric Bastiat does use Robinson Crusoe as a man 'accidentally cut off from civilization' (cf. Marx's phrase 'a civilized man . . . driven into the wilderness by accident'), though Bastiat cites Robinson simply as one illustration of the many possible forms of the human social condition, rather than as a starting point for any of his arguments. Bastiat and Marx agree that Robinson Crusoe on his island is not really outside society:

One of the most popular philosophers . . . has shown us man surmounting by his energy, his activity, his intelligence, the difficulties of absolute solitude. For the purpose of setting clearly before us what are the resources of that noble creature, the author has exhibited him as accidentally cut off from civilization. It was part of Defoe's plan to throw Robinson Crusoe into the Island of Juan Fernandez alone, naked, deprived of all that the union of efforts, the division of employment, exchange, society, add to the human powers.

And yet . . . Defoe would have taken away from his tale even the shadow of probability if, too faithful to the thought which he wished to develop, he had not made forced concessions to the social state, by admitting that his hero had saved from shipwreck some indispensable things . . . a decisive proof that society is the necessary medium in which man lives. . . . (Bastiat (1851), 101.)

In *Capital*, i, Marx himself does not hesitate to use the situation in *Robinson Crusoe* as an example of a form of production different from that carried on in modern capitalist society. Bastiat had claimed that economic laws 'will be found to act on the same principle, whether we take the case of a numerous agglomeration of men . . . or even of a single individual'. (Bastiat (1851), 196.) Marx, however, disputes that view in the *Introduction* (1857) and in *Capital*, i, arguing that economic laws are not 'eternal', but differ according to the mode of production. The mysteries, laws, and concepts peculiar to political economy would never arise, according to Marx, in Robinson's world:

[The categories of bourgeois economy] are socially applicable, hence objective forms of thought for the relations of production of that historically determinate social mode of production, commodity-production. All the mysticism of the world of commodities, all the magical apparitions which cloud the products of labour [in a system] based on commodity-production, disappear as soon as we fly to another form of production.

Since the political economists are in love with stories *à la Robinson Crusoe*, let us look, first of all, at Robinson on his island . . . All the relations between Robinson and the things which form his self-created wealth, are clear and transparent here. . . . (KAP i. 45–6; cf. CAP i. 47–8. Marx also refers the reader to his own criticisms of Ricardo in *A Contribution to the Critique of Political Economy* (1859) for his anachronistic treatment of the primitive hunter and fisher.)

The criticism in the *Introduction* (1857) that 'production by an individuated individual outside society . . . is just as absurd as the development of language without individuals living *together*' applies more directly to Carey's use of Robinson Crusoe to introduce the notion of value, since Carey does not bother to mention Crusoe's social legacy of ideas and techniques:

An individual of mature age, thrown upon and sole occupant of an island, or of an extensive body of land of average fertility, finds himself provided with land, fruits, and flowers, in quantity that is practically unlimited . . . His first object is to supply himself with food . . . His next desire is to provide himself with a place in which he shall be sheltered from summer's heat and winter's cold . . . He has now acquired various species of property, to which he attaches the idea of *value*. (Carey (1837), i. 7.)

Marx's reference to language as a necessary part of the notion of social existence ('living *together* and talking together') repeats, in abbreviated form, a view which appears in the *Economic and Philosophical Manuscripts* (written in 1844):

However, even if I am active *scientifically* etc., an activity which I can seldom pursue in direct association with others, I am still active *socially*, because I am active as a *man*. Not only the material of my activity—like the language itself in which the thinker is active—is given to me as social product, my *own* existence *is* social activity. (MEW Ergänzungsband i. 538; cf. ET 150.)

This view concerning the essentially social nature of language, and of institutions such as property-ownership, is developed by Marx in a later manuscript of 1857–8, published in the *Grundrisse*:

An isolated [*isoliertes*] individual could as little own property in land as he could speak . . . Language itself is just as much the product of a communal way of life as it is in another respect the existence of the communal way of life—its self-expressing existence. (GR 385, 390; cf. PCEF 81, 88.)

But the theory that language is a social product is not, of course, uniquely Marx's; Bastiat writes that

. . . Robinson Crusoe carried with him into solitude another *social* treasure . . . I mean his ideas, his recollections, his experience, above all, his language without which he would not have been able . . . to think. (Bastiat (1851), 101–2.)

H

The other side of Marx's view (that language is the existence of the community expressing itself) seems to follow from the epistemological position, and the thesis on the relation between material production and the production of language, expressed in the *German Ideology*:

The production of ideas, conceptions, of consciousness, is, to begin with, immediately involved in the material activity and the material interaction of men, the language of real life. Conceiving, thinking—the intellectual interaction of men—still appear here as the direct emanation of their material affairs. The same is true of intellectual production, as it is presented in the language of politics, law, morals, religion, metaphysics etc. of a people. (MEW iii. 26; cf. GI 37.)

Later in the same work he presents his thesis on material production (his declared subject in the later *Introduction* of 1857) and its effect on these intellectual products: 'men, developing their material production and their material inter-action, alter—along with this, their actuality—their thinking and the products of their thinking'. (MEW iii. 27; cf. GI 38.)

Proudhon, like Carey, uses what Marx considers a Robinson-type situation to introduce a discussion of value, in this case, a distinction between use-value and exchange-value:

Since among those objects which I need, a very large number occur in nature only in a small quantity, or even do not occur at all, I am forced to assist in the production of what I lack; and since I cannot put my hand to so many things, I shall suggest to other men, my collaborators in various functions, that they give me part of their products in exchange for mine. I shall always have around me, of my own product, no more than I consume; just as my equals will have around them of their respective products, no more than they use. This tacit agreement is achieved through *commerce*. At this juncture, we point out that the logical sequence of the two types of value appears even better in history than it does in theory, men having spent thousands of years . . . before their industry gave rise to any exchange.

So the particular capacity which all products have, be they natural or industrial, to aid the subsistence of man, is termed use-value; the capacity that they have to be accepted for each other, exchange-value. (Proudhon (1846), i. 34.)

In his *Poverty of Philosophy* (1847) Marx complains that Proudhon begins with one Robinson talking to his 'collaborators', and that in doing so, Proudhon simply presupposes what he said that he would prove historically:

In order to emerge from the condition in which everyone produces in isolation and to arrive at exchange, 'I turn to my collaborators in various functions', says M. Proudhon . . . The collaborators and the various functions, the division of labour and the exchange it implies, are already to hand . . . That is a sample of the '*historical and descriptive method*' of M. Proudhon. . . . (PP 34–6; cf. GR 983.)

In the *Introduction* (1857) Marx once again singles out Proudhon for a special attack, this time for his allegedly pseudo-Hegelian method (developing the source of an economic relation 'historico-philosophically'); this is criticized at length in the *Poverty of Philosophy*:

Economists express the relations of bourgeois production, the division of labour, credit, money, etc., as fixed, immutable, eternal categories. M. Proudhon, who has these ready-made categories before him, wants to explain to us the act of formation, the genesis of these categories, principles, laws, ideas, thoughts . . . Just as from the dialectic movement of the simple categories is born the group [according to M. Proudhon], so from the dialectic movement of the groups is born the series, and from the dialectic movement of the series is born the entire system.

Apply this method to the categories of political economy, and you have the logic and metaphysics of political economy, or, in other words, you have the economic categories that everybody knows, translated into a little-known language which makes them look as if they had newly blossomed forth in an intellect of pure reason. . . . (PP 116, 120–1.)

Marx also thinks very little of Proudhon's treatment of society as analogous to an individual, whom Proudhon calls Prometheus; Marx's complaint (of 1857) that Proudhon 'mythologizes' the origin of social institutions carries on the sarcastic criticism of the earlier 'Anti-Proudhon':

What now follows belongs to classical antiquity. It is a poetical narrative intended to refresh the reader after the fatigue which the rigour of the preceding mathematical demonstrations must have caused him. M. Proudhon gives the person, Society, the name of *Prometheus*, whose high deeds he glorifies. . . . (PP 109; cf. Proudhon (1846), i. 77ff.)

In part (1) of the *Introduction* (1857) Marx gives a short account of the historical development of the human social individual which resembles his discussions of the development of modern private property and the modern class structure in the *German Ideology*, the *Communist Manifesto* (1848), and the section of the *Grundrisse* (written after the *Introduction* of 1857) lately translated into English as *Pre-capitalist Economic Formations*. Some information about the sort of historical, anthropological thinking which lies behind Marx's distinction between the 'dependent' individual of the primitive community (which 'arose from the antagonisms and mergers of tribes') and the 'individuated individual' of modern bourgeois society appears in one of his articles of 1853 on India, written in English for the New-York *Tribune*. The pre-modern community, in Marx's view, held man in subjection. The post-modern community (about which Marx has much less to say) would be a form of social organization in which man's capacity for conscious control over, and appropriation of, the human, natural world, would become a reality:[2]

These small stereotype forms of social organism [Hindu villages] have been to the greater part dissolved, and are disappearing, not

[2] See for example ET 156–7, and CAP i. 50, 789.

so much through the brutal interference of the British tax-gatherer
and the British soldier, as to the working of English steam and
English Free Trade ... Now, sickening as it must be to human feeling
to witness those myriads of industrious patriarchal and inoffensive
social organizations disorganized and dissolved into their units ...
we must not forget that these idyllic village-communities, inoffensive
though they may appear, had always been the solid foundation of
Oriental despotism, that they restrained the human mind within the
smallest possible compass, making it the unresisting tool of supersti-
tion, enslaving it beneath traditional rules, depriving it of all
grandeur and historical energies ... We must not forget that these
little communities were contaminated by distinctions of caste and
by slavery, that they subjugated man to external circumstances
instead of elevating man [to be] the sovereign of circumstances. ...
(NYT xiii (no. 3804, 25 June 1853). 5; see also Karl Marx, *Surveys
from Exile*, ed. David Fernbach (Harmondsworth, 1973), 305–6.)

In bourgeois society, Marx writes, the individual appears
detached from natural bonds which had formerly tied him to
a 'determined, delimited, human conglomerate', and in that
society men come to see social relations themselves in a new
way as the 'mere means' for 'private purposes', as 'external
necessity'. This view is discussed at length in Marx's *On the
Jewish Question*:

None of the so-called rights of man goes beyond egoistic man,
man as a member of bourgeois society ... The single link which
connects them [individuals in bourgeois society] is natural necessity,
need and private interest. . . . . (MEW i. 366; cf. ET 104.)

This account of the modern individual is indebted to Marx's
critical reading of Hegel, especially the *Philosophy of Right* (1821),
in which Hegel gives an account of the family and then the
transition into civil or bourgeois [*bürgerliche*] society, where
social life takes on these characteristics:

In civil or bourgeois society each is himself an end; all the others are
nothing to him. But without a relationship to others he cannot reach

the [full] range of his ends; hence the others are a means to the end of the particular person. (Hegel (1821), 263; cf. PR 267.)

Marx's view of man as producer, which he repeats in the *Introduction* (1857) as the basis of his historical account of the development of the modern individual, is traceable to his critical reading of Hegel's *Phenomenology* (1807), as Marx himself makes plain in the 1844 *Manuscripts*; in those writings he develops the view that the human individual is in essence the producing individual:

The practical production of a *world of objects*, the *working-up* of inorganic nature, is the confirmation of man as a conscious species-being, i.e. a being which relates to the species as his own being, or to himself as a species-being . . . Hence only in the working-up of the world of objects is man actually confirmed as a *species-being*. This production is his species-life in action. (MEW Ergänzungsband i. 516–17; cf. ET 139–40.)

Hegel, Marx writes, recognizes the importance of the 'self-production of man', but his account in the *Phenomenology* is one-sided and limited:

The important thing in Hegel's *Phenomenology* . . . is that Hegel understands the self-production of man as a process . . . [but] the only labour which Hegel knows and recognizes is *abstractly intellectual*. (MEW Ergänzungsband i. 574; cf. ET 164.)

In the *Introduction* (1857) Marx also argues that the epoch which produces a particular point of view, that of the individuated individual, is the 'epoch of the most developed social relations up to now', and that from the point of view of that epoch (i.e. from the bourgeois point of view) the most developed social relations are general relations—relations found in all societies. (Marx is thinking here of theses like Bastiat's and Carey's,[3] that economic laws are universal.)

[3] See the passages quoted on p. 94 above and p. 103 below.

But how can an epoch 'produce' a point of view? By point of view Marx seems to mean a general presupposition about man, used as the basis for more detailed arguments and claims. In this passage he is applying one of his own theses on the relation between ideas, beliefs, and points of view, and the social organization of production; the thesis appears in the *German Ideology*:

We begin with actual active men, and from their actual life-process we present the development of the ideological reflexes and echoes of that life-process. (MEW iii. 26; cf. GI 37–8.)

And again in the 'general result' formulated in the *Preface* (1859) to *A Contribution to the Critique of Political Economy*:

The totality of the relations of production forms the economic structure [*Struktur*] of society, the real basis, on which a legal and political superstructure [*Überbau*] arises, and to which correspond definite social forms of consciousness. (MEW xiii. 8; cf. SW i. 503.)

In this opening section of the *Introduction* (1857) Marx began his discussion of material production with an attack on various political economists. They have not, in his view, presented the situation—'individuals producing in society'—in a way that is historically accurate and philosophically sound. In the next section he investigates (in particular) the *concept* or category of production, and criticizes the way in which certain political economists have treated production and distribution.

Eternalization of the historical relations of production.
—Production and distribution in general.—Property.

Having found the work of various political economists to be unsatisfactory, Marx sets himself a problem which is practical and constructive, yet philosophical: how does one talk about production correctly? How does one talk about production without contradicting general truths or matters of historical or contemporary fact? His first point is that the discussion must not be about a mythical or inaccurately conceived time in the past, nor must it be about individuals who are alleged to be non-social in some sense.

Next he proposes two ways in which the discussion of production might proceed correctly. One is a genetic account (tracing the 'historical process of development in its various phases'); the other is an account which sticks to one particular period, such as 'modern bourgeois production', which, he notes, is 'our proper subject'.

There is, however, a third possibility noted by Marx: a discussion of *production in general*, i.e. the abstraction, or logical universal, which represents what is common to all forms of production, or those features which are necessary in order to conceive of production at all (he does not distinguish between those two views).

It soon becomes apparent that his interest in the correct formulation of the concept 'production in general' is not simply an interest in solving a problem in logic, but an interest in distinguishing what is common to all epochs of production from what is different, and more particularly, from what constitutes their *development*. According to Marx, political economists generally fail to make those distinctions because of their careless or insufficient consideration of historical fact, and because they do not always distinguish logical universals from universal truths about all epochs of production. Marx later contends that the truths which they cite are, in any case, uninteresting, inane, or platitudinous. Furthermore, he charges the political economists with ignoring historical and contemporary evidence which reveals, in his view, that social forms and relations of production have changed and developed in the course of human social history. He parodies the reasoning of political economists who have made that sort of mistake and have therefore come to the conclusion (convenient, he says, for the bourgeoisie and their apologists) that capital is 'a general, eternal, natural relation'.

Marx does not dispute that capital is an 'instrument of production' and also 'past, objectified labour', both of which are features common to all forms of production and therefore 'determinations' or concepts necessary in order to conceive of production at all; both are determinations of the logical universal 'production in general'. For Marx, however, the significance of capital is that it is not entirely the same as those two 'common determinations'; the conditions (the 'specifics') which make 'instrument of production' and 'accumulated labour' into capital are the very conditions which interest him, the conditions of 'modern bourgeois production'. Those conditions, he claims, are not eternal conditions, but the product of various processes of social change which have been under way since the sixteenth and seventeenth centuries. He singles out Carey as an example of an economist who postulates eternal laws and consequently puts economic change down to government interference.

Carey does argue that there are universal laws of nature, but he attributes only certain sorts of change (e.g. increasing poverty and misery, as opposed to increasing wealth) to 'interference':

We think there is abundant evidence that the prosperity of nations and the happiness of the individuals composing them, are in the ratio in which the laws of nature have been allowed to govern their operations, and that the poverty, misery, and distress, that exist are invariably to be traced to the interference of man with those laws, and that they exist in the ratio of that interference . . . [W]henever the laws of nature shall be accurately traced by the political economist it will be found that they *are universally true, and universally applicable*. . . . (Carey (1837), i. p. xvi.)

By contrast, Steuart's approach to this question (the alleged universality of the laws of political economy) is more cautious and pragmatic:

If one considers the variety which is found in different countries, in the distribution of property, subordination of classes, genius of people, proceeding from the variety of forms of government, laws, and manners, one may conclude, that the political oeconomy in each must necessarily be different, and that principles, however universally true, may become quite ineffectual in practice, without a sufficient preparation of the spirit of a people. (Steuart (1767), i. 3.)

At the beginning of this discussion Marx suggests that there are three correct ways of 'talking about production'; he closes with his conclusions on what sorts of production do not exist (e.g. 'production in general', since it is an abstraction), and what sorts actually do.

Production, he explains, may be said to exist in two ways: as 'a *particular* branch of production', or as 'the *totality* of production', not as 'general production'. Nevertheless he does not confine himself to a discussion of the concrete aspects of production which he has identified ('political economy', he writes, 'is not technology'), but declares his interest in investigating ('elsewhere') the relation between the 'general determinations of production' (the 'common features' represented by the logical universal 'production in general') and the 'particular forms of production' at a given stage of social development. He leaves—to part (3)—the problem of the 'relation of scientific presentation to real movement', but reiterates the distinction between his presentation of production and any idealist notion that production is (or may be said to be) in some way independent of man. For Marx, 'production in general' (i.e. the 'general determinations' of production), 'particular branches of production', and 'totality of production' are three meaningful senses of the term, so long as the place of production in the human social world is kept clearly in focus, i.e. there is always a 'social subject' doing the producing.

Having distinguished production as a logical universal from the 'so-called general conditions of production', and what production is (a '*particular* branch of production', or the '*totality* of production') from what it is not (some activity called 'general production'), Marx returns to the work of particular political economists in order to put them right when they generalize about production. His thesis is that their generalizations are tautological, false, or irrelevant, and that the political economists are often (consciously or unconsciously) apologists for 'bourgeois relations'.

He begins by attacking the opening chapter (entitled 'Of the Requisites of Production') of J. S. Mill's *Principles of Political Economy* (1848). Mill claims that 'the requisites of production are two: labour, and appropriate natural objects', but later adds:

there is another requisite without which no productive operations, beyond the rude and scanty beginnings of primitive industry, are possible: namely, a stock, previously accumulated, of the products of former labour . . . termed Capital. (J. S. Mill (1848), i. 29, 67.)

Marx puts Mill's discussion of those 'requisites' down as a collection of tautologies, charging that Mill has simply defined production, or rather outlined what we presuppose when we talk about production, but has not in any sense explained it or even said anything interesting about it.

Marx's second target is Adam Smith, who gives—not the general conditions for any production at all, but—those conditions which cause some nations to be better supplied with 'all the necessaries and conveniences' than others:

But this proportion [between produce for consumption and the number of consumers] must in every nation be regulated by two different circumstances: first, by the skill, dexterity and judgement with which labour is generally applied in it; and, secondly, by the proportion between the number of those who are employed in useful labour, and that of those who are not so employed . . . The abundance or scantiness of this supply too seems to depend more upon the former of those two circumstances than upon the latter. (Smith (1776), i. 1-2.)

The allusion in the *Introduction* (1857) to 'Adam Smith's progressive and stagnant state[s] of society' is probably a reference to his distinction between 'subsistence' and 'the progress of opulence':

As subsistence is, in the nature of things, prior to conveniency and luxury, so the industry which procures the former, must necessarily be prior to that which ministers to the latter. The cultivation and improvement of the country, therefore, which affords subsistence, must, necessarily, be prior to the increase of the town . . . The town, indeed, may not always derive its whole subsistence from the country in its neighbourhood . . . but from very distant countries; and this . . . has occasioned considerable variations in the progress of opulence in different ages and nations. (Smith (1776), i. 460–1; cf. GR 983.)

Marx suggests that what Smith says may or may not be so, depending on the results of further historical investigations into 'the [different] *degrees of productivity* in the development of a single people'; that problem, in Marx's view, does not fit into his subject (the study of 'modern bourgeois production'), except for the link between increasing productivity and the 'development of competition, accumulation etc.'—certain developments which explain why bourgeois society is more productive than any previous social arrangement.

However, Marx is probably thinking of J. S. Mill in this discussion, since he moves from the critique of the 'general conditions' of production to a critique of various theories about why some nations are so much more productive than others, just as Mill advances, in the passage below, from the 'requisites' of production to the factors which determine their 'degree of productiveness':

We have concluded our general survey of the requisites of production. We have found that they may be reduced to three: labour, capital, and the materials and motive forces afforded by nature . . . We now advance to the second great question in political economy; on what the degree of productiveness of these agents depends. (J. S. Mill (1848), i. 119.)

Mill goes on to specify the factors which affect productivity: 'natural advantages' (e.g. fertility of soil, favourable climate, minerals, good maritime situation) and various qualities of the 'human agents' (e.g. regular and habitual energy of labour, skill, knowledge, moral qualities of the labourers, their probity—or the lack of it, and the consequent need for a police force—and the degree to which persons and property are secure). Then he offers a disquisition on how the English and Anglo-Americans differ from other peoples.

Marx puts all this down, somewhat hastily, as tautologous, saying that Mill refers only to the subjective and objective conditions for the creation of wealth. However, he levels a more serious charge against Mill—that his work 'is the occasion for passing off, in an underhand way, *bourgeois* relations as irrevocable natural laws of society in the abstract'. This happens, according to Marx, because Mill's principles of production, which cover labour, 'natural agents', capital, division of labour etc., are presented as 'eternal natural laws independent of history'. According to Mill:

The laws and conditions of the production of wealth, partake of the character of physical truths. There is nothing optional, or arbitrary in them . . . But howsoever we may succeed in making for ourselves more space within the limits set by the constitution of things, those limits exist; there are ultimate laws, which we did not make, which we cannot alter, and to which we can only conform. (J. S. Mill (1848), i. 239–40.)

Mill goes on to contrast the 'ultimate laws' of production with an apparently arbitrary state of affairs in distribution:

It is not so with the Distribution of Wealth. That is a matter of human institution, solely. The things once there, mankind, individually or collectively, can do with them as they like . . . Further, in the social state, in every state except total solitude, any disposal whatever of them can only take place by the general consent of society . . . The distribution of wealth, therefore, depends on the laws and customs of society. The rules by which it is determined, are what the opinions and feelings of the community make them, and are very different in different ages and countries; and might be still more different, if mankind so chose. (J. S. Mill (1848), i. 240.)

Marx accuses Mill of crudely separating production from distribution, and also objects that Mill might just as well have applied his 'method' to distribution as to production. Marx gives another parody of this method—seizing on those features which all forms of something have in common and then formulating *general human* laws'; his complaint is that it confounds or extinguishes 'all historical differences'.

Actually Mill's position is not quite as Marx represents it, since Mill backs away from the view that the distribution of wealth is entirely a matter of chance; his conclusion is that distribution is a consequence of 'the fundamental laws of human nature', which, he says, are part of the 'general theory of human progress, a far larger and more difficult subject of inquiry than political economy'. (J. S. Mill (1848), i. 240–1.) Marx's parody might not have been necessary, since Mill seems to adopt much the same position (ultimately) with distribution as with production; the critique of Mill's treatment of production 'as framed in eternal natural laws independent of history' might also have applied to that economist's treatment of distribution, had Mill ever produced a study of the 'fundamental laws of human nature'.

In rebutting the preliminary arguments of various political economists Marx offers his own definition of production as 'the appropriation of nature on the part of the individual within and by means of a determinate form of society'; this is an abbreviated version of the view presented in his earlier work *Wage-labour and Capital* (1849):

In production men are not related to nature alone. They only produce by working together in a determinate way and by exchanging their activities against one another. In order to produce they enter into determinate relationships and relations with one another and only within those social relationships and relations does their relationship to nature—does their production [itself]—take place. (MEW vi. 407; cf. GR 983.)

The same point (that production necessarily involves both the material and the social worlds) appears in Marx's 'general result' of 1859; in the later work he has, characteristically, condensed *and* elaborated his view:

In the social production of their life men enter into determinate, necessary relations independent of their will, relations of production which correspond to a determinate level of development of their material powers of production. (MEW xiii. 8; cf. SW i. 503.)

Marx notes that the political economists (e.g. J. S. Mill) discuss property and its protection under *distribution*, but his first criticism is of the suggestion that property is a condition of production—and *private* property at that. Carey, for instance, links security and private property with the advantageous application of man's powers 'to the production of the necessaries of life':

In the infancy of society population is widely scattered over the earth. Man is dependent for food upon the superior soils . . . His hand is against every man, and every man's hand is against him . . . Upon the establishment of a government, were each individual to state what he would desire to obtain from its formation, as likely to enable him to apply most advantageously his powers to the production of the necessaries of life . . . it would be found that *every one* would ask for *himself*,
First that he should be *secure in his person* . . . Second, he would desire to feel that *his property was secure*. . . . (Carey (1837), ii. 9–12.)

Bastiat simply declares that private property is part of human nature:

Such [private] property is legitimate, unassailable; no Utopia can prevail against it, for it enters into the very constitution of our being. (Bastiat (1851), 219.)

Marx's view is that property, like production and distribution, has a complex history (not a simple linear development), and that it is essentially social; forms of property, beginning with some sort of common property, have been different in different sorts of societies. In the *German Ideology* he develops at greater length the views on the history of property later expressed in the *Introduction* (1857):

The different levels of development of the division of labour are just so many different forms of property, i.e. in each case the level of the division of labour also determines the relations of individuals to one another with respect to the material, instrument, and product of labour.

The first form of property is tribal property . . . The second form is ancient communal and state-property, which derives from the union of diverse tribes into a city . . . Movable, and later also immovable private property is developed alongside communal property, but as an abnormal form subordinated to communal property . . . With the development of private property there occur, for the first time, the same relations which we will find again with modern private property, only on an expanded scale . . . The third form is feudal property, or the property of the [various] estates of the realm. (MEW iii. 22–4; cf. GI 33–5.)

Later in the *Grundrisse*, in passages written after November 1857, Marx continues his investigation of the history of forms of production and property, developing a more complex acccount.[4] However, in the *Introduction* (1857) he notes that some of the older forms of property still exist at the same time as the newer forms; he returns to this in part (3).

J. S. Mill's account of the history of property is quite different from Marx's, though Mill, too, claims to base his view on historical fact:

[4] See Hobsbawm's discussion of this material in PCEF 27–59.

Private property, as an institution, did not owe its origin to any of those considerations of utility, which plead so strongly for the maintenance of it when established. Enough is known of rude ages, both from history and from analogous states of society in our own time, to show, that tribunals (which always precede laws) were originally established, not to determine rights, but to repress violence and terminate quarrels. With this object chiefly in view, they naturally enough gave legal effect to first occupancy. . . . The preservation of the peace, which was the original object of civil government, was thus attained; while, by confirming to those who already possessed it, even what was not the fruit of personal exertion, a guarantee was incidentally given to them and others that they would be protected in what was so. (J. S. Mill (1848), i. 241–2.)

Marx also objects to Mill's presentation of property as a 'question in social philosophy', claiming that it is a tautology to state that there can be no talk of social production in (hypothetical) circumstances 'where no form of property exists'; his point seems to be that any notion of social production presupposes *some* form of property—hence property is neither a prior condition of production, nor is it logically separable from production.

Marx's comment that private property is an 'antithetical form' recalls his discussion in the *Holy Family* (1845) of the 'contradictory essence' of private property, as revealed by Proudhon in opposition to the political economists who preceded him. Marx's assessment of Proudhon was not entirely negative:

Up to now political economy has proceeded from the *wealth* which the movement of private property allegedly produces for the *nations*, to observations on them which apologize for private property. Proudhon proceeds from the opposite side (sophistically concealed in political economy), from the poverty produced by the movement of private property to his observations negating private property. The first critique of private property derives naturally from the fact whereby its contradictory essence appears in the most perceptible, most flagrant form, which shocks human feeling most directly—from the fact of poverty, of wretchedness. (MEW ii. 36; cf. HF 49–50.)

Part of Marx's 'refutation' of the views of the political economists on the relation between private property and government consists in claiming that the economists unwittingly provide evidence for the thesis that 'each form of production produces its own legal relations [e.g. private property], form of government etc.' He had previously expressed that view in the *German Ideology*:

But not only the relationship of one nation to others, but also the whole inner arrangement [*Gliederung*] of that nation itself depends upon the level of development of its production and upon its internal and external commerce. (MEW iii. 21; cf. GI 32.)

Marx's method of reducing 'trivialities' to their 'real content', and his conclusion that 'they express more than their preachers realize', echo a passage from Hegel's *Logic*:

What emerges from this consideration is, therefore, first, that the law of identity or of contradiction which purports to express merely abstract identity in contrast to difference as a truth, is not a law of thought, but rather the opposite of it; secondly, that these laws contain *more* than is *meant* by them. . . . (Hegel (1812), 416.)

In the *Introduction* (1857) Marx adds to his thesis (on production and the relations of production) the 'natural' occurrence of crises; in the *Communist Manifesto* he explains that changes in the two spheres—forms of production and the corresponding social conditions—are neither perfectly synchronized nor peaceful:

For decades the history of industry and of trade has been but the history of the rebellion of modern forces of production against modern relations of production, against property relations, which are vital conditions for the bourgeoisie and its domination. It will suffice to mention the trade crises which, with their periodic recurrence, place the existence of the whole of bourgeois society more and more seriously in question. (MEW iv. 467–8; cf. SW i. 113.)

Marx also directs (in the 1857 text) a methodological criticism at the economists, implying that one of the reasons why their views are so limited, biased, and superficial (e.g. on the nature and functioning of the modern legal system and police) is that they do not develop their concepts and pre-suppositions thoroughly and correctly; he says that their thinking displays a crude, mechanical quality (*Begriffslosig-keit*), and the use of the 'simple connection based on reflection'. These are terms from Hegel's *Logic*; Marx's criticism of the political economists resembles some of Hegel's criticisms of other (unnamed) philosophers. Hegel complains that some logicians, in attempting to reduce logic to mathematics, and to formulate universally valid propositions, have failed to see the limitations of their results:

[In conventional logic] . . . determinations are accepted in their unmoved fixity and are brought only into an external relation with each other. In judgements and syllogisms the operations are in the main reduced to and founded on the quantitative aspect of the determinations; consequently everything rests on an external difference, on mere comparison and becomes a completely analytical procedure and mechanical [*begriffloses*] calculation. (Hegel (1812), 52.)

In the first place, reflection is the movement of nothing to nothing and is the negation that coincides with itself. This coincidence with itself is, in general, simple equality-with-self, immediacy . . . The *categories of reflection* used to be taken up in the form of *propositions*, in which they were asserted to be *valid for everything*. These proposi-tions ranked as *the universal laws of thought* that lie at the base of all thinking . . . [A]lthough the determinations of reflection have the form of equality-with-self and therefore of being unrelated to an other and without opposition, yet they are *determinate against* one another . . . their form of reflection, therefore, does not exempt them from transition and contradiction. (Hegel (1812), 400, 409–11.)

Marx concludes very briefly by stating that he admits the existence of common determinations or logical universals, such as the features which all forms of production have in common; but, in his view, those 'abstract moments' do not give a full account of any particular form of production which has actually existed.

Having argued that the political economists are confused about the logic of some of the basic concepts of their subject, as well as about the pertinent historical and contemporary facts, he moves on in the *Introduction* (1857) to clarify the logic of the economic categories for himself. This inquiry into the nature and interrelations of production, consumption, distribution, and exchange represents an important stage in the development of his critical work on political economy.

(2) THE GENERAL RELATION OF PRODUCTION TO DISTRIBUTION, EXCHANGE, CONSUMPTION

Marx pursues his investigation of 'modern bourgeois production' by considering 'the different rubrics which the economists set alongside it'; more specifically, he investigates the interrelations of four economic categories—production, distribution, consumption, and exchange—the subject-matter of political economy, as outlined by James Mill in his classic study:

It thus appears, that four inquiries are comprehended in this science.

1st. What are the laws, which regulate the production of commodities:

2dly. What are the laws, according to which the commodities, produced by the labour of the community, are distributed:

3dly. What are the laws, according to which commodities are exchanged for one another:

4thly. What are the laws, which regulate consumption. (James Mill (1826), 4.)

In the *Introduction* (1857) Marx summarizes the conventional wisdom of political economy about the economic process, and then undertakes his own analysis of this conception in terms related to Hegel's work in the *Phenomenology* and the *Logic*. Marx's comments that in production the person is objectified and materialized, and that in consumption the thing is subjectified in the person, recall Hegel's discussion of the development of individuality through action and work, and the changed significance of the object on which the action or work is performed:

Hence the individual does not know what he is, until he is brought to actuality through action. . . . Whether taken in one way or another there is, just the same, an action and work, a presentation and expression of an individuality. . . . To begin with, the work which has come into existence is to be considered for itself. It has received the whole nature of individuality. . . . The thing . . . now has its meaning through self-consciousness and for it alone; on this rests the distinction between a thing and a fact. (Hegel (1807), 306, 308, 310, 315; cf. PM 422, 424, 426, 431, and GR 983.)

In the course of his investigations Marx places the economic categories into an Hegelian syllogism, as outlined in the *Logic*:

The first syllogism is, therefore, strictly the *formal* syllogism . . . The Notion, differentiated into its *abstract* moments, has *individuality* and *universality* for its extremes, and appears itself, as the *particularity* standing between them. (Hegel (1812), 666.)

Marx's account of consumption, as conceived by the political economists, is also presented in Hegelian terms; he writes that consumption is understood as 'ultimate goal' and as 'ultimate purpose' so that it is technically outside political economy, but is still one of its presuppositions. Hegel gives a similar presentation when he describes a conscious action:

But it appears from this that the purpose of the action cannot be determined until it has been done; at the same time, however, the individual must, in that he is consciousness, have the matter at hand as wholly his own, i.e. as purpose. The individual who is embarking on an action appears to be situated in a circle, in which each moment presupposes the other. . . . (Hegel (1807), 306–7; cf. PM 422.)

Marx's summary of the way in which the political economists present production, distribution etc. (production is determined by natural laws, distribution by social change, and so forth) tallies with his earlier critical presentation of the work of J. S. Mill. Mill's *Principles of Political Economy* was nicely adapted to Marx's plan for a critique of the classic conceptions of political economy, since Mill regarded his book as a re-survey of the principles of the subject, incorporating the latest improvements, as well as his own views on their practical application. (J. S. Mill (1848), i. p. iii.)

Having made his own criticisms of the way in which the economic categories are understood by the political economists, Marx considers their 'opponents', and finds their work no better. The trouble with their points of view, according to Marx, is that they either treat the economic categories as a unity (without differentiating them correctly), or they treat them as separate and autonomous (without explaining the extent to which they are interrelated). Besides being philosophically inept, the opponents of the political economists are at the same time, in his view, *too* philosophical in the idealist sense, in that they look for a 'dialectical equation of concepts' rather than the 'apprehension of real relations'.

Marx's critical presentation of the general interrelations of the four economic categories[5] forms a basis for the consideration of the relationships of three of them—consumption, distribution, and exchange—to production, in three sections marked (a_1), (b_1), and (c_1).

[5] I think that Marx's investigations into the logical interrelations of various concepts can be followed without a 'philosophy of internal relations'. (Ollman (1971), 28–42, and *passim*.)

(a_1) [[*Consumption and Production*]]

He begins by presenting the notion, detected in the work of the political economists, that production and consumption are identical; the economists, according to Marx, admit this, and introduce the concept productive consumption. That identity, he comments, is 'tantamount to Spinoza's proposition: determination is negation', since assigning a determination to production results in its negation (productive *consumption*). The reference is probably to a letter of 2 June 1674 where Spinoza writes:

As to the doctrine that figure is negation and not anything positive, it is plain that the whole of matter considered indefinitely can have no figure . . . For he who says, that he perceives a figure, merely indicates thereby, that he conceives a determinate thing . . . This determination, therefore, does not appertain to the thing according to its being, but, on the contrary, is its non-being. As then figure is nothing else than determination, and determination is negation, figure, as has been said, can be nothing but negation.[6] (Benedict de Spinoza, *Chief Works*, ii, trans. R. H. M. Elwes (London, 1884), 369-70.)

Marx's comment should be interpreted with heavy emphasis on the word 'tantamount', since the particular case of 'productive consumption' merely reminds him of a 'tag' version of Spinoza's phrase.

[6] Hegel discusses the same passage in his *Logic*:
   Determinateness is negation posited as affirmative and is the proposition of Spinoza: *omnis determinatio est negatio*. This proposition is infinitely important; only, negation as such is formless abstraction. However, speculative philosophy must not be charged with making negation or nothing an ultimate: negation is as little an ultimate for philosophy as reality is for it truth. (Hegel (1812), 113.)
   Hegel is probably quoting from memory, since the Latin text reads: '*Quia ergo figura non aliud quam determinatio, et determinatio negatio est. . . .*' (Benedict de Spinoza, *Opera*, ed. C. H. Bruder (Leipzig, 1843), ii. 299; cf. GR 984 which misprints Bender for Bruder.)

Marx continues by charging that the economists only introduce the term 'productive consumption' in order to separate two supposedly different kinds of consumption: 'productive consumption' and 'consumption proper' (the latter is the 'nullifying antithesis of production'). The economists, in his view, have postulated the identity of production and consumption in the concepts productive consumption and consumptive production, and the non-identity of the two in the concepts production proper and consumption proper. The last two, Marx claims, are supposed to cancel each other.

Storch, whom Marx mentions later in part (2) of the *Introduction* (1857), characterizes consumption as sometimes destructive (i.e. the opposite of production) and sometimes not:

Consumption is at one time *destructive*, and at another it is not; destruction is, in its turn, at one time *slow*, at another time *swift*, according to the nature of the things and the use for which we intend them. (Storch (1823), i. 51.)

James Mill puts this view—that consumption is essentially destructive, but productively and unproductively so—more clearly:

Of Consumption, there are two species . . . These are, 1st, Productive consumption; 2dly Unproductive Consumption . . . by productive consumption, nothing is lost: no diminution is made of the property, either of the individual, or of the community; for if one thing is destroyed, another is by that means produced. The case is totally different with unproductive consumption. Whatever is unproductively consumed, is lost. (James Mill (1826), 220–2.)

Marx finds this conception of the relation between production and consumption unsatisfactory because, he says, it posits their identity or immediate unity (e.g. productive consumption) and their essential difference or duality (e.g. unproductive consumption, or 'consumption proper') at the same time. He then investigates the logical relations between the two categories for himself, drawing on concepts and distinctions remembered from Aristotle and Hegel—an example of the strictly logical aspect of his mode of investigation. In doing so, he concludes that production and consumption, as categories, are related in a way that requires a complex description: (1) each is immediately the other, (2) each is immediately the opposite of the other, (3) each mediates the other, (4) one (production) attains its 'last finish' (? i.e. final stage in its creation) in the other, (5) each is a necessary condition for the other.

Furthermore, he claims that consumption produces production in two ways, and that production produces consumption in three ways. In the first way in which consumption is said to produce production Marx offers a view about when certain objects count as products, and when they do not—e.g. 'a house which is not lived in, is in fact not a real house'. The second way contains a thesis on the reasons, purposes, motives, and needs which he infers that people have and develop when they engage in productive activities—e.g. 'consumption creates the need for *new* production'.

In both arguments Marx contends that products cannot be identified simply as objects of this or that material kind, but must be defined and described in the human social context as objects with a purpose and, correspondingly, objects which are purposefully made. His view is that products only *become* products in consumption, and that consumption, in a sense, creates the object, since it figures in production as a 'purpose-defining object.'

He also claims that production may be said to produce consumption, the opposite of the previous proposition, because, firstly, 'production supplies the material, the object for consumption', and secondly, 'not only the object of consumption but also the mode of consumption is produced by production'.

In his remark that civilized hunger is, in a sense, different from primitive hunger, he seems to recall part of a passage from Hegel's *Logic*, in which Hegel takes the 'instruments of eating, the teeth and claws' (Marx mentions 'hand, nail, and tooth') to be 'vital points of animal individuality'. (Hegel (1812), 805–6.) Marx has assimilated the animal characteristics to the human situation, contrasting an animal-like with a civilized mode of life, and the correspondingly different modes of production. He has not simply borrowed from Hegel, nor is he simply under Hegel's influence; rather Hegel's work has been thought over by Marx and employed in putting across certain views and distinctions.

The third way in which production produces consumption, according to Marx's account, is that 'production produces the products . . . as a need in the consumer'. He also adds the corresponding third point to the two ways, previously noted, in which consumption produces production: '. . . consumption produces the *disposition* of the producer, since consumption requires him to determine a need purposefully'.

Marx summarizes his investigations of the ways in which production and consumption may be said to be identical: immediate identity; each appears as a means to the other; each of the two creates the other. Yet the point of the discussion, in his view, is not that production and consumption are identical, as some writers ('socialist *belletristes*' and 'prosaic economists') had stated. Here he may have been thinking of Proudhon, since in the *Poverty of Philosophy* he quotes this passage from Proudhon's *Philosophy of Poverty*:

And since, after all, to consume for him [Prometheus, i.e. society] is to produce, it is clear that every day's consumption, using only the product of the day before, leaves a surplus for the next day. (PP 110; cf. Proudhon (1846), i. 78, and GR 984.)

The editors of the *Grundrisse* have suggested that Marx was thinking of Karl Grün, a German socialist whom he had criticized in the *German Ideology*, where he quotes this passage from Grün's *Social Movement in France and Belgium* (1845):

Production and consumption may be temporally and spatially

separated in theory and in *external reality*, but in essence they are one. . . . In a word, *activity* and *enjoyment* are one, but a perverted world has torn them apart and thrust the concept of *value* and *price* between the two, [and] through this concept it has torn man down the middle, and with man, society. (MEW iii. 503; cf. GI 580; Karl Grün, *Die soziale Bewegung in Frankreich und Belgien* (Darmstadt, 1845), 191–2; and GR 984.)

After the quotation from Grün's book, Marx (in the *German Ideology*) moves from a refutation of the notion that production and consumption are identical to an important general thesis about different, contradictory relations between production and consumption at 'different stages of production', and how the contradictions will be overcome in practice:

Thus far Herr Grün has convinced himself that in order to consume, something must be produced. . . . His real difficulty begins when he wants to prove that he produces when he consumes . . . His insight is that his consumption, i.e. his demand, produces a new supply. But he forgets that his demand must be *effective* [Italics in original—TC] . . . in order to call forth new production. The [political] economists likewise refer to the inseparability of consumption and production and the absolute identity of supply and demand . . . but they never say anything as inept and trivial as Herr Grün . . . Herr Grün has no idea that with the different stages of production there are different relations of production to consumption, different contradictions of the two, and that these contradictions are to be understood only with respect to solving them through a *practical alteration of the prevailing mode of production* [my italics—TC] and of the whole [set of] social circumstance[s] based on it. (MEW iii. 504–5; cf. GI 581–2.)

In the *Introduction* (1857) Marx singles out J.-B. Say as a 'prosaic economist' and accuses him of positing 'production and consumption [as] identical'. In his *Treatise* Say writes:

Thus, the terms, to *consume*, to *destroy* the *utility*, to *annihilate* the *value* of any thing, are as strictly synonymous as the opposite terms, to *produce*, to *communicate utility*, to *create value*, and convey to the mind precisely the same idea. (Say (1821), ii. 222.)

But Marx is thinking particularly of Say's consideration of a whole people:

Opulent, civilized, and industrious nations, are greater consumers than poor ones, because they are infinitely greater producers. They annually, and in some cases, several times in the course of the year, re-consume their productive capital, which is thus continually renovated. . . . (Say (1821), ii. 229.)

Marx takes the work of Storch as proof that Say's view is wrong, since Storch adopts a straightforward distinction between capital (as stock to be consumed in production) and stock for consumption alone:

We understand by the term *stock* all accumulated supply of riches. . . . When stock is devoted to material production, it takes the name *capital*.

I specify when it is intended for material production, because stock accumulated to be used or consumed in another fashion does not constitute capital: this we call *stock for consumption*. (Storch (1823), i. 207.)

And in a later work Storch argues at length against Say's view:

If we grant that the revenue of a country is equal to its gross production—that is to say that there is no capital to deduct from it, we must also grant that the country can spend unproductively the entire value of its annual production without doing the least damage to its future revenue. . . . We see that the clear revenue of the producers and the excess revenue of the investors are the only portions of the original revenues of which a country might freely dispose— for *spending* (in procuring amusements and possessions), or for *saving* (in increasing capital). (Storch (1824), 147, 159.)

In any case, to consider society as if it were one human

agent or 'subject' is, in Marx's view, 'to consider it falsely, speculatively'.

Thus far Marx has treated the categories production and consumption as equals; neither is, as yet, said to be in any way prior to the other and to be the 'transcending' moment. However, he concludes his critical investigation of production and consumption by stating that production is 'the real starting point' and that 'consumption appears as a moment of production', whether production and consumption are considered as 'activities of one subject' or of many individuals. According to Marx, 'productive activity is the starting point of realization', since the individual produces an object and through its consumption 'returns again as himself', but as a productive and 'self-reproducing' individual.

This is a restatement of the view of man developed in the 1844 *Manuscripts* and the *German Ideology*. In the *Introduction* (1857) Marx appeals to his conception of man as *homo laborans* as evidence for the logical priority of one 'economic category' over another—production over consumption; production, he claims, is the 'real starting point' of a process fundamental to human life and its development. He recognizes, however, that his conclusion is a statement of what is the case with respect to human life in general, not a report on the actual workings of society, or even a conception which, as yet, takes society explicitly into account. In the next two sections of part (2) he investigates the relation of production to two other categories, distribution and exchange, which necessitate the consideration of the relationship of the human subject to 'other individuals'.

(b₁) Distribution and Production

He makes the transition from a discussion of production and consumption to one of production and distribution by bringing up the relations of the producer to the product in society: is the product immediately obtainable by the producer? Is the product produced for his immediate appropriation? If the product is produced in society, his answer to both questions is 'no'. He concludes that distribution 'steps between' production and consumption, and then poses a question about the logical independence of distribution from production: is distribution 'an autonomous sphere alongside and outside production'? The answer will obviously be negative, since he has already condemned the view taken by some of the political economists and their 'opponents' that 'distribution dwells next to production as an autonomous, independent sphere'.

Marx compares the 'rubrics' or sub-categories of distribution, as presented by various political economists (e.g. Ricardo, J. S. Mill, and Say), with the rubrics of production, and concludes that those of distribution (interest, profit, wages, and ground rent) are not applicable to all societies, but are functions peculiar to a system in which capital, wage-labour (rather than, for example, slaves), and large-scale landed property (rather than 'simple earth') are agents of production. He claims that the political economists have committed the same fallacy with the economic rubrics of distribution that they have with the rubrics of production and with the 'individuated individual'; they have, according to Marx's argument, attempted to 'pass off' present conditions as general conditions, and to expand these into general truths about the past, present, and future. He also draws the stronger conclusion consistent with his thesis that production is the 'real starting point': 'the arrangement of distribution is completely determined by the arrangement of production'.

He then considers a number of ways in which distribution *appears* 'to precede production and to determine it'; Ricardo, Marx says, was taken in by the *appearance* and so declared distribution to be the 'exclusive subject of [political] economy'. In his *Preface* to the *Principles of Political Economy and Taxation* (3rd edn., 1821) Ricardo identifies the laws of distribution as his 'principal problem':

The produce of the earth—all that is derived from its surface by the united application of labour, machinery, and capital, is divided among three classes of the community. . . . But in different stages of society, the proportions of the whole produce of the earth which will be allotted to each of these classes, under the names of rent, profit, and wages, will be essentially different. . . . To determine the laws which regulate this distribution, is the principal problem in Political Economy. . . . (Ricardo (1821), p. v.)

Marx claims that the reality in each of his examples (social distribution of labour, distribution of the instruments of production, certain kinds of changes in the mode of production) belies the appearance, and that production in each case precedes and determines (or conditions) distribution. In considering these apparent counter-examples to his thesis that the mode of production conditions or determines other aspects of social life (e.g. various kinds of distribution), he takes certain historical cases (conquest, revolution, the caste-system, legislation) into account, and offers arguments that his view is correct. The evidence adduced in the *Introduction* (1857)—or in the longer versions of these case-studies found in the *German Ideology*[7]— can hardly be said to prove his point, but the text does demonstrate that he at least considered situations in which production does not appear to be the determining factor for other aspects of social life (and even cases where production itself appears to be determined by other factors), and that he was probably aware that particular cases might not agree with his theory. He seems to draw a distinction between truths which are general, yet take historical and contemporary developments into account (e.g his thesis that production determines various other phenomena), and contrary effects which might turn up in individual examples.[8]

---

[7] See for example GI 34-5, 91-2, where Marx discusses conquest.

[8] Cf. Professor Plamenatz's view that the particular cases overthrow the alleged general truth. (John Plamenatz, *Man and Society* (London, 1963, repr. 1968), ii. 282-3.)

(c₁) EXCHANGE, FINALLY, AND CIRCULATION
EXCHANGE AND PRODUCTION

Marx quickly disposes of the category circulation as only 'a determinate moment of exchange', in agreement with political economists such as Storch:

In a more extensive sense, the word circulation comprehends not only the circular movement of capital, but in general the circulation of all commodities, that is to say of everything which is exchanged. (Storch (1823), i. 405.)

In considering the relation of exchange to production, and to distribution as well, Marx concludes that exchange, in its various forms, is a 'mediating moment' between production and distribution, or a 'moment of consumption', or a direct and an essential part of production, or an act 'comprised in production', or an activity 'determined by production'. His reference to the 'so-called exchange between dealers and dealers' could be a reference to J. S. Mill's discussion of the

great dealers or merchants, who only buy [goods] to sell again . . . to the retailers, to be by them further distributed among the consumers. Of those various elements is composed the Distributing Class, whose agency is supplementary to that of the Producing Class. . . . (J. S. Mill (1848), i. 49.)

Or to Adam Smith, as Kautsky has suggested:

The circulation of every country may be considered as divided into two different branches; the circulation of the dealers with one another, and the circulation between the dealers and the consumers . . . The value of the goods circulated between the different dealers, never can exceed the value of those circulated between the dealers and the consumers; whatever is bought by the dealers, being ultimately destined to be sold to the consumers. (Smith (1776), i. 389–90; cf. Kautsky (1903), 744, and GR 984.)

Only the 'last stage' of exchange—'the stage where the

product is immediately exchanged for consumption'—seems to present any difficulty for Marx, since exchange *appears* at that point to be 'independent alongside, indifferent towards production'. It takes him only a few sentences to refute this appearance to his own satisfaction and to draw the same conclusion for exchange that he had drawn for consumption and distribution: exchange is 'either directly comprised in production or determined by it'.

The result of his inquiry into the interrelations of the economic categories production, distribution, consumption, and exchange is given in two stages: firstly, that they are not simply identical, but are 'members of a totality, differences within a unity'; and secondly, that one category, production, clearly 'transcends' all the others. Consumption and exchange, he claims, were never serious rivals to production as the transcending or overriding moment, since 'the process always begins anew from production'. By 'transcending moment' Marx seems to mean that one moment or aspect of economic life is logically prior to the others and determines them (as a general rule).

The one category at which he takes a closer look is distribution 'as distribution of the agents of production', but his final word is that production not only determines the specific forms of the other processes (consumption, distribution, and exchange) but also determines their relationships to one another.[9]

For Marx this is a general truth about production, albeit one which does not 'extinguish or confound' historical differences. In the consideration of particular cases, where production and the other categories take a 'one-sided' form, he expects the results to be more varied. In his *Logic* Hegel gives this definition of 'one-sided':

The commonest injustice done to a speculative content is to make it one-sided, that is, to give prominence only to one of the propositions into which it can be resolved. (Hegel (1812), 91.)

[9] In their discussions McLellan and Ollman seem to miss this concluding point. (McLellan (1971b), 68. Ollman (1971), 16–18.)

K

Marx's one-sided forms are immediately recognizable as versions of the economic categories which apply more immediately to measurable economic phenomena than the four general concepts: 'extent' of production (for production), 'the market' (for exchange), 'distribution of population' and 'concentration of capital' (for distribution), 'needs of consumption' (for consumption). Where phenomena are considered in a limited, one-sided way, his general truth about production determining (i.e. limiting, restricting, conditioning) consumption, distribution, exchange, and their interrelations does not necessarily hold; rather he predicts a 'reciprocal' effect between the different one-sided forms.

Why should Marx be so interested in general truths about production, distribution, exchange, and consumption, taken in their most abstract, general senses? The one-sided forms, by contrast, get only a brief mention.

The exercise is probably a part of his method of investigation, since the economists seem to him to be (among other things) logically muddled. Their generalizations about the basic categories of their subject are, according to Marx, incorrect, unhistorical, misleading, or biassed, or some combination of these. He investigates the logical relations that obtain among those categories in order to see the theoretical, factual, and methodological 'errors' of the political economists more clearly, and to get a thorough grasp of the science—but on his own terms.

After criticizing and investigating the most general categories of political economy, he turns to the methods which political economists have used in presenting the content of their works. In part (2) of the *Introduction* (1857) he has investigated what economic categories *are*—they are abstractions which, in his view, pick out what is common to different forms of, for example, production. And he has looked into what can be derived from them: he thinks that they are mostly used to express tautologies or superficial truths and do not demonstrate very much in themselves. In part (3) he develops his arguments and conclusions in more detail, using additional material from political economy and further distinctions drawn from his studies in philosophy and logic, in order to criticize and clarify the work of the political economists and to determine for himself the way to re-present their material correctly and informatively.

(3) THE METHOD OF POLITICAL ECONOMY

Marx begins by commenting on a general approach: how to consider 'a given country in the manner of political economy', and where to start, e.g. with 'population'. He may have had in mind works such as Steuart's *Inquiry into the Principles of Political Oeconomy*, in which the author takes up the 'complicated interests of domestic policy', beginning with *population* and agriculture, and proceeding through trade and industry, money and coin, credit and debts, public credit and taxes. To start with population (i.e. 'the real and concrete', the presupposition which actually exists), Marx argues, is only *apparently* correct, though it is true that a population is 'the basis and subject of the whole social act of production'.

However, he notes that population is a complex concept, and that it is merely an 'abstraction' unless we introduce numerous simpler concepts, e.g. class, wage-labour, capital, and value, in order to grasp the actually existing population of a given country. To obtain the simpler concepts, he writes, one proceeds 'analytically'.

The process of breaking down a complex, concrete conception like population into simpler, more abstract concepts (or determinations) corresponds to the philosophical method of analysis, in which something complex is resolved or broken up into simple elements. Marx seems to have used the standard terminology of nineteenth-century logic (derived, in both English and German, from concepts and procedures of ancient and medieval philosophy) with reasonable precision and consistency. Synthesis proceeds in the opposite direction in order to reproduce the concrete in a conception which is, as he says, 'a rich totality of many determinations and relationships'.

An apparent contradiction arises when he identifies population as real and concrete, and then suggests that it is an abstraction. His point seems to be that it *is* an abstraction, i.e. a *conception* removed from a particular, concrete example, unless the conception has been built up along the synthetic lines which he indicates. Once the correct synthesis is performed, the conception would represent the 'reproduction of the concrete by means of thinking'. It would be the 'conceptualized concrete', and hence an abstraction only in the sense that as a conception it exists as an *idea*. But at the same time it would *not* be abstract, in the sense that it would not be at a remove from a concrete example (either by being too simple, or by being a 'chaotic' combination of related concepts), but would be its correct, synthetic, conceptual representation. Perhaps a simpler way of putting this point is to say that population is an abstraction (i.e. a conception which is too simple) unless other contextual elements (e.g. classes etc.) are included in it in the proper synthetic way. In general, he regards population as the 'actual presupposition', a presupposition which actually exists, rather than the starting or finishing point for his critical presentation; population or society, he explains, is the 'real subject', i.e. that which accounts for activity, development, and change.

The distinction between logical analysis and synthesis derives from classical philosophy; in his *Logic* Hegel presents his own interpretation of it:

The relation contained in something concrete, in a synthetic unity, is *necessary* only in so far as it is not just given but is produced by the spontaneous return of the moments back into this unity—a movement which is the opposite of the analytical procedure, which is an activity belonging to the subject-thinker and external to the subject matter itself. (Hegel (1812), 75.)

Later Hegel develops a distinction between analytic and synthetic cognition for which there is no parallel in Marx's text, but it is not difficult to imagine the latter's views on certain metaphysical aspects of the Hegelian philosophical consciousness and its aim of 'comprehension'. Nevertheless Marx obviously admired and used some of the methodological details of Hegel's work, for example:

... analytic congnition is merely the *apprehension* of what *is*. Synthetic cognition aims at the *comprehension* of what *is*, that is, at grasping the multiplicity of determinations in their unity. (Hegel (1812), 794.)

Much of Marx's lengthy discussion of the economic categories in part (2) of the *Introduction* (1857) was devoted to 'grasping the multiplicity of determinations in their unity', though he sought to do this independently of Hegel's metaphysics. At the end of part (2) Marx had, of course, moved beyond this 'grasping' of determinations as a unity to the conclusion that one (production) was prior to the others and their 'transcending moment.'

In part (3) he divides up the history of political economy according to whether the analytic or synthetic method was employed, citing as his first example 'the economists of the seventeenth century'. Here he may have been thinking of works like William Petty's *Political Arithmetic* (1690), or Boisguillebert's *Détail de France* (1695.)

Marx contrasts the analytic character of seventeenth-century works with the synthetic character of later ones which 'ascend from the simple [moment], such as labour, division of labour, need, [and] exchange-value, up to the state. . . .' He may have been thinking of standard works by James and John Stuart Mill (for their treatment of labour), Adam Smith (for his treatment of the division of labour), J.-B. Say (for need), and Ricardo (for exchange-value).

In the *Introduction* (1857) Marx comes down on the side of synthesis as the 'scientifically [*wissenschaftlich*] correct method'; synthesis, in his view, is the way to reproduce 'the concrete' (e.g. complex, real-world phenomena) 'by means of thinking'. When he writes that 'the concrete is concrete, because it is . . . a unity of diversity', he very nearly quotes Hegel's *Logic*, though he clearly rejects a view of the 'subject' as 'self-related universality':

> The concrete totality which makes the beginning contains as such within itself the beginning of the advance and development. As concrete, it is *differentiated within itself*; but by reason of its *first immediacy* the first differentiated determinations are in the first instance merely a *diversity*. The immediate, however, as self-related universality, as subject, is also the *unity* of these diverse determinations. (Hegel (1812), 830.)

Marx develops the view that his concrete result, achieved by a process of synthesis, is also the 'actual starting point', the starting point which actually exists; in other words, to perform the synthesis properly, he must, at the beginning, presuppose actuality, in order to arrive at the summarized, conceptualized concrete. In a sense, he must presuppose his result; the point, presumably, is that synthesis cannot proceed solely from isolated, context-less abstractions. Similarly, Hegel begins his *Logic* with the 'universal' (the 'concrete totality' which is not yet 'for itself'), and proceeds from 'simple determinations' to those which are 'ever richer and more concrete'. The concrete universal is, as a result which contains its beginning, both beginning and end:

> First of all, this advance [in cognition] is determined as beginning from simple determinateness, the succeeding ones becoming ever *richer and more concrete*. For the result contains its beginning and its course has enriched it by a fresh determinateness. The *universal* constitutes the foundation. . . . (Hegel (1812), 840.)

It is apparent that these notions—proceeding from the abstract to the concrete, from the simple to the complex; and the appearance of the concrete as a result, while it is at the same time a beginning or presupposition—were developed by Marx with Hegel's *Logic* (and probably other Hegelian works) in mind. He evidently thought that Hegel had had an insight into the 'reproduction of the concrete' through logical thinking, even though Marx was at pains in the *Holy Family* (and elsewhere) to point out that Hegel had, in his philosophy, stood 'the world on its head':

Because Hegel places *self-consciousness* in place of *man*, the *most varied* human reality appears as only a *determinate* form, as a *determinateness of self-consciousness* . . . Hegel makes man into the *man of self-consciousness*, instead of making self-consciousness into the *self-consciousness of man*, of real man, hence also of man living in a real world of objects and conditioned by it. He stands the world on its *head*. . . The whole *Phenomenology* is intended to prove that *self-consciousness* is the *sole reality* and *all* of it. (MEW ii. 203–4; cf. HF 253–4, and GR 984.)

In the *Introduction* (1857) Marx charges Hegel with confusing logical synthesis, which is carried out by the human mind, with a metaphysical conception of reality such that 'thinking' somehow *produces* 'the real'. According to Marx, Hegel is guilty of hypostatization; in the Hegelian world, as Marx sees it, concepts have a life of their own, or rather 'Being', 'Spirit', or some other Hegelian 'demiurgos' (e.g. the 'self-delivering concept') is the active subject in his account of reality, not men producing in society. In Marx's work, concepts may be said to exist only in man's thoughts, speech, and written language; concepts are very much man's products, and any development or change in them is traceable to man, not to 'Spirit', the 'Idea', or the 'concept thinking outside or above [human] perception and conceptualization'. Marx concludes that 'the method of ascending from the abstract to the concrete is merely the way for thinking to appropriate the concrete, to reproduce it as a mental concrete'; and thinking, as he goes on to explain, is merely *one* way of 'appropriating' the world—other ways are the artistic, religious, and practical-mental modes of appropriation.

The distinction between 'thinking' and 'practical-mental' appropriation suggests a contrast between thought un-accompanied by action (e.g. working out logical relations) and practical activities involving forethought (e.g. 'taking in' the facts of a practical situation).

But in the *Preface* to *A Contribution to the Critique of Political Economy* Marx did not speak of 'ascending from the abstract to the concrete' but of 'ascending from the individual to the general' (*von dem einzelnen zum allgemeinen aufzusteigen*). (MEW xiii. 7; cf. SW i. 502.) What was behind this change?

The 1859 formulation may be a result of an alteration in Marx's plans which occurred between April and November 1858; he had changed the organization of his presentation of the category 'capital' from 1. Value, 2. Money, 3. Capital (as outlined in the letter to Engels of 2 April) to 1. The Commodity, 2. Money or Simple Circulation, 3. Capital in General. This change probably took place in November, since Marx wrote to Lassalle on 12 November 1858, 'I shall be finished in about four weeks, since I have really just begun to write' (MEW xxix. 567), and to Engels on 29 November, 'the first part has grown much larger, since the first two chapters, of which the *first*: *The Commodity*, has not been written at all in rough draft. . . . ' (MEW xxix. 372.) In the *Contribution* and *Capital*, i (1867), Marx stated that the individual commodity (*die einzelne Ware*) represents the elementary form or unit of capitalist wealth; the series no longer began with value, which he had described in the *Introduction* (1857) as an 'abstract, general relationship'. (MEW xiii. 15; cf. CCPE 27. KAP i. 1; cf. CAP i. 1.)[10]

He seems to have chosen the distinction individual/general to cover the new series commodity/money/capital, but he did not explain why he made either of the changes. Probably

[10] In *Theories of Surplus Value*, iii, Marx distinguishes between the initial treatment of the commodity as the 'simplest *element* of capitalist production', and its actual occurrence in capitalist society as the '*general* form of the product'. (MEW xxvi(3). 108; my italics; cf. TSV iii. 112.)

neither is of great significance, since his presentation of 'the commodity' included his critical material on 'value'.

But it is possible to speculate on his reasons for the alteration. Commodity/money/capital are more nearly the same sort of thing than value/money/capital, since value cannot be a tangible thing in quite the same way as money or capital. 'From the abstract to the concrete' does not describe the progression of the new series especially well, since all three may be abstractions *or* concrete objects. Hence he may have shifted to a distinction between the individual (or unit) and the general (or conglomerate), resolving what may have been some confusion between relative theoretical simplicity, and the relatively simple *elements* of the process of production in capitalist society. But the formula 'from the simple to the complex' was probably rejected (if it were even considered) because he went to great lengths in his published works to explicate the 'mysterious' notions of the commodity and value, which, he claimed, were not at all simple.

Marx's mode of presentation, as it emerged in *A Contribution to the Critique of Political Economy* and *Capital*, i, resembles philosophical synthesis more than analysis, as discussed in the *Introduction* (1857). But his presentation, which opens with the complexities of the individual commodity, does not conform throughout to the 'scientifically correct method' (ascending from the abstract to the concrete, from the simple to the complex) recommended in the 1857 text, though his overall progression in *Capital* from the commodity, to money, capital, accumulation and circulation of capital, and the 'process as a whole' corresponds to this intention.[11] Similarly, his mode of investigation (tracing the 'inner link' of his material) is more like analysis, as discussed in the *Introduction* (1857), than

[11] Marx gives a brief recapitulation of the structure of *Capital* in the second volume, where he argues that in order to understand 'commodity-capital' and the 'capitalist process of production', one must analyse the 'circulation of commodities', and before that, the commodity itself. (KAP ii. 383; cf. CAP ii. 389.)

synthesis; but again, the two are not exactly comparable, nor are the two modes (investigation and presentation) absolutely distinct in his work, since his presentation undoubtedly reproduces some of the investigation.

In part (3) of the 1857 text he makes two further points about 'the concrete', after his remark that it is 'the sum of many determinations' and 'a unity of diversity'. 'The concrete', he writes, is 'the actual starting point of perception and conceptualization'—that with which perception and conceptualization begin. Perception does not begin, in his view, with 'mind' or 'consciousness' on its own.

He also states that the mental reproduction of the concrete through logical synthesis is to be distinguished from the *actual* genesis of the concrete. In logical synthesis he says that he proceeds from an abstract relationship like exchange-value towards a complex, concrete phenomenon like population or world market. But something like exchange-value, in his view, could never be said to exist outside a 'given, concrete, living whole'; this point is presumably directed against political economists who spoke of exchange-value without taking 'certain sorts of familial or communal or political existence' into account.

Marx does say that exchange-value 'as a category' (i.e. an idealist category) exists in the 'antediluvian' past; this is probably a derogatory reference to Proudhon's work on the economic categories, where he uses, according to Marx, pseudo-Hegelian methods and expressions. Marx continues his attack on philosophical idealism and traces the root of that view to what he sees as a strange conception of man and the world; for idealists, 'conceptual thinking is the actual man and hence the conceived world as such is the only actuality'. With that view, he argues, the 'movement of categories' in logic seems more real than actual activities, such as production.

Marx's own view, expressed in the 1844 *Manuscripts* and *Capital*, i,[12] that man distinguishes himself in practice from the

[12] See ET 139-40, and CAP i. 156-7.

animals by his conscious, imaginative mode of production, was developed in opposition to Hegel's dictum that 'it is *thinking* which distinguishes man from beasts', though Marx does not deny this obvious point—he puts it into a different philosophical framework, and expands it. (Hegel (1812), 31.) Hence in the *Introduction* (1857) he takes 'socially determined production' as his starting point, and puts the real world 'outside the head', i.e. not in the 'thought-world' as conceived by idealists. For Marx the real world is the everyday world of experience, and the only 'thought-world' is the world of thoughts (a man-made world) inside the head. The 'concrete totality' as a 'thought-totality' is not, in Marx's view, the product of 'the concept thinking outside or above perception', but of actual thinking ('the working up of perception and conception into concepts'), something done every day by actual men.[13]

The trouble with the idealists, according to Marx, is that they regard man as really 'the head', and the 'thought-world' as the real world; hence Hegel sees the real subject, something which accounts for activity and development and change, as the 'movement of categories'. Marx, on the other hand, says that he is concerned with the 'actual man' and the 'actual act of production'; hence he concludes that 'with the theoretical method' we must stand on our feet in the real world where the real subject is society as it exists 'outside the head', i.e. *not* as it is in the head (where it is a concept), but as it is in actuality. For Marx, the real subject (i.e. agent) is not a concept or category as such or 'self-motivating thinking' (but actual society—men), and what the head does (it acts theoretically, or speculatively) is not the actual act of material production.

He seems to have considered Hegel's contribution to logic and the 'theoretical method' a valuable one, so long as the

[13] Stanley Moore cites passages from this section of the *Introduction* (1857) out of context to support his claim that Marx rejected the epistemological position outlined in his early works. ('Marx and the Origin of Dialectical Materialism', *Inquiry*, xiv (Oslo, 1971), 422.)

idealist presuppositions and conclusions were thoroughly exposed and corrected. The *Introduction* (1857) represents, in part, one of his attempts to sort out the rational element in Hegel's method, and put it to use. Marx mentions this project in a letter to Engels of 16 January 1858, when he was working on the remainder of the *Grundrisse*:

> If there is ever again time for such work, I would very much like to make accessible, in two or three printer's sheets . . . what is *rational* in the method which Hegel discovered but has mystified. (MEW xxix. 260.)

And on 31 May 1858 he wrote to Lassalle in the same vein, saying that the dialectic must be freed from the 'mystical appearance' that it has in Hegel's works. (MEW xxix. 561.)

Later, in his *Afterword* (dated 1873) to the second edition of *Capital*, i, Marx returned to the subject in one of his most puzzling and frequently quoted assessments of the relation of his own work to Hegel's:

> With him [Hegel] it [the dialectic] is standing on its head. It must be inverted, in order to discover the rational kernel in the mystical shell. (KAP i. p. xix; cf. CAP i. p. xxx.)

By 'rational kernel' he might be referring to Hegel's insight into logic and conceptual analysis; the 'mystical shell' might be Hegel's confusion between 'the conceived world' (or 'the movement of categories') and actuality (or in this case, 'the actual act of production').

Marx's dialectic, like Hegel's, grasps the 'positive' and the 'negative' of things, but on a different basis:

> In its mystified form the dialectic became a German fashion because it appeared to transfigure the existing state of affairs. In its rational form it is a scandal and an abomination to the bourgeoisie and its doctrinaire spokesmen, because it includes in the positive understanding of the existing state of affairs the understanding of its

negation, its necessary downfall . . . (KAP i. p. xix; cf. CAP i. pp. xxx-xxxi.)

In his *Logic* Hegel explains that his dialectic grasps 'the positive in the negative'; these passages reveal what Marx and Hegel shared in their understanding of the dialectic:

> It is in this dialectic as it is here understood, that is, in the grasping of opposites in their unity or of the positive in the negative, that speculative thought consists. (Hegel (1812), 56.)
>
> . . . it [dialectic] usually takes the following more precise form. It is shown that there belongs to some subject matter or other . . . presence in *this* place, absolute negation of space; but further, that with equal necessity the opposite determination also belongs to the subject matter. . . . (Hegel (1812), 831.)

The following passage, in which Hegel distinguishes between his dialectic method and 'formal thinking' (which deals with propositions, not dialectical accounts), must have impressed Marx; his attack on J. S. Mill for the 'crude sundering of production and distribution and their actual relation', his criticism of the political economists generally for the 'crudeness and the mechanical character of their thought . . . in haphazardly relating to one another things which belong together organically', and his investigation of, for example, the relations which obtain between the categories production and distribution, all recall Hegel's account of the dialectic method:

> . . . this unity can be expressed as a proposition . . . for example, the *finite is infinite, one is many, the individual is the universal.* However, the inadequate form of such propositions is at once obvious . . . the *positive* judgement, is incapable of holding within its grasp speculative determinations and truth. The direct supplement to it, the *negative* judgement, would at least have to be added as well. . . . It may be taken in the first instance as a simple determination, but in its truth it is a *relation* or *relationship*; for it is a negative, *but the negative of the positive*, and includes the positive within itself . . . [T]herefore it includes *its* own other within it and is consequently *as contradiction*, the *posited dialectic of itself.* . . . But formal thinking makes identity its

law, and allows the contradictory content before it to sink into the sphere of ordinary conception . . . in which the contradictories are held *asunder* in juxtaposition and temporal succession and so come before consciousness without reciprocal contact. (Hegel (1812), 834–5.)

In his *Afterword* to *Capital*, i, Marx distinguishes between his 'coquetting' with 'modes of expression' peculiar to Hegel (e.g. his use in *Capital*, i, of terms such as 'assemblage of many properties', 'germ' of the money form, and the two 'poles' of the expression of value) and the 'rational form of the dialectic'. The latter is a substantial adaptation (or correction) by Marx of a method (not simply a mode of expression); according to Marx, Hegel was the *first* to present it, though in a mystified form. Some of Marx's closest preliminary work with that method takes place in the *Introduction* (1857), where—in part (2), for example—he criticizes various political economists for taking certain economic categories to be simply identical or simply antithetical, rather than interrelated in a complex but specifiable way.[14] His view of the relations between the economic categories does include their 'reciprocal contact' (though in their 'one-sided forms'). But in his conclusion about their logical relations, which is not a thesis in 'simple determination' (a conception which Hegel found inadequate), he nevertheless overrides the Hegelian view of 'reciprocal contact' by assigning to production a determining role.

Having refuted, to his own satisfaction, the idealist standpoint, and developed a distinction between categories (some are simple and abstract, others are complex and concrete), Marx is in a position to take up specific questions about the 'mental concrete' and the actual origin of 'the concrete itself', e.g. do simple categories have an 'independent historical or natural existence' *before* the categories which are more concrete?

[14] See pp. 119–20 above. Marx refers to his 'critical mode' of applying Hegel's methods, in a letter to Kugelmann of 27 June 1870. (MEW xxxii. 686.)

He argues that possession is indeed, as Hegel claimed in the *Philosophy of Right*, 'the subject's simplest relationship to do with rights':

Right is, at first, the immediate existence which freedom is given in an immediate way.
(a) possession, which is property ownership. . . . (Hegel (1821), 92; cf. PR 38.)

Marx notes that 'possession does not exist before the family', a point with which Hegel agrees:

It cannot be said, for example, that property existed before the family. . . . (Hegel (1821), 83; cf. PR 233.)

What Marx objects to here is Hegel's equation of possession with *property* ownership, a relation of right or legal relationship which, according to Marx, only appears in developed societies. Hegel, in Marx's view, does not distinguish correctly between simple, primitive societies, and those which are more complex and developed.

When Marx writes that possession is not 'developed historically into the family', he does not necessarily contradict Hegel:

But it is to be noted that the moments . . . precede it [the result] as conceptual determinations in the scientific development of the idea, but do not go before it in temporal development as forms [of experience]. (Hegel (1821), 82; cf. PR 35.)

And when Marx writes that 'possession always implies that "more concrete category of right" [i.e. the family]', he does not disagree with Hegel's view:

Thus the idea, determined as the family, presupposes the conceptual determinations whose result will be the family. . . . (Hegel (1821), 82; cf. PR 35.)

Marx's quarrel with Hegel is that the latter does not seem to take seriously forms of possession which do *not* imply a development towards modern property rights. Hegel gives this impression when he explains:

But that these inner presuppositions [of, e.g. the family] are seen present as forms [of experience], as property rights . . . etc.—this is the other side of development which is brought to the properly formed existence of its moments only in a higher, more complete [social] formation. (Hegel (1821), 82; cf. PR 35.)

Marx did have strong convictions concerning the direction of the (allegedly) necessary development of capitalist society, but his view of historical situations in relation to his own capitalist society was not that of a consistent historicist, since he seems to chide Hegel for seeing *in* possession a relation of right (i.e. a *legal* relation) and for implying that there is some inevitable or necessary historical development from primitive to 'higher' forms of social organization. But what is perhaps surprising here is the extent to which Marx follows Hegel's account without disagreeing.

In the *Introduction* (1857) Marx draws a complex conclusion about the existence of simple categories as expressions of social relationships or practices in more or less developed societies: simple categories, such as possession, may, in his view, be expressions of a less developed (i.e. familial or tribal) form of society where more complex categories (such as property) have not come into existence; possession continues to exist, however, in more developed societies (e.g. modern bourgeois society) as a 'subordinate relation'.

Money, he argues, is another example of a simple category existing (as the expression of certain social relations) *before* more complex categories (such as wage-labour and capital). The simple category money expresses a 'subordinate' relation in modern times, much as in the previous example, but a 'dominating' relation in a pre-modern society, so simple categories are not, in his view, necessarily the expression of unimportant or subsidiary relations.

He concludes that his two examples (possession/property and money/capital) demonstrate a historical development from simple forms to combined forms, and that 'thus far the path of abstract thinking . . . corresponds to the actual historical process', where abstract thinking follows the synthetic method. This represents the first, affirmative part of his answer to the question whether the simple categories have an 'independent historical or natural existence' *before* the more concrete categories.

But his next example is chosen to support a negative answer. Complex economic forms (e.g. co-operation, developed division of labour) have existed before the simpler ones (e.g. money), according to Marx, in the Inca civilization. In 1851 he had read Prescott's *Conquest of Peru* (1847), and he may have had passages such as the following in mind. The first refers to co-operation (Marx understood this as many labourers working on the same project), and the second to the absence of money:

Those who may distrust the accounts of Peruvian industry, will find their doubts removed on a visit to the country. The traveller still meets . . . with memorials of the past, remains of temples, palaces, fortresses, terraced mountains, great military roads, aqueducts, and other public works. . . . (W. H. Prescott, *History of the Conquest of Peru* (London, 1847), i. 57; cf. CAP i. 324–6.)

For they [the Incas] were not a commercial people, and had no knowledge of money. In this they differed from the ancient Mexicans, who had an established currency of a determinate value. (Prescott, i. 141–2; see also CHR 110.)

Marx's argument is that the simpler economic forms of life do not necessarily exist before the more complex ones, nor are the simpler ones (e.g. the type of exchange which is associated with money) necessarily part of the constituent elements of pre-modern societies. His example for the latter point is the Slavic commune, where commodity-exchange and money first appeared, according to Marx, in contacts with other peoples,

L

but not within the commune itself. Furthermore, he argues, the simple form may achieve its 'complete development' (e.g. a system of exchange based on money, rather than payment in kind) during the *dissolution* of a particular type of society (e.g. ancient Greece and Rome), or it may be one of the *presuppositions* of a society (e.g. modern capitalist society).

Marx introduces further refinements into his discussion of how simple economic forms may be said to exist before those which are more complex. Simple forms may exist in the premodern world in what *appears* to be the modern form (e.g. in 'trading nations'), but there is still a difference between the existence of a simpler form in pre-modern times and its existence in modern bourgeois society; the simple form does not exist multi-nationally, or as the presupposition of a society, or in the complete array of forms which it takes in modern society (it 'does not appear historically in its intensiveness'), or it does not permeate so many other economic relations, e.g. taxation, or all forms of labour. It is this sort of investigative, philosophical thinking about existence—the ways in which something may be said to exist—that lies behind Marx's jibe in *A Contribution to the Critique of Political Economy* that the political economists have not thought matters through; they have not, in his view, grasped the historical development of money, nor have they understood that economic categories are the expression (in different ways) of different sorts of social relations— relations which involve people and things:

All the illusions of the monetary system derive from the fact that money[15] is not regarded as representing a social relation of production, but is considered in the form of a natural object with determinate properties. Modern economists, who look down on the illusions of the monetary system, reveal the same illusions as soon as they set to work on the higher economic categories, e.g. capital. This emerges from their confession of naïve astonishment when what they crudely imagined to be pinned down as an object appears

[15] In 1859 Marx changed 'money' (*Geld*) to 'gold' (*Gold*). (MEW xiii. 22.)

presently as a social relation, and what they had just fixed as a social relation teases them again as an object. (MEW xiii. 22; cf. CCPE 35.)[16]

Marx's conclusion is that simple and complex economic forms (e.g. money and co-operation, respectively) may exist more or less intensively and extensively in more or less developed societies; however, simple categories (e.g. money) only obtain their 'complete intensive and extensive development' in a complex, modern society. He notes that a more concrete category (e.g. co-operation) has existed in a more completely developed form in pre-modern societies than in some later societies, but he does not commit himself here to the view that co-operation will attain its 'complete intensive and extensive development' in an even more complex future society, though there is evidence in *Capital*, i, that he may have been thinking along those lines:

Finally, let us take, for variety, an association of free men who work with the social means of production and expend their individual labour-powers self-consciously as a social labour-power. . . . The form of the social life-process, i.e. the material process of production, only strips off its mystical veil[17] when it stands as the product of freely associated men and is under their conscious control according to a plan. (KAP i. 48–9; CAP i. 50.)

His discussion of the category labour introduces further complexities into his consideration of the ways in which economic categories may be said to exist as expressions of social relations. He begins by granting that labour *appears* to be a

[16] The English version cited for comparison misses the contrast established by Marx in this passage between social relations and the physical properties of things. In the *perverted* world of political economy, according to Marx, certain social relations (e.g. exchange-value) *appear* as the (allegedly) natural properties of things, just as weight *is* a natural property of e.g. iron. (MEW xiii. 21–2; cf. CCPE 34–5.)

[17] Marx suggests that this is a society which does not produce ideology, at least of the economic sort.

simple category, and that it has been understood as a simple category for a very long time; yet, he argues, labour is a modern category 'in the same way as the [social] relations which produce that simple abstraction'. Next he gives a short history of the understanding of the category labour at different points in the development of political economy, beginning with the monetary system, then mentioning the manufacturing or commercial system, the physiocratic system, and Adam Smith's *Wealth of Nations*. The conclusion which Marx draws is typically complex: it might *appear* as if an abstract expression for an old and simple relationship had been discovered, 'the relationship in which men—in whatever form of society— emerge as producing'. He argues that this is correct (since men have developed a conscious awareness of the simple category labour), but claims that this apparent conclusion omits several important points.

This discovery, or formulation of a simple category, was not, in Marx's view, a purely intellectual process, but rather the result of certain changes in the social organization of labour. The development of the concept labour, in its most abstract and general form, presupposes, according to Marx, a society in which the division of labour is highly developed and in which one particular form of labour is not dominant over the others, i.e. a society in which men do not conceive of labour as essentially one sort of labour rather than another. His development of the simple category labour or 'labour in general' resembles his work in part (1) on the category 'production in general'—both are sensible abstractions in so far as they 'actually pick out what is common'. But he notes that general production does not actually exist as an activity; 'labour in general', however, exists 'in the category' and 'in actuality', as in the United States, where he sees an 'indifference towards the determinate form of labour', a situation in which labour 'has ceased being attached to individuals as a determination in a particular situation' (as opposed to the feudal organization of society). (Cf. CAP i. 327–63.)

Marx is careful to clarify the epistemological implications of his claim that the conception of labour in the abstract only emerges in a particular sort of society. It is not, in his view, the simple fact that labour has become diversified that produces the conception of labour as the economic category 'labour in general', but the way in which people conduct their activities— what he calls the practical existence of the category. This represents a specification of his general thesis on the social determination of ideas as expressed in the *German Ideology*.[18]

Marx has come to a conclusion about labour similar to his conclusion about money: simple categories only come to their 'complete intensive and extensive development' as expressions of practical social relations in modern, complex societies. But in the case of labour he has explained why he thinks that this occurs, and he has traced the history of the category as it appears in works of political economy, together with its development as the expression of a social relationship in practice. The example of labour seems to show more clearly than that of money that the 'most general abstractions generally develop only with the richest concrete development'. He seems concerned to refute the notion that the members of simple societies have simple, abstract conceptions; such conceptions, in his view, only develop in complex, advanced societies.

However, he does consider an apparent counter-example to his thesis: Russian 'barbarians' *seem* just as indifferent to particular forms of labour as American workers. But by drawing a distinction between a 'disposition to be assigned to every-thing', and the more consciously active way in which 'civilized men assign themselves to everything', he justifies his conclusion to himself.

In summary, Marx declares that the most abstract categories, though valid (in the sense that they are logical universals) for all forms of society, are nevertheless very much the products of a long historical process of development. They can only be

[18] See pp. 96, 101 above, and Marx's further application of this thesis to the category labour in CAP i. 44–5.

formulated at a late historical stage when social life has become diverse and complex, and only in a developed society do they possess their 'full validity', their full range of connotations and denotations.

After developing the view that the most abstract categories are only formulated and only possess their full validity in modern societies, Marx claims that in consequence the present provides a key to the past—if it is used carefully. Fragments and elements of less developed, extinct forms of society and of animal life persist, in his view, in the more developed forms which exist at present; hence the categories which express 'an insight' into the arrangement of the higher forms also express an insight into the lower, and the categories of the higher forms are therefore applicable, in a sense, to the lower forms ('in the anatomy of man there is a key to the anatomy of the ape'). Marx explains this point further by claiming that the hints of the higher types of animal life can be seen in the lower *only if* the higher types are already understood. We can comprehend the significance of past epochs, according to Marx, only from the viewpoint of the present, though there is no suggestion of a strictly linear view of historical development. He does see a process of development, and some developmental links and relations between epochs, and he claims that we can only comprehend the past in the light of the present; perhaps his point is that 'simple' societies are not simple to understand on their own terms. He seems to have subscribed, though with the usual anti-Hegelian reservations, to the view (expressed in the *Preface* to the *Philosophy of Right*) that the owl of Minerva flies only at dusk, but there is little of the Hegelian sense of strict historical necessity, viz. the view that specific epochs *must* have succeeded each other in order to produce the present (Hegel sometimes gives this impression). Marx seems to query such a view in section (7) of part (4) of the *Introduction* (1857), and to refer to his own, more flexible approach in section (5). (See pp. 83–4 above; cf. CAP i. 46–7.)

He applies his conclusion by suggesting that we can understand the developmental significance of economic forms in pre-modern societies (he takes tribute and tithes as examples) if we are acquainted with the modern economic form, ground rent. 'However', he warns, 'one must not identify them [with each other]'; and furthermore, the differences between modern and pre-modern economic forms may be of great significance. In his view, not only are pre-modern forms not identical with the bourgeois forms, but some of the forms which occur in bourgeois society are themselves pre-modern (though distorted), e.g. communal property (Marx might be thinking here of Russia or India, where capitalist relations had made an impact on older forms).

He goes on to draw a distinction: '*one-sided*' *criticism* obliterates historical differences and 'demonstrates' that past economic forms are 'really' those of the present, but in an undeveloped way (this was also his complaint—in part (1)—about the political economists); but '*objective*' *understanding* only develops when writers see their own societies critically. Historical development, in his view, does not mean the linear progress of history to its culmination in present-day society, but the development of the past *through* the present; hence only after criticism of the present (i.e. seeing its 'positive' aspects, and those leading to its negation) do we understand the past—and Marx's critique of political economy was for him nothing if not the beginning of his critique of the present.

He then explains what he means by a 'historical social science'. In doing so, he introduces a distinction between the understanding of categories (they 'express forms of being . . . single sides of that determinate society') and their scientific understanding and presentation. Scientific understanding begins from his anti-idealistic standpoint: 'as in actuality, so in the head [i.e. in theoretical constructs], the subject [i.e. agent] [which] is here modern bourgeois society, is given. . . .' Furthermore, his scientific account presents the categories in a particular order, so that their interrelations are presented in a particular light.

The first step is their proper 'disposition'; he begins with a particular category selected according to a theory which he states and then illustrates and supports with analogies from the physical sciences and with historical examples. His view that 'in all forms of society there is a determinate [form of] production which directs all the others, and . . . all the other relations' incorporates and expands the conclusion to his investigations in part (2) into the relation of production to the other economic categories. Production determines the other economic categories, and *one* form of production determines the other forms.

Marx dismisses the idea of beginning with what is thought to be 'in accord with nature', i.e. with ground rent and landed property. Instead, he cites three sorts of society, in which three different forms of production are, in turn, the determining factor for the other economic forms; these are the examples cited to support his thesis that there is one form of *production* which determines the other forms of production and all the other economic relations.

Firstly, he takes a society of herdsmen, in which 'a certain form of cultivation of the earth comes to the fore, a *sporadic* form . . . Landed property is thereby determined'. The determination of this form, according to Marx, depends on the mode of production (i.e. tending animals), but whether or not the corresponding form of property persists, depends on whether those people 'cling to their tradition, e.g. the communal property of the Slavs'. Marx was no advocate of a strict technological determinism.

Secondly, he claims that with peoples who have developed a *settled* form of agriculture, as in Roman times, industry and property have the character (more or less) of landed property; and similarly in the middle ages, urban industry imitates the country, and capital (so far as it is not pure money-capital) has certain characteristics of landed property.

Thirdly, bourgeois society, in Marx's view, represents an age in which the 'historically-created' (as opposed to the 'natural') element is predominant. Capital dominates agriculture and ground rent, in fact, the whole of society: capital is the economic power of bourgeois society, the power ruling over everything'. When Marx wrote in the *Preface* to *A Contribution to the Critique of Political Economy* of 'results still to be proved', this may have been one of the things he had in mind. (MEW xiii. 7; cf. SW i. 502.)

He does not propose to treat these categories of political economy 'in the sequence in which they were the determining categories historically' (though this does not commit him to an unhistorical presentation), but in an 'order of succession . . . determined by the relationship which they have to one another in modern bourgeois society', i.e. 'their arrangement within modern bourgeois society'; he tells us that this means capital first, then landed property, then their 'reciprocal relationship'.

Marx's work in the *Introduction* (1857) bears comparison with the 'general result', as formulated in the *Preface* to the *Contribution*. The thesis on the 'determining' relation of production to consumption, distribution, and exchange, and the 'dominating' rôle of capital within the relations of production of bourgeois society, represents a preliminary specification of half of his general result of 1859 (the half to do with the 'economic structure'), though the other half of the general result (concerning 'definite social forms of consciousness' corresponding to the economic structure) is presupposed and used in the 1857 text.[19] (MEW xiii. 8; cf. SW i. 503.) His view of production as the determining factor seems to follow from the special ontological status assigned to production in the 1844 *Manuscripts* and the special rôle it plays in his theory of history, as outlined in the *German Ideology* and other works. The theory that capital is the 'dominating' (or 'ruling') factor in bourgeois society is something of an innovation in the 1857 text, but a development of earlier views (c.f. the *Communist Manifesto* on the rôle of the bourgeoisie as ruling class) rather than a departure.

In the *Introduction* (1857) Marx uses his conclusion that capital

---

[19] Cf. MEW iii. 26; GI 37–8. The 'general result' is also formulated in *Capital*, iii, where Marx discusses the 'capitalist process of production' as an 'historically determinate' instance of the 'social process of production generally'. (KAP iii(2). 353; cf. CAP iii. 789.) See also CAP i. 54 n.

is the dominating factor or ruling element in bourgeois society to elucidate some of his views on pre-modern societies. Capital in its modern, dominating form is not to be confused with the appearance of capital in its pure, abstract form (trading or money-capital), as with the Phoenicians, Carthaginians, Lombards, and Jews. The activities of those peoples, and even the early appearance of joint-stock companies, demonstrate, for Marx, that capital existed before modern society, but that it occupied a different, less dominant place in pre-modern times, so it did not exist in *quite* the same way: the same categories take different places 'in different stages of society'. Earlier in part (3) he had argued that money had put in an appearance, so to speak, in pre-modern times as a 'dominating relation' of certain societies, but that in modern bourgeois society it was a subordinate relation—subordinate, we learn, to capital. In this discussion he distinguishes between the existence of an economic category (capital) in an abstract form (as with the ancient trading nations, who appear exceptional against the predominance of agricultural peoples) and its existence as a 'ruling element' in bourgeois society.

The trading nations appear less exceptional after the seventeenth century, and, Marx notes, the concept of national wealth crept into the political economy of the day, where the state was considered as 'only a means to the production of wealth'. Marx may have been thinking of Steuart, who refers to this view in his *Inquiry*:

I have said, that when nations contented themselves with their own productions, connections between them were not very intimate. While trade was carried on by the exchange of consumable commodities, this operation also little interested the state. . . . But so soon as the precious metals became an object of commerce, and . . . by being rendred [*sic*] an universal equivalent for every thing, it became also the measure of power between nations. . . . (Steuart (1767), i. 327; cf. GR 984.)

At the end of part (3) Marx gives his five-part plan for a

critique of political economy, which deals not only with the economic categories in their abstract forms (as they apply to all societies), but also with the particular categories, beginning with capital, which 'constitute the inner arrangement of bourgeois society and on which the three fundamental classes are based'. The further sections of his plan indicate that the critique of political economy was a way of approaching the critique of bourgeois society and of the state, and of understanding the impact of capitalist relations of production on the rest of the world and the consequent crises, which we know that Marx linked with a working-class revolutionary movement.

(4) PRODUCTION, MEANS OF PRODUCTION ETC.

The final section of the 1857 text includes some brief notes to the effect that certain fundamental problems raised by his investigations must eventually be dealt with: definitions of production, means of production, relations of production, relations of commerce; accounts of 'imported' relations of production, and forms of consciousness (e.g. various forms of historiography and philosophical materialism) with respect to the relations of production, and other social relations. Marx at least recognized that certain sorts of questions presented a challenge to his views on the rôle of production in history and human life in general, even though he never actually dealt with all the difficulties, or satisfied all his critics.

In the *Introduction* (1857) he comments that certain economic relations and relationships developed earlier (and more clearly) in the army than in the remainder of bourgeois society—an example, previously used in *Wage-labour and Capital*, of the influence of what Marx called 'material relations' on a social organization:

With the invention of a new instrument of war, the fire-arm, the whole internal organization of the army was necessarily altered, the relations within which individuals form an army and can work as an army were transformed, and the relation of different armies to each other was also altered. (MEW vi. 407–8; cf. GR 984; see also Marx to Engels, 25 September 1857, MEW xxix. 192–3.)

But the theme which occupies his attention in the bulk of part (4) is the exact relation between material production (and its development) and some of the phenomena (and their development) which he takes to be determined by it, e.g. education. He considers 'artistic production' at length, and briefly mentions the 'really difficult point', legal relations, a subject to which he returned in detail some months later. The problem, as formulated in the *Introduction* (1857), is to explain 'how the relations of production enter as legal relations into unequal development . . . for example, the relation of Roman civil law . . . to modern production.' In answering this question Marx claims that certain relations of production are similar in Roman and modern bourgeois societies, and that the elaboration of a legal system is to be distinguished from its enforcement:

The usage of exchange-value [*Tauschwertprozess*], developed in circulation, does not only respect liberty and equality, rather they are its product; it is their real basis. As pure ideas they are the idealized expressions of its different moments; as developed in legal, political, and social relationships, they are only reproduced in another power. This has been confirmed historically. Not only was the trinity of property, liberty, and equality formulated theoretically at first, and formulated on this basis [*Grundlage*], by the Italian, English, and French [political] economists of the seventeenth and eighteenth centuries. [But] they [property, liberty, and equality] were [also] first realized in modern bourgeois society. The ancient world, for which exchange-value did not serve as the basis of production . . . produced a liberty and equality of completely contradictory and essentially merely local content. On the other hand, since in the ancient world in the realm of free men the moments of simple circulation, at least, were developed, then it is explicable that in Rome . . . the determinations of the legal person, the subject of the exchange-process, were developed. The legal arrangements [*Recht*] of bourgeois society [were] elaborated according to its essential determinations; above all, however, [they] must be enforced—as opposed to the middle ages—as the legal arrangements of the rising industrial society. (GR 915–16.)

But the chief problem turns out to be another case of disproportionate or unequal development. He seems quite certain that he has established a general truth about production and other phenomena or activities in social life, but feels obliged to investigate its validity as an explanation for specific cases of historical development—a more complex concept, he notes, than simple progress. Not surprisingly, his view is that the general truth does hold as a thesis about historical development, but he is also concerned to avoid a simplistic determinism, as when he asks how to reconcile his view, which appears to be a view of necessary development, with contingent phenomena and counter-examples.

The instance which he takes up in the *Introduction* (1857) is the problem of the achievement of an 'unreachable' artistic standard by a society, such as that of ancient Greece, whose mode of production was much less developed than the mode of production of modern society. He states with confidence that any contradictions with his thesis are only apparent contradictions, and that they will disappear 'as soon as they have been specified'.

His account of the Greeks' 'mythologizing relation to nature . . . [and] to social development' is probably derived, in part, from Hegel's discussion of the Greek world in the *Philosophy of History* (1837), especially the notion that both the human and the natural worlds were treated by the Greeks as subjects for mythology:

The interpretation and explanation of nature and of natural changes . . . is the act of subjective spirit, to which the Greeks assigned the name μαντεία. We can grasp this generally as the way in which man relates to nature. . . . It is also to be observed that the stirrings of the spirit are at first external, natural events, but that

inner changes which take place in man himself . . . are also interpreted intelligibly only through the μάντις. (Hegel (1837), 310–11;
cf. PH 235–6.)

Marx concludes that 'Greek art and epic poetry are tied up
with a certain social form of development'—a reassertion of his
thesis that a particular mode of production establishes the conditions for particular kinds of artistic production, e.g. epic poetry.

But for Marx the difficult problem is not to establish the
relation between Greek art and the Greek mode of production,
but to account for the relation of Greek art to his own society.
His explanation of this phenomenon (that modern society
takes Greek art as a norm) is couched in historical and aesthetic
terms; the 'charm' of Greek art, according to Marx, 'is inseparably connected with the fact that the immature social
conditions under which it originated, and alone could originate,
can never recur'. Perhaps a Marxian contribution to aesthetics
would not have been as relentlessly socio-economic as some have
feared.

After writing the *Introduction* (1857) Marx went on to the
detailed studies recorded in the *Grundrisse*. He does not seem to
have revised the 1857 text at a later date, though there is
evidence to suggest that he re-read it or looked it over. In the
Preface to *A Contribution to the Critique of Political Economy* he
comments, 'I am suppressing a general introduction which I
had dashed off' (MEW xiii. 7; cf. SW i. 502), but the *Introduction* (1857) is best regarded as a rough study towards such
an introduction, or even as a compendium of preliminary
investigations.

In the 1857 text Marx criticizes various political economists
and philosophers on both philosophical and historical grounds.
But when he argues that their work is unhistorical, his objection
is not, as a rule, that they have missed particular points of fact
(though he does make this sort of criticism occasionally), but
that they do not grasp that human nature and social life have

changed and developed in the past, and that this is still happening in the present. Moreover, he argues that if various practices in human life have changed (particularly practices related to material production) then so have some of the concepts used to pursue and explain those activities; new concepts have arisen, and old ones have been given new content. These views were derived, in part, from his critical reading of Hegel, but he also takes Hegel to task for overlooking certain historical changes and for his philosophical orientation (as Marx construes it).

Marx also taxes the political economists with a number of other methodological errors: taking society as analogous to a single person, presenting the economic categories with insufficient philosophical sensitivity and thoroughness, failing to grasp human nature in the correct way. But what is perhaps surprising in this text is the detail into which he goes in his criticisms; some of the points in logic and history are complex and subtle, though by no means conclusive. Doubtless some of the political economists were not as historically inaccurate and insensitive as Marx claims, and much of his own historical work consists, in any case, of assertions, rather than fully argued and documented accounts. Furthermore, he has a view of human nature (albeit a view of it as largely self-creating) which he never seriously questions. Nonetheless his historical and philosophical work distinguishes him from the writers whom he criticizes: he is deeply suspicious of 'eternal' laws and 'universal' truths, scorning them as trivial, misleading, or false. Change and development (and the ways in which they take place) are what interest him; he generalizes about these processes, and draws general conclusions. These are confidently stated, but do not seem, for Marx, to constitute 'general human laws' in the sense that they represent some reality which can, of necessity, only be discovered, not changed; rather, they seem to be generalizations about human social development, past and present. The theses on the determination of various phenomena by production and their domination by capital (though neither term is thoroughly defined in the 1857 text) seem to be generalizations of this type—true generalizations, as Marx would have it. His work on production seems to include two sorts of claim: (1) A claim that certain general aspects of economic life (distribution, consumption, exchange) are determined or conditioned by production (taken in its most general sense), as a general rule. (2) A claim that various aspects (both 'universal' and historically specific) of social life are determined or conditioned by production in some particular form, as a general rule.

He seems to have considered his own work more scientific than that of the political economists and philosophers whom he criticizes—but why? His conception of man and society (his 'real premisses'), which he takes to be verified by sensory and intellectual experience, and his attempts to develop a detailed, complex understanding (in logical and historical terms) of selected concepts drawn from political economy, are certainly part of the answer. Both these aspects of his methodology are employed and developed by Marx in the *Introduction* (1857).

PART II

Marx's *Notes* (1879–80) *on Adolph Wagner*

M

Editor's Preface

'. . . pray let us go in, that I may prove myself to belong to the place, to be a true citizen of Highbury. I must buy something at Ford's. It will be taking out my freedom.—I dare say they sell gloves.'

'Oh! yes, gloves and every thing. I do admire your patriotism. You will be adored in Highbury. You were very popular before you came, because you were Mr. Weston's son—but lay out half-a-guinea at Ford's, and your popularity will stand upon your own virtues.'

—*Emma*

Marx's *Notes* (1879-80) *on* *Adolph Wagner*

The *Notes on Adolph Wagner* (*Randglossen zu Adolph Wagners Lehrbuch der politischen Ökonomie*), probably written between the latter half of 1879 and November 1880, represent Marx's last comments on the criticism of political economy before his death on 14 March 1883. The book which prompted his 'marginal notes' was the second (improved and enlarged) edition of Adolph Wagner's *General or Theoretical Political Economy, Part One, Foundations* (*Allgemeine oder theoretische Volkswirthschaftslehre, Erster Theil, Grundlegung*), published in Leipzig and Heidelberg in 1879 as the first volume of a completely revised version of the *Manual of Political Economy* (*Lehrbuch der politischen Ökonomie*) by Karl Heinrich Rau,[1] Wagner's late mentor.

[1] Marx once referred to him as 'Rau-Rau—the German [Jean-Baptiste] Say', and noted that his own views 'figured' in the 1860 edition of the first volume of Rau's *Lehrbuch*. (Marx to Engels, 7 May 1861, MEW xxx. 162, 718.)

Marx's *Notes* were found among his last excerpt-notebooks, and were first published in a Russian translation, edited by D. B. Ryazanov, in the Marx-Engels *Arkhiv* for 1930. The German text appeared in the Marx-Engels *Werke*, xix ([East] Berlin, 1962), 355–83, and it is from that version that the present translation was taken.[2]

The *Notes* of 1879–80 demonstrate Marx's continuing concern, even at this late stage of his career, with some of the problems on which he had worked as early as 1844: e.g. what are the correct presuppositions about man, social life, and language, for a critical study of political economy and of life in capitalist society? What is the correct understanding of the basic concepts and categories of political economy; how are they related; what is 'hidden' beneath them? Some of these questions were also pursued at length in the *Introduction* (1857) to the *Grundrisse*; however, in the *Notes on Wagner*, Marx's work was no longer a preliminary investigation for his critique of political economy but a commentary on the published volume, *Capital*, i (particularly the crucial opening chapters), which he once described as the 'quintessence' of his critique. (Marx to Kugelmann, 28 December 1862, MEW xxx. 639.)

In the course of his comments on Wagner, Marx dealt with the method of that political economist, as well as the content of his book, and with Wagner's paraphrases and criticisms of Marx's own published work. According to Marx, Wagner and other political economists, such as Rau and Rodbertus, were guilty of holding the wrong point of view, and of propounding bad history, bad philosophy, bad logic, and bad political economy; Marx seems to have found this enraging, rather than surprising. A philosophical side of his own method was revealed with particular clarity, since one of his principal complaints about Wagner and others was that they ignored or conflated important distinctions, especially those to do with labour and value. Marx regarded that aspect of his own presentation as

[2] For further information on the manuscript, excerpt-notebook, published texts, and other translations into English, see p. 221 below.

all-important for a clear, critical understanding of the science of political economy and of the society which had produced it, and he had gone to considerable trouble in *Capital*, i, and elsewhere, to try to explain exactly what was involved in certain concepts (e.g. commodity, labour, and value) which had been taken over from the language of contemporary economic life and then used, and allegedly explained and clarified, by the political economists.

As his critical study of political economy progressed, Marx had become more knowledgeable about (and critical of) the technical details of political economy; that sort of criticism was not omitted from the *Notes* of 1879–80. But it is mistaken to assume that he had lost interest in the basic logical and philosophical 'errors' of the political economists, or that he had changed his point of view or method in some fundamental, 'anti-philosophical' way. He was never (after 1843, at any rate) interested in doing philosophy for its own sake, nor did he necessarily consider his philosophical and logical corrections to the work of philosophers and political economists his only (or even primary) achievement, since he prided himself that some of his critical work on, for example, the theory of money, would be 'interesting for specialists'. (Marx to Engels, 13–15 January 1859, MEW xxix. 383.) In addition he pursued detailed historical investigations which were not, perhaps, directly connected with his critical work on political economy, though some of his results did appear in the critique *passim*. His hostility to academic philosophy, and his scorn for bad philosophy and bad logic when he found them on the printed page, were never tantamount to a rejection of philosophical and logical arguments as an essential part of his scientific method, which also included historical research.

Marx's attacks on spurious conceptual 'derivations' were in no way incompatible with an interest in a correct account of concepts in general and of particular concepts, considered as 'social forms', i.e. expressions or concepts of certain social relations (which involve persons, concepts, and things) which

are also in use within those relations. In fact, he stated in
Capital, i, that an understanding of 'the commodity' (i.e. an
understanding of his own account of this 'social form') was
absolutely necessary for the solution of the 'riddle' presented
by money and for a correct account of the formation of capital.
This view, that concepts (specifically the basic concepts of
political economy) must be examined and understood in the
context of the social, material world, was thoroughly rehearsed
and extensively employed in the *Notes on Wagner*.

Since Marx has paraphrased Wagner and quoted him at
length, while inserting his own comments and views, the *Notes*
require careful reading, so that Wagner's work, Wagner's
version of Marx's work, Wagner's version of the work of other
political economists, and Marx's comments on these and on his
own published work can be separated. What emerges most
clearly from the text are Marx's concern with the exact wording
of the definitions and distinctions fundamental to his critique
of political economy, particularly his work on labour and value,
and his lengthy attack, using the methods of the nineteenth-
century philosopher, logician, and historian, on two or three
sentences in which Wagner gave an account of the way in which
'man' comes to ascribe value to 'goods, with respect to things
in the external world'. Other passages in the *Notes* reveal
Marx's keen interest in some of the more practical aspects of
political economy: e.g. credit, prices, costs, the effects of various
discoveries and inventions on industrial technology, and the
practice of speculating in commodities.

Marx's opening criticism was of Wagner's 'point of view', the
'*socio-legal point of view*', to which he strenuously objected.
According to Marx, Wagner had inverted the real relationship between economic activities and social, legal relations; in
Wagner's work the latter were treated as a presupposition of
the former, whereas Marx had been arguing exactly the reverse
since at least 1845–6.[3] In the *Notes* of 1879–80 Marx commented

[3] See, for example, the passage from the *German Ideology* quoted above p. 96.

that with Wagner there was 'first, the law, and then commerce', but that in reality it was the other way round: 'at first there is *commerce*, and then a *legal order* develops out of it'. That thesis found further expression in Marx's summary (in the *Notes on Wagner*) of his own work on the formation of capital from the exchange of equivalent commodities: the capitalist need not, in theory, rob the workers (though Marx collected a great deal of evidence that this did occur), but could obtain 'with full rights, i.e. the rights corresponding to that mode of production, the *surplus value*'. Marx commented that he presented the capitalist 'as the necessary functionary of capitalist production', not, of necessity, as a robber or cheat. This passage does not, however, support a view that Marx's scientific presentation ruled out value-judgements altogether. Rather he was concerned to dissociate his critical work from accounts which criticized capitalists for behaving as such; he thought this approach an obvious waste of time. He seems to have aimed at the clearest possible understanding of capitalist society, an understanding uncluttered with preaching and simplistic schemes for reform; but his own hostility towards that society, and his conviction that the evils therein would be overcome, were implicit even in the most 'economic' sections of the first volume of *Capital*:

The form of the social life-process, i.e. of the material process of production, strips off its *mystical veil*, only when it stands as the product of freely associated men, [and is] under their conscious control in accordance with a plan. For that, however, a material foundation for society is required, or a set of material conditions of existence, which are themselves the spontaneous product of a long and agonizing historical process of development.

To be sure, political economy has analysed, even if incompletely, value and the quantity of value, and has discovered the content hidden in those forms. But it has simply never put the question *why* this content takes on that form, *why* labour is presented in value, and *why* the measure of labour by time is presented in the quantity of value of the labour-product. These are formulas upon whose brow[4] it is written that they belong to *a social formation in which the process of production governs men*,[5] but man does not yet govern the process of production; these formulas are considered by the bourgeois consciousness [to be] as much a self-evident natural necessity as productive labour itself. (KAP i. 49–51; cf. CAP i. 51–3; my italics.)

And at the end of the work he gave an explicit opinion on capitalists and a graphic view of their fate:

With the continuously decreasing number of capitalist magnates who usurp and monopolize all the benefits of this process of transformation [i.e. the accumulation of capital] . . . grows . . . the revolt of the ever-swelling working class, united, organized, schooled by the mechanism of the capitalist process of production itself. . . . The hour of capitalist private property strikes. The expropriators are expropriated. (KAP i. 790; cf. CAP i. 788–9.)

It should come as no surprise that Marx also attacked Wagner's conception of man and of human social life, since for many years this had been a standard Marxian line of criticism. According to Marx, Wagner's conception, as it emerged from his 'derivation' of the economic categories, presented some abstract 'man' whose social (or non-social) situation was not specified, whose relation to the external world was curiously stationary and theory-oriented, and whose vocabulary somehow included the concepts which Wagner had set out to 'derive'. All of these points had been made by Marx against Feuerbach in the *Theses* of 1845 and against various political

---

[4] Probably a Biblical allusion; cf. Rev. 14:1, 17:5. There are other more explicit allusions to the Book of Revelation in CAP i. 58, 355. Marx quoted Rev. 17:5 in GI 156.

[5] Cf. a passage from the 1844 *Manuscripts* where Marx describes two aspects of 'the alienation [*Entfremdung*] of practical human activity, labour': (1) 'the relation of the labourer to the *product of labour* as an alien [*fremden*] object, an object exercising power over him', and (2) 'the relation of labour to the *act of production*', i.e. 'the relation of the labourer to his own activity', as 'an activity turned against him, independent of him, not belonging to him'. (MEW Ergänzungsband i. 515; cf. ET 138.)

economists, beginning in 1844. (See SW i. 13–15, and, for example, ET 133–4, 138–40.)

Marx conceived of man (with respect to the critique of political economy) as a social language-user necessarily engaged in active, productive relations with the things of the external world. This view was as clearly expressed in the *Notes on Wagner* as in the 'early writings' of nearly forty years before (and in CAP i. 156–64), though in the *Notes*, the account of the development of language (of a certain sort) had been worked out in more detail. He took the view that men begin by 'relating themselves actively' to the external world (by eating, drinking etc., just as animals do), and that they take hold of things and satisfy their needs. 'Through the repetition of this process', they, like animals, come to distinguish certain things which satisfy their needs from all other things, but unlike animals, they come eventually to 'christen these things linguistically', because they 'stand continually in the production process . . . in active association among themselves and with these things'. Language, he wrote, comes to express 'what repeated corroboration in experience has accomplished'.

Besides attacking Wagner for starting out on historically and philosophically dubious grounds, Marx took him to task for the details of his treatment of labour, value, economic goods, capital, and other categories of political economy. According to Marx, Wagner's assertions were tautological, false, circular, spurious, confused, illogical, and/or apologetic for the German state and social order. Here Marx the student of logic was very much in evidence, as well as Marx the committed critic of capitalist society and of theorists who, in his view, took that society too much on its own terms.

Marx claimed that Wagner had missed an important distinction under '*labour*': the distinction between types of labour which are different in concrete ways, and labour in its most abstract form, common to all types of labour (as discussed, e.g. in the *Introduction* of 1857). While writing the *Grundrisse* in 1857–8 he developed the more precise view that this 'abstract general labour' was the expenditure of labour-power in the abstract. The 'twofold character of labour'—concrete useful labour and simple abstract labour—was considered by Marx to be one of his most important critical clarifications of the categories of political economy:

The best things in my book [*Capital*] are 1. (on which *all* understanding of the facts is based) the *twofold character of labour*, emphasized in the very *first* chapter, expressed, as it is, in use-value or exchange-value; 2. the treatment of *surplus value independent of its particular forms*, like profit, interest, ground rent etc. This is shown in the second volume in particular. (Marx to Engels, 24 August 1867, MEW xxxi. 326.)

And in the first chapter of *Capital*, i, he remarked:

I was the first to demonstrate critically this twofold nature of the labour contained in the commodity. Since this is the point on which the understanding of political economy turns, we must look at it more closely. (KAP i. 8; cf. CAP i. 8.)

Wagner, on the other hand, disputed this 'clarification' of the labour theory of value, claiming that Marx's definition of value-creating labour was unwarranted and politically tendentious. If, as Marx claimed, the expenditure of simple abstract labour-*power* produces value, then the economic 'services' of capitalists and civil servants begin to look dispensable; Wagner advocated a 'broad' understanding of labour such that capitalists and civil servants may be said to labour, to create value, and hence to be in direct line for a share in the value created. (Cf. Wagner (1879), 24, 111.) Marx's 'twofold character of labour' tended to undercut any suggestion that capitalists and civil servants justifiably claim a share in value for any but purely conventional, transitory reasons (e.g. legal entitlement). He expressed this view in a letter to Kugelmann of 11 July 1868:

With the insight into the [social] context [of exchange-value] all theoretical belief in the permanent necessity of existing circumstances collapses, before the practical smash-up. (MEW xxxii. 553–4.)

As one would expect, Marx and Wagner differed in their views on the social question. Wagner favoured government intervention and regulation to rectify abuses deriving from the free market and exploitative employers. Marx agreed that capitalist society lacked conscious regulation, but argued (at length) that the very presuppositions and fundamental practices of a capitalist, commodity-producing society (e.g. the commodity, exchange-value, private organization of the production process) were historically peculiar (albeit necessary for a time) and destined to be superseded by a better way of organizing and understanding economic life. 'The point of bourgeois society', he wrote (somewhat dogmatically) is 'that *a priori* there is no conscious social regulation of production'. (MEW xxxii. 553; my italics.)

But his chief quarrel with Wagner concerned the latter's treatment of Marx's own work on value, as published in *Capital*, i. In his comments Marx made it quite clear that he had never treated value as equivalent to price of production or market price, but that he *distinguished* them from one another; furthermore, his consideration of value was not directed exclusively towards the determination of its quantity in any given situation, or in general. Rather, he began with 'the commodity', 'the simplest economic concretum', 'the *concrete social form* of the labour-product', 'the simplest social form in which the labour-product is presented in contemporary society'; and from the commodity he moved on to discuss usefulness or utility, use-value, exchange-value, and value itself. Hence he remarked in the *Notes* that neither value nor exchange-value were his subjects, but *the commodity*, and claimed that he did not start from 'concepts' (his own quotes) but from a concrete, historically specific 'social form'. Marx's view was very much that distinctions (and 'social forms') spring 'from real life into the textbooks', such as textbooks on political economy. (Cf. *Introduction* (1857), p. 58 above.)

But when Marx investigated and discussed the commodity

as a 'social form', he was nonetheless dealing with a concept (albeit the concept of a concrete social thing). The point of his distinction between starting from 'concepts' and starting from a 'social form' (or 'social thing', or 'given economic form') was, I think, that Wagner and others had attempted to define and relate economic concepts in some nebulous, arbitrary way; Marx dismissed this in the *Notes* of 1879–80 as 'helter-skelter quibbling' over concepts or words. His own method was to attempt to elucidate and explain the (given, but confused) theory and the physical and social reality of the commodity, taking into account the historical development of economic life and the assumptions and practices (as he saw them) involved in a certain sort of society, one where men do not simply produce use-values, i.e. useful things, but use-values for others, use-values for exchange, social use-value, *commodities*. (KAP i. 7–8; cf. CAP i. 7–8.)

Marx did not only define and discuss commodity-producing societies, but gave examples of societies where, in his view, labour-products did *not* become commodities, or did so only in limited circumstances. He contrasted the development of the deliberate production of social use-values for others (commodities) in certain societies, with the more 'primitive' (though not necessarily extinct) social arrangements where exchange, understood as exchange between 'private owners', did not exist. Surplus products, as he explained in the *Grundrisse*, did exist in 'primitive' societies; however, such products were regarded not as the disposable property of individuals, but as the property of the tribe, commune, family, or despot. (GR 377–8 etc.; cf. PCEF 70–1 etc.) A compressed version of Marx's views on 'primitive' societies and a society of commodity-producers appeared in *Capital*, i:

The first way in which a potential object of need is exchange-value is its existence [*Dasein*] as non-use-value, as the quantum of use-value exceeding the immediate needs of its possessor. In and of themselves, things are external [*äusserlich*] to man and therefore alienable [*veräusserlich*]. To make this alienation [*Veräusserung*] mutual, men need only confront each other tacitly as private owners of alienable things, and in that way, as persons independent of one another. Such a relation of mutual estrangement [*Fremdheit*] does not yet exist for the members of a spontaneous community-life [*Gemeinwesens*], whether it has the form of a patriarchal family, an ancient Indian commune, an Inca state etc. The exchange of commodities begins where community-life leaves off, at the point of contact with foreign communities or members of foreign communities.[6] (KAP i. 57–8; cf. CAP i. 59–60.)

Or, as he had written a few pages earlier:

This division of a labour-product into a useful thing and a thing of value is only manifested in practice so soon as exchange has gained such sufficient extent and importance that useful things are produced for exchange, and the *value*-character of the materials *comes into consideration in their very production*. From this moment the private labours of the producer acquire *in actuality* a twofold social character. (KAP i. 42; cf. CAP i. 44; my italics.)

In Marx's view, the first manifestations of commodity-exchange are to be distinguished historically and logically from later, more complex developments, such as the explicit formulation of the notion (necessarily hidden from, e.g. Aristotle) that 'in the value-form of the commodity all labours are expressed as equal human labour':

However, Aristotle could not read off from the value-form itself that in the form of commodity-values all labours are expressed as equal human labour and hence regarded equally, because Greek society was founded on slave-labour; hence it had for its basis the inequality of men and of their labour-powers. The *secret of the expression of value*, the equality and the equal standing of all labours, because and in so far as they are human labour in general, can only be deciphered, as soon as the concept of human equality already possesses the strength of a popular prejudice. But this is only possible

[6] Cf. *Introduction* (1857), p. 75 above.

in a society in which the commodity-form is the general form of the labour-product, hence also the relation of men to one another as commodity-possessors is the prevailing social relation.[7] (KAP i. 27–8; cf. CAP i. 29; my italics.)

In a similar way, and for similar reasons, he distinguished feudal and peasant economies from commodity-production, but made the additional point that labour and its products appear to the members of those societies in some particular, natural form, rather than in some 'fantastic form', e.g. human labour as value-producing labour-power, and useful labour-products as commodities (which have value):

Personal dependence characterizes social relations [in the middle ages in Europe] just as much as the spheres of life founded on it. But just because relations of personal dependence form the given social basis, labour and its products need not take on a fantastic form *different from their reality*. They enter into the workings of society as services and payments in kind. The natural form of labour, its particularity, and *not*, as at the basis of commodity-production, its generality, is here its immediate social form. . . . For the consideration of common, i.e. directly associated labour, we need not go back to its spontaneous form, which we encounter at the historical threshold of all civilized peoples. The rural, patriarchal industry of a peasant family forms an example closer to us; they produce corn, cattle, yarn, linen, and articles of clothing etc. for their own needs. These different things confront the family as different products of their family-labour, but *not* in their mutual relations, as commodities. (KAP i. 46–7; cf. CAP i. 48–9; my italics.)

In *Capital* and in the *Notes on Wagner* Marx did not disown concepts, any more than he could have rejected the use of words, but rather scorned the pretence that an account of economic phenomena could be given 'from concepts', rather than from historical and contemporary facts (including 'social forms', such as the commodity) about human social life and

[7] This sort of appearance/dominance distinction is developed and employed by Marx in e.g. the *Introduction* (1857), cf. pp. 79–81 above.

about life in particular sorts of societies—the 'economically-given social period' which he mentioned in the *Notes*.

In presenting his analysis of the commodity, he reasoned that since, in certain societies, commodities exchange for one another, then they are replaceable by one another, and are 'equal to one another'. (KAP i. 3–4; cf. CAP i. 3–4.) But equal in virtue of what? What, he asked, do all commodities, as interchangeable commodities, have in common?[8] In the *Notes on Wagner* his answer was the same as in *Capital*, i, but he put it more forcefully:

Nowhere do I speak of '*the common social substance of exchange-value*', but [I] say, rather, that exchange-values (*exchange-value* does not exist unless [there are] at least two of them) represent something *common to them* [commodities] which is wholly independent 'of their use-values' (i.e. here, of their natural form), namely '*value*'.

The next question for Marx was 'What is value?', and his answer was a 'clarification' of Adam Smith, Ricardo *et al.*: commodities are all products of human labour in the abstract. When *regarded* (in the theory and practice of capitalist society) as 'crystals of this social substance common to them', useful products of labour are '*values*, commodity-values'—a round-about (and mystifying) way, according to Marx, of expressing the fact that human labour-power has been expended on useful products. (KAP i. pp. xxiv, 5; cf. CAP i. 5.) For Marx, value was a purely social property (but alleged by some political economists to be a natural property) of the useful products of human labour, and, *a fortiori*, a 'real' property of the 'social form': 'the commodity'. In Marx's view, the terms value and

[8] Marx may be subject to criticism here along lines indicated by Wittgenstein, e.g. 'Don't say: "There *must* be something common . . ."—but *look and see* whether there is anything common to all.—For if you look at them you will not see something that is common to *all*, but similarities, relationships, and a whole series of them at that.' (Ludwig Wittgenstein, *Philosophical Investigations*, trans. G.E.M. Anscombe (Oxford, 1953, repr. 1958), §66.)

commodity were, strictly speaking, neither generally applicable to all societies, nor neutral in their connotations:

We saw how in the simplest expression of value, x commodity A = y commodity B, the thing, in which the quantity of value of another thing is presented, *appears* to possess its form as an equivalent independent of this social relationship, [i.e.] as a natural property. We have pursued the establishment of this *false appearance*. It is completed as soon as the general form of the equivalent has coalesced with the natural form of a particular type of commodity, or has crystallized into the form of money. (KAP i. 63; cf. CAP i. 65; my italics.)

The measurement of the *quantity* of value (in terms of the 'normal amount of labour which the production of an object costs', or 'socially necessary labour-time') was, for Marx, a problem *separate* from the elucidation and explanation of the *nature* of value and money. In the *Notes on Wagner* he pointed to Ricardo as an example of an economist who had concerned himself only with the quantitative determination of value and 'for that reason found no connection between his theory of value and the nature [*Wesen*] of money'. The latter, for Marx, was an important problem, and his clarification of it an important achievement: 'the *value* of one commodity is presented in the *use-value* of another, i.e. in the natural form of another commodity'. Early in *Capital*, i, he stated the problem:

Everyone knows, even if he knows nothing else, that commodities possess a common value-form—the money-form—which is in striking contrast to the motley natural forms of their use-values. Nevertheless there is something to be done here, which was never attempted by bourgeois [political] economy, namely, to identify the genesis of that money-form, hence to trace the development of the expression of value contained in the value-relation of commodities from its simplest, inconspicuous form up to its dazzling money-form. With that, the *riddle* of money will disappear. (KAP i. 15; cf. CAP i. 15; my italics.)

But Marx did not rest with a definitional 'clarification'; he considered the money-form not only dazzling but 'peculiar' in three significant ways:

The first peculiarity which stands out in the consideration of the equivalent form [of value] is this; use-value is turned into the *form of appearance of its opposite*, of value . . . Hence there is a second peculiarity of the equivalent form, that concrete labour is turned into the *form of appearance of its opposite*, abstract human labour. . . . Hence there is a third peculiarity of the equivalent form, that private labour is turned into the *form of its opposite*, into labour immediately social in form. (KAP i. 24–6; cf. CAP i. 25–8; my italics.)

These 'peculiarities' lead ultimately to Marx's theory of the 'fetish-character' of commodities, his way of specifying and summarizing the 'absurd', 'mystical' character of the 'life-process' in capitalist society:

Here [in the religious world] the products of the human mind *appear* endowed with a life of their own; [they *appear* as] independent forms standing in relations among themselves and with men. So [it is] in the commodity-world with the products of the human hand. This I call the fetishism[9] which adheres to labour-products as soon as they are produced as commodities, and hence [it] is inseparable from commodity-production. (KAP i. 41; cf. CAP i. 43; my italics.)

The upshot is this:

The latter [amounts of value] change continually, *independent of the will, foresight, and action of the exchangers*. Their own social movement [*Bewegung*] possesses for them the form of a movement of things,

---

[9] Marx understood 'fetishism' in this eighteenth- and nineteenth-century sense: 'By writers on anthropology (following C. de Brosses, *Le Culte des Dieux Fétiches*, 1760) . . . An inanimate object worshipped by savages on account of its supposed inherent magical powers, or as being animated by a spirit.' (OED *s.v.* Fetish 1b.) Cf. Marx's reading for 1842 discussed on p. 11 above.

N

under whose control they stand, instead of controlling them. (KAP i. 44; cf. CAP i. 46; my italics.)

Hence he poured scorn on Wagner and Rodbertus for missing or conflating these distinctions between use-value and value, value and exchange-value, value and the various 'value-forms' (including the 'money-form'), and value and costs and prices, and for depending on etymological coincidences and alleged 'German usage' for their definitions and explanations, rather than on the theory (i.e. political economy) and practice of commodity-producing societies as far back as the time of Aristotle.[10] In the *Notes on Wagner* Marx contrasted Rodbertus's complaints of 'illogical procedure' with his own account of a 'fact', or rather artifact, of contemporary economic life, the price-list, where, Marx claimed, the distinctions which he had traced out in *Capital*, i, occur in real life. In the list, commodities appeared as use-values (i.e. useful products of human labour, such as cotton and yarn), which are by nature qualitatively different from one another; yet at the same time, in the list, they appeared to be qualitatively the same as equivalent (i.e. exchangeable, or mutually interchangeable) commodities, but different from each other only quantitatively in terms of price. In the opening chapter of *Capital* he had concluded that a peculiar though historically necessary organization of production ('private labours, carried on independently') was at the root of this characteristic and transitory way of dealing with the useful products of human labour and at the root of the uncertainties, panics, and crises to which the capitalist system was subject.

One of the difficulties with Marx's 'economics' (i.e. his critical re-presentation of political economy) is that much of it does

[10] Marx distinguished, of course, between societies where some commodity-production takes place and capitalist society, where, in his view, commodity-production becomes general and dominating. See, for example, CAP i. 123.

not resemble economics as generally understood and practised today, since he developed many of his distinctions and arguments for reasons other than the immediate establishment of relationships expressible (and testable) in quantitative terms. It seemed important to him to understand and present the presuppositions of capitalist, commodity-producing society, in particular, how certain uncomplicated things and relations come to appear there in 'fantastic', 'mysterious' forms (e.g. useful products of human labour *appear* there as commodities), before he dealt with money, capital, profit etc., which were more susceptible to quantification and mathematical treatment:

In order to find out how the simple expression of the value of a commodity is hidden in the value-relation of two commodities, we must consider the latter, to begin with, *entirely independent of its quantitative aspects* . . . [Note:] The few economists who, like S. Bailey, have concerned themselves with the analysis of the value-form, could not obtain a result, because, in the first place, they confused the value-form and value, and in the second place, under the coarse influence of the practical bourgeois, they *confined* their attention from the outset exclusively to the quantitative definition. (KAP i. 16–17, 17 n.; cf. CAP i. 17, 17 n.; my italics; see also TSV iii. 139 etc. for further remarks on Bailey.)

My conclusion is not that Marx was exclusively (or even primarily) a philosopher and logician, but that he applied the techniques of philosophy and logic (among others) to the criticism of political economy. Few modern economists would expend any effort on explaining in detail what a commodity is (and is not), how things have come to be commodities, how it is that we have come to deal with them in monetary terms, and what exactly is involved in the notions of value, exchange-value, and price; yet Marx thought that these were all extremely interesting and important problems. In his discussion of them he claimed to provide an insight into the special nature of capitalist society (and how it was different from earlier societies, and from contemporary societies which he thought were organized on a different basis), and to support his conviction that the capitalist system was a transitory form of social organization. He seems to have taken the view that his critical work on the commodity and value contained an explanation of the necessary relations 'hidden' under the apparently accidental movement of prices, and an explanation for some of the worrying phenomena of capitalist life, e.g. reductions in the labour-force or shifts in labour from one branch of production to another (with more or less 'friction'), and sudden crashes in the market prices of various commodities. (See, for example, CAP i. 11, 46, 66, 74–5.) In addition he expected to clear up a great deal of confusion among specialists in political economy, and in doing so, to demonstrate the 'absurd' character of a society in which the 'life-process' was out of man's control and not subject to conscious, rational planning.

Some of Marx's work on the nature of commodity-production (and various contrasting forms of production) is still of interest, though his 'clarification' of the labour theory of value is perhaps a museum-piece: not specifically because of its limited applicability to modern economic studies, but because the exchangeability of commodities may not, after all, presuppose a common 'something' in quite the way he maintained.[11] However, he also held the view that the mere exposure of incorrect ideas, and the formulation of correct ones, was not sufficient for social change, though correct ideas would presumably be incorporated into the revolutionary social practice which he saw growing out of the capitalist economy itself.

[11] For a detailed discussion of this point see my forthcoming article 'Marx's Commodity Fetishism', *Inquiry* (Oslo, 1975).

Notes (1879–80) on Adolph Wagner

1. Herr Wagner's point of view is the '*socio-legal point of view*' (p. 2).[1] On that [he] finds himself in '*accord with Rodbertus, Lange, and Schäffle*' (p. 2).[2] For the '*main, fundamental points*' he refers to *Rodbertus and Schäffle*. Herr Wagner himself speaks of *piracy* as 'illegal acquisition' by *whole peoples*, and says that it is only robbery, if 'a *true international law* [jus gentium] is assumed to exist' (p. 18, n. 3).

Above all he is seeking the '*conditions of economic life in a community*', and he '*defines, according to the same conditions, the sphere of the economic freedom of the individual*' (p. 2).

'The "drive for satisfaction" . . . does *not* and should not operate, as a *pure force of nature*; rather it stands, like any human drive, under the guidance of reason and conscience. Any act resulting from it is consequently an *accountable* act and is always liable to a *moral judgement*, but that is itself, to be sure (!), subject to *historical change*' (p. 9).

[1] Marx's citations refer to Wagner (1879). These page references, like all other insertions by Marx, appear in parentheses; insertions by the editors of MEW xix are enclosed in double square brackets.

Wagner writes: 'My standpoint is characterized most briefly as that of a *socio-legal* understanding of the matter . . . It is near to the standpoint of the young German "*ethical*" or "*realistic*" *school*, [or] better, the "*socio-political*" *school* . . . particularly in the critique of the system of free competition. . . .' (Wagner (1879), 2; cf. MEA I. v. 380 n. .)

[2] Johann Karl Rodbertus (Jagetzow) (1805–75); political economist; see above p. 18, and TSV ii. 15–160. Wagner was a co-editor of Rodbertus's posthumously published works.

Friedrich Albert Lange (1828–75); political economist and philosopher; author of the *Labour Question*, Duisburg, 1865, and the *History of Materialism*, Leipzig, 1866.

Albert Friedrich Eberhard Schäffle (1831–1903); author of *Capitalism and Socialism*, Tübingen, 1870; (anon.) *Quintessence of Socialism*, Gotha, 1875; and *Structure and Life of the Social Body*, 4 vols., Tübingen, 1875–8. (Cf. MEW xix. 638, 645; TP no. 5, p. 63.)

Under *'labour'* (p. 9, §2) Herr Wagner does not distinguish between the *concrete character of each* [type of] *labour*, and the *expenditure of labour-power* common to all those concrete types of labour (pp. 9, 10). [See CAP i. 4–5.]

'Even the *mere administration of assets* for the *purpose of drawing revenue* always necessitates activities which belong *under the concept labour*, and it is the same with the *utilization* of the income obtained, for the satisfaction of needs' (p. 10, n. 6).

The *historico-legal* [categories] are, according to Wagner, the *'social categories'* (n. 6, p. 13).[3]

'In particular, *natural monopolies of location* have an effect, especially in *urban* relations' (! A natural monopoly—location in the City of London!) 'then, under the influence of *climate*, [there are,] for the *agricultural production* of whole countries, further *natural monopolies* of the *specific fertility of the land*, e.g. in especially good vineyards, and, indeed, even between different peoples, e.g. with the *sale of tropical products* to the countries of the temperate zone' ('*Export duties* on products in some sort of natural monopoly form a contribution— they are imposed in many countries (southern Europe, tropical countries) [Wagner's parentheses] in the safe assumption of throwing them on to foreign consumers' (n. 11, p. 15). (If Herr Wagner deduces export duties in southern European countries from this, it indicates that he knows nothing of the *'history'* of those duties)—'[such] that *goods* at least *partially free by nature* are, on acquisition, requited in the highest possible degree for *purely economic* [goods]' (p. 15).[4]

The domain of *regular* exchange (*sale*) of goods is their *market* (p. 21).

[3] Wagner writes: 'The distinction [between 'economic' and 'free' goods] introduced here is a consequence of the division of the *purely economic* or *purely natural* and the *historico-legal*, with respect to the social categories.' (Wagner (1879), 13 n. 6; cf. MEA I. v. 380 n. 3.)

[4] Marx has miscopied 'form an example' (*Belegfall bilden*) as 'form a contribution' (*Beitrag bilden*), and has changed 'laying them on' (*zu wälzen*) to 'throwing them on' (*zu werfen*). (Wagner (1879), 15 n. 11; cf. MEW xix. 356; TP no. 5, p. 63; MEA I. v. 381 n. 1.) See also Wagner (1879), 42.

[Wagner includes] *under economic goods*: '*Relations to persons and things (incorporeal things)* [res incorporales],[5] whose objective isolation [in political economy] is based on an abstraction: (a) *out of completely free commerce*: the cases of *goodwill, firms*, and the like, where profitable relations to other men, which are formed through human activity, can be acquired and sold *for payment*; (b) on the basis of certain *legal restrictions on commerce*: exclusive trading rights, real equities, privileges, monopolies, patents etc.' (pp. 22, 23).

Herr Wagner subsumes '*services*' under '*economic goods*' (p. 23, n. 2, and p. 28). What he really succumbs to here is his desire to present Privy Councillor [*Geheimrat*] Wagner as a '*productive labourer*'; for he says

'the response is prejudicial for a judgement [in Wagner's text: an economic judgement] on all those classes which exercise *personal services professionally*, hence on *servants*, on members of the *liberal professions*, and consequently even on the *state* [service]. Only if their services are also reckoned as economic goods, are the [above] mentioned classes *productive* in the economic sense' (p. 24).

The following is very characteristic of the manner of thought of Wagner and consort:

Rau had remarked: it depends on the '*definition of assets*, and, in the same way, on the definition of economic goods', whether '*services* also belong there or not'. Then *Wagner*: '*such a definition*' of '*assets*'—would have to '*be adopted*, which *includes services under economic goods*' (p. 28).

But the '*decisive reason*' would be 'that the *means of satisfaction* could not possibly consist only in material goods, because *needs are not merely* related *to such* [things], *but to personal services* (in particular, those of the state, like *legal protection* etc.) [Wagner's parentheses]' (p. 28).

Assets:

1. '[taken] *purely economically* . . . the *supply of economic goods to*

[5] The Latin term is Wagner's, as are the parentheses.

hand at a moment in time, *as real stock for satisfying needs*', '*assets as such*', 'parts of the total or national assets or the assets of a people'. [Wagner (1879), 32.]

2. 'As an *historico-legal concept* . . . a *fixed supply of economic goods*', '*possession of assets*', '*in the possession, with respect to* the *property of a person*' (p. 32). The latter is an '*historico-legal, relative concept of property.* Property gives only a *certain authority for disposal* and a *certain authority for the exclusion* of others. The *extent* of this authority *changes*' (i.e. historically) (p. 34). 'Every asset in the second sense is an *individual asset*, the asset of a physical or legal person' (loc. cit.).

Public assets,

'principally the *community-controlled economic* assets, hence particularly the *state, district,* [and] *communal assets.* These assets [[are]] determined for *general use* (like roads, rivers etc.) and . . . property therein is assigned to the state etc. as to the legal *representative of the whole* (people, inhabitants of a locality etc.) or it is *state and communal assets* proper, particularly *administrative assets*, which serve for the establishment of state services, and *financial assets*, which are used by the state for the acquisition of revenue, as means for the establishment of its services' (p. 35).

Capital, capitale, is a translation of κεφάλαιον, by which the debt of a sum of money was designated, in contrast [to the debt] of *interest* (τόκος). In the middle ages capitale, caput pecuniae came into use as the main thing, the essential, the primary [thing] (p. 37). In German the word Hauptgeld [principal] was used (p. 37).

'*Capital, capital invested for earnings, an interest-bearing stock of goods: a movable stock of the means of acquisition.*' On the other hand: '*stock for use*: a quantity of the movable means of gratification collected in any respect*' (p. 38, n. 2). [Wagner is quoting Rau.]

Circulating and fixed capital (p. 38, 2(a) and 2(b)).

Value. According to Herr Wagner, Marx's theory of value is '*the cornerstone of his socialist system*' (p. 45). Since I have never promulgated a *'socialist system'*, this is a fantasy of Wagner, Schäffle, and all such [*e tutti quanti*].

Furthermore: Marx

'finds the *common social substance* of *exchange-value*, which is solely what he has in mind here, in *labour*, [and he finds] the *quantitative measure of exchange-value* in socially necessary labour-time' etc.

Nowhere do I speak of *'the common social substance of exchange-value'*, but [I] say, rather, that exchange-values (*exchange-value* does not exist unless [there are] at least two of them) represent something *common to them* [commodities] which is wholly independent 'of their use-values' (i.e. here, of their natural form), namely *'value'*. This means: 'The common something, which is represented in the exchange-relation or the exchange-value of commodities, is therefore *their value*. The course of the inquiry will take us back to exchange-value as the necessary mode of expression or form of appearance of value, which is to be considered, at first, *however, independent of that form*' (p. 13).[6]

Therefore I do not say that the 'common social substance of exchange-value' is 'labour'; and since I deal extensively in that particular section [CAP i. 1–55] with the *value-form*, i.e. the development of exchange-value, it would be strange to reduce that 'form' to a 'common social substance', labour. Also, Herr Wagner forgets that neither 'value', nor 'exchange-value' are my subjects, but *the commodity*.[7]

---

[6] See CAP i. 4–5. Marx's page references to *Capital*, i, refer to the second German edition, dated 1872.

[7] In *Capital*, i, Marx writes: 'If we remove from consideration the use-value of the material bodies of commodities [*Warenkörper*], then there remains only one more attribute, that of [being] the products of labour ... Along with the useful character of the products of labour there disappears [in the exchange of commodities] the useful character of the labours represented in them, hence the different concrete forms of those labours also disappear; they are no longer distinguished [from one another], but are all reduced together to equal human labour, abstract human labour

Further:

'This' (Marxian) 'theory is, however, not so much a general theory of value as a *theory of costs*, connected *to* [that of] *Ricardo*.' (loc. cit.)

Herr Wagner [[could]] have acquainted himself with the difference between me and Ricardo from *Capital*, as well as from *Sieber's work*[8] (if he knew Russian); in fact, he [Ricardo] concerned himself with labour only as the *measure of the quantity of value* and for that reason found no connection between his theory of value and the nature [*Wesen*] of money.

When Herr Wagner says that that would not be a 'general theory of value', then in his sense [of the term] he is quite right, since he understands by a general theory of value a musing over the word 'value', which enables him to stick with the traditional German academic confusion of 'use-value' and 'value', since both have the word 'value' in common. But when he says further that it is a '*theory of costs*', then either he runs to a tautology: commodities, so far as they are values, only represent a *social* something, labour, and, in particular, so far as the *quantity of value* of a commodity is determined, according to my account, through the *quantity of labour-time contained in it* etc., then [it is determined] through the normal amount of labour which the production of an object costs etc.; and Herr Wagner proves the opposite by asserting that this theory etc. of value is not 'the general [theory]', because this is not Herr Wagner's view of the 'general theory of value'. Or else he says *something false: Ricardo* (following [Adam] Smith), lumps value and costs of production

. . . As crystals of this social substance common to them [labour-products], they [labour-products] are—values, commodity-values . . . The common something which is presented in the exchange-relation or exchange-value of commodities, is therefore their value'. (KAP i. pp. xxiv, 4–5; cf. CAP i. 4–5.)

8 Nikolai Ivanovich Sieber (or Ziber') (1844–88); Russian political economist; author of *David Ricardo's Theory of Value and Capital*, Kiev, 1871. (Cf. MEW xix. 596; and TP no. 5, pp. 63–4.) See also CAP i. p. xxvi, where Marx praises Sieber's book.

together; I have already in *A Contribution to the Critique of Political Economy* [1859] and likewise in the notes to *Capital* [1867, 1872–5] expressly pointed out that *values* and *prices of production* (which merely express costs of production in money) do *not* coincide. Why not? I have *not* said [what he says I said] to Herr Wagner.[9]

Moreover, I 'proceed' 'arbitrarily', if I

'reduce these costs only to the so-called productivity of labour in the strictest sense. That always presupposes a demonstration, which is lacking up to now [in Marx's work], that the process of production would be possible wholly without the mediating activity of *private capitalists* forming and utilizing capital' (p. 45).

Instead of burdening me with such future proofs, Herr Wagner would, on the contrary, have first to verify that *a social process of production*, to say nothing of the process of production generally, *did not exist* in the numerous communities which *did exist* before *the appearance of private capitalists* (the ancient commune of India, the family-commune of the southern Slavs etc.). Besides, Wagner could only say: the exploitation of the working class by the capitalist class, in short, the character of capitalist production, as Marx presents it, is correct, but he errs by considering this economy as transitory, while, on the contrary, Aristotle erred by having considered the *slave economy* as *non*-transitory.[10]

'So long as such a proof is *not* established' (alias, so long as the capitalist economy exists), 'then *in fact*' (here the club-foot or ass's ear makes its appearance) '*profit* is also a "constitutive" element of

[9] In *Capital*, i, Marx comments: 'The possibility of quantitative incongruence between price and the quantity of value, or the deviation of price from the quantity of value, lies therefore in the price-form itself. This is not a defect of that form, but on the contrary makes it a form suited to a mode of production in which order can be imposed only as the blind working of the law of averages'. (KAP i. 73; cf. CAP i. 75; see also CAP i. 144 n., 550 n., and CAP iii. 157, 165.)

[10] Aristotle, *Politics*, 1254b39–1255a2 etc.

value, *not* merely a *deduction* or "robbery" on the labourer, as the socialists understand it' (pp. 45, 46).

What a '*deduction on the labourer*' is, a deduction of his hide etc., cannot be made out. In fact, in my presentation, profit is *not* 'merely a *deduction* or "robbery" on the labourer'. On the contrary, I present the capitalist as the necessary functionary of capitalist production and show very extensively that he does not only 'deduct' or '*rob*', but forces the *production of surplus value*, therefore the deducting only helps to produce; furthermore, I show in detail that even if in the exchange of commodities *only equivalents* were exchanged, the capitalist—as soon as he pays the labourer the real value of his labour-power—would secure with full rights, i.e. the rights corresponding to that mode of production, *surplus value*. [See CAP i. 166–80.] But all this does not make 'profit' into a '*constitutive*' *element* of value, but only proves that in the value not '*constituted*' by the labour of the capitalist, there is a portion which he can appropriate 'legally', i.e. without infringing the rights corresponding to commodity-exchange.

'That theory considers too one-sidedly only this one value-determining moment' (1. Tautology. The theory is false, because Wagner has a 'general theory of value' with which it does not agree; his 'value' is determined through 'use-value', as is proved by the academic salary in particular; 2. Herr Wagner substitutes for value the actual 'market price' or the commodity-price divergingfrom it, which is something very different from value), '[it considers] the *costs*, not the other [moment], the usefulness, the *uses*, the moment of *demand*' (i.e. it [Marx's own account] does not lump 'value' and *use-value* together, which is so desirable for a born Confusius[11] like Wagner).

'Not only does it not correspond to the *formation of exchange-value* in *present-day commerce*'[12]

[11] A pun on Confucius and confusion.
[12] In Wagner's text: 'present-day free commerce'. (Wagner (1879), 45; cf. MEW xix. 360; MEA I. v. 385 n. 1.)

(he has in mind the *formation of prices*, which alters absolutely nothing in the *determination of value*: after all, the *formation of exchange-value* certainly *takes place in present-day commerce*, as any speculator, swindler etc. knows; it has nothing in common with the *formation of value*, but has a sharp eye on value [already] 'formed'; anyway, I proceed, e.g. with the determination of the *value of labour-power*, from this [assumption], that its value is actually paid for, which, *as a matter of fact*, is *not the case*. [See CAP i. 176, 214, and 251 etc.] Herr Schäffle is of the opinion, in *Capitalism* etc., that it would be 'magnanimous' [to pay labour-power at its real value] or something similar. He only refers to a scientifically necessary procedure),

'but also, as *Schäffle* in the *Quintessence* and particularly in the *Social Body* proves to perfection and indeed conclusively (!), [it does] not [correspond] to the relations, as they *would necessarily have to take shape, in Marx's hypothetical social state*'. [p. 45.]

(Hence the social state which Herr Schäffle was so kind to 'shape' for me, is transformed into '*the Marxian*' [social state] (not the 'social state' falsely attributed to Marx in Schäffle's hypothesis).)

'This may be *strikingly* demonstrated, particularly in the example of grain and the like, whose *exchange-value* would necessarily have to be regulated *other* than *merely according to costs*, *even* in a system of "*social assessment*" ["Socialtaxen"], because of the influence of variable harvests with much the same demand.' [p. 45.]

(So many words, so much idiocy. Firstly, I have nowhere spoken of '*social assessment*', and in the *inquiry into value* I deal with bourgeois relations, not, however, with the application of that theory of *value* on the 'social state' never constructed by me, rather by Herr Schäffle for me. Secondly: if the price of corn rises after a bad harvest, then, in the first place, its *value* rises, because a given quantity of labour is *realized in less product*; in the second place, its *selling price* rises still more. What has this to do with my theory of value? To the degree that corn[13] is *sold* above *its value*, other commodities, whether in their natural form or in their money-form, are, to the same degree, sold *below their value*, and, to be sure, even if their own money price does *not* fall. The *sum of values* remains the same, even if the expression of that total *sum of values* were to grow in money [terms], hence the sum of 'exchange-value' rises, according to Herr Wagner. This is the case, if we assume that the *fall in price* in the sum of the other commodities does not cover the *over-valued price* (excess price) of corn. But in that case the exchange-value of money has, to the same degree [*pro-tanto*], fallen below its value; the sum of values of all commodities not only remains *the same*, it even remains the same in *monetary expression*, if money is reckoned among the commodities. Furthermore: the rise in the price of corn, as a result of the bad harvest, over its rise in value, is, in any case, smaller in the 'social state' than with present-day profiteering in corn. Then again, the 'social state' will direct production from the outset so that the yearly grain supply depends only to the very minimum on the variations in the weather; the sphere of production—the supply- and the use-aspects thereof—is rationally regulated. Finally, what is 'social assessment' to prove for or against my theory of value, supposing Schäffle's fantasies on that score were realized? As little as the rule of force encountered in the struggles for the means of life on board ship, or in a fortress, or during the French Revolution etc., which pay no attention to *value*; and how ghastly for the 'social state' to infringe the *law of value* of the 'capitalist (bourgeois) state', and hence also the theory of value! Nothing but childish twaddle!)

This same Wagner cites, with approval, from Rau:

'In order to eliminate misunderstandings, it is necessary to set down what is meant under *value pure and simple* [Wert schlechthin], and *it is in conformity with German usage* to choose *use-value* for this' (p. 46).

---

[13] The editors of MEW xix suggest the reading 'corn' for 'corn-price' in the manuscript. (MEW xix. 361.)

Derivation of the concept of value (p. 46 et seq.).

According to Herr Wagner, *use-value and exchange-value* are to be derived at once [*d'abord*] from the *concept of value*, not as with me, from a *concretum* [Konkretum], *the commodity*, and it is interesting to pursue this *scholasticism* in its latest '*Foundations*' [*Grundlegung*—the title of part one of Wagner's work].

'It is a *natural* tendency of man to bring the *relation* in which intrinsic and extrinsic *goods* stand to his *needs*, into *clear consciousness* and *understanding*. This happens through the *assessment* (the *assessment of value*) [Schätzung (Wertschätzung)],[14] whereby *value* is *ascribed* to goods, with respect to things in the external world, and is *measured*' (p. 46), and this signifies, *p. 12*: 'All means for the satisfaction of needs are called *goods*.'

If in the first sentence we insert for the word 'good' its Wagnerian *conceptual content*, then the first sentence of the quoted passage reads:

'It is a *natural tendency* of "*man*" *to bring* the *relation*, in which the intrinsic and extrinsic' means for the satisfaction of his needs 'stand *to his needs*, into *distinct consciousness* and *understanding*'. We could simplify this sentence somewhat by dropping 'the *intrinsic* means' etc. as Herr Wagner does 'with respect to' in the sentence which immediately follows.

'*Man*'? If the category 'man' is meant here, then he has, in general, 'no' needs; if it is man who confronts nature as an individual [*vereinzelt*], then he is to be understood as a non-herd animal; if it is man situated in any form of society—and Herr Wagner implies this, since, for him, 'man', even if he does not have a university education, has language at any rate—, then the determinate character of this social man is to be brought forward as the starting point, i.e. the determinate character of the existing community [*Gemeinwesens*] in which he lives, since production here, hence his *process of securing life*, already has some kind of social character.

[14] Wagner's parentheses.

But with a schoolmaster-professor the relations of man to nature are not *practical* from the outset, that is, relations established by action; rather [for Wagner] they are *theoretical* relations, and two relations of that sort are interlocked in the first sentence.

Firstly: since in the following sentence the '*external means for the satisfaction of his needs*' or '*external goods*' are transformed into '*things of the external world*', then the first interlocked relation takes the following form: man stands *in relation to the things of the external world* as means for the satisfaction of his needs. But on no account do men begin by 'standing in that theoretical relation to the *things of the external world*'. They begin, like every animal, by *eating*, *drinking* etc., hence not by 'standing' in a relation, but *by relating themselves actively*, taking hold of certain things in the external world through action, and thus satisfying their need[s]. (Therefore they begin with production.) Through the repetition of this process, the property of those things, their property 'to satisfy needs', is impressed upon their brains; men, like animals, also learn to distinguish 'theoretically' from all other things the external things which serve for the satisfaction of their needs. At a certain stage of this evolution [*Fortent-wicklung*], after their needs, and the activities by which they are satisfied, have, in the meantime, increased and developed further, they will christen these things linguistically as a whole class, distinguished empirically [*erfahrungsmässig*, i.e. by ex-perience] from the rest of the external world. This happens necessarily, since they stand continually in the production process—i.e. the process of appropriating these things—in active association among themselves and with these things, and soon have to engage in a battle with others over these things. But this linguistic designation only expresses as an idea what repeated corroboration in experience has accomplished, namely, that certain external things serve men already living in a certain social connection (this is a necessary presupposition on account of language) for the satisfaction of their needs. Men assign to these things only a particular (generic) name, because they already know that they serve for the satisfaction of their needs, because they get hold of them through activity which is repeated more or less often, and they also seek to retain [them] in their possession; perhaps they call them 'goods', or something else which expresses the fact that they need these things practically, that these things are useful for them, and they believe that this useful character is possessed by the thing, although it would scarcely appear to a sheep as one of its 'useful' properties that it is edible by man.

Therefore: men begin, as a matter of fact, by appropriating certain things of the external world as the means for satisfying their own needs etc. etc.; later they *also* come to designating *them linguistically* as what they [the things] are for them [men] in practical experience, namely, as *means for satisfying their needs*, as things which 'satisfy' them. If one calls this circumstance, that men do not only deal with such things practically as the means of satisfying their needs, but also that they designate them in ideas, and moreover, in language, as things '*satisfying*' their needs, hence things '*satisfying*' *them themselves* (so long as the need of man is not satisfied, he is in *conflict* with his needs, hence with himself); if one calls this 'ascribing' a '*value*' to them 'according to German usage', then one has proved that the general concept '*value*' arises from the behaviour of men towards the things found in the external world which satisfy their needs, and consequently that this is the *generic concept* [Gattungsbegriff] of '*value*' and that all other sorts of value, as e.g. the chemical value [valence] of the elements, are only a subspecies.[15]

It is 'the natural tendency' of a German professor of political economy to derive the economic category 'value' from a

[15] [[Crossed out in the manuscript:]] But with Herr Wagner this 'deduction' is still prettier, because he is dealing with '*man*', not with '*men*'. Herr Wagner expresses this very simple 'deduction' thus: 'It is a *natural* tendency of man' (read: of German professors of political economy), [to bring into clear consciousness and understanding] 'the relation', by which the things of the external world are not only [recognized] as the means for satisfying human needs, but are recognized as such linguistically, and hence also serve [end of fragment]. (MEW xix, 364.)

'*concept*', and he achieves this by re-christening what in political economy is commonly [*vulgo*] called 'use-value' as '*value*' pure and simple, 'according to German usage'. And as soon as 'value' pure and simple has been found, it serves in turn for *deriving* '*use-value*' again from 'value pure and simple'. For that, one has only to replace the fragment 'use', which has been dropped, in front of 'value' pure and simple.

In fact it is Rau (see p. 88),[16] who says plainly that it 'is necessary' (for German schoolmaster-professors) 'to establish what is meant under *value pure and simple*', and who naïvely asserts: 'and for this it is *in accordance with German usage—to choose use-value*'. (In chemistry, the *chemical value* of an element means the number in which one of its atoms can be combined with the atoms of other elements. But the compound weight of the atoms also signified equivalence, the equivalent value of different elements etc. etc. Hence one must first define the concept 'value pure and simple' etc. etc.)

If man relates himself to *things as 'means for satisfying his needs'*, then *he* relates *himself to them as 'goods'*, *witness* [teste] *Wagner*. He ascribes to them the attribute 'good'; the *content of this operation* is in no way altered by Herr Wagner's re-christening this in [the phrase] '*to ascribe value*'. His own addled consciousness comes forthwith 'to understanding' in the next sentence:

'This happens through the *assessment* (the assessment of *value*), by which *value* is *ascribed to the goods, with respect to* the *things of the external world*, and is measured.'[17]

We do not want to waste words on Herr Wagner's derivation of *value* from the assessment of *value* (he himself adds to the word *assessment* the [phrase] 'assessment of *value*' in parenthesis, in

---

[16] Karl Heinrich Rau (1792–1870); political economist; Wagner's mentor; the page reference is to Rau's *Manual of Political Economy*, Heidelberg, 1826–37 etc., which went through numerous editions. (Cf. Wagner (1879), 46; MEW xix. 644; TP no. 5, p. 63.)

[17] The parentheses are Wagner's. (Wagner (1879), 46; cf. MEA I. v. 389 n. 3)

order 'to bring' the matter 'to clear consciousness and understanding'). '*Man*' has the 'natural tendency' to do this, to
'assess' goods as '*values*', and this permits Herr Wagner *to
derive* the result, promised by him, of the 'concept of *value* in
general'. Wagner does not smuggle in '*with respect to*' the '*things
of the external world*', under the word 'goods' for nothing. He sets
out from this: Man 'relates' himself to 'things of the external
world', which are the means for satisfying his needs, as '*goods*'.
He *assesses* these things just by relating himself to them as
'goods'. And we have already had the earlier 'paraphrase' for
this 'assessment', reading, for example:

'Man stands as a *needy* being [*Wesen*] in continuous contact with
the *external world around* him, and discovers that in that external
world lie *many conditions of his life and well-being*' (p. 8).

This means nothing more than that he '*assesses* the things
of the external world' so far as they satisfy his 'needy being',
so far as they are the means for satisfying his needs, and for
that reason, as we heard earlier, he relates himself to them as
'goods'.

Now, one can, particularly if one feels the 'natural' professorial
'tendency' to derive the concept of value in general, [do] this: to
ascribe to 'the things of the external world' the attribute 'goods',
even *to name* [them], [is] to '*ascribe value*' to them. One could also
have said: Since man relates himself to the things of the
external world, which satisfy his needs, as 'goods', he 'prizes'
['*preist*'] them, hence he ascribes '*Price*' ['Preis'] to them, and
then the derivation of the concept '*price* pure and simple' would
be offered ready cut[18] to the German professor [*Professor
germanicus*] through the methodology of '*man*'. Everything that
the professor cannot do for himself, he lets '*man*' do, but he is in
fact nothing but *professorial man*, who thinks to have conceived
the world, when he arranges it under abstract rubrics. But so
far as 'to ascribe *value*' to the things of the external world is here

[18] Marx uses the English phrase 'ready cut'; possibly a reference to tailoring
or cloth manufacture.

only another way of stating the expression to ascribe to them the attribute *'goods'*, then, as Wagner wants to insinuate, *'value'* is certainly not ascribed to the *'goods' themselves* as a determination different from their 'good-ness' [*'Gutsein'*]. It is only the word 'value' substituted for the word 'good'. (As we see, the word *'price'* could also be substituted. The word *'treasure'* ['Schatz'] could also be substituted; since *'man'* stamps certain 'things of the external world' as *'goods'*, he 'treasures' [*'schätzt'*] them and relates himself to them as a *'treasure'* ['Schatz']. Hence we see how the three economic categories *value*, *price*, [and] *treasure* [or riches, wealth etc.] can be conjured up at a stroke by Herr Wagner from 'the natural tendency of man' to offer the professor his blockheaded conceptual (imaginary) world.) But Herr Wagner has the hidden urge to escape from his labyrinth of tautologies and to obtain a 'further something' or 'something further' by false pretences. Hence the phrase: 'by which *value* is *ascribed* to the goods, *with respect to* the things of the external world etc.' Since the stamping of 'things of the external world' as *goods*, i.e. ditto the *labeling* and *fixing* of them (in ideas) as the *means for satisfying* human needs, has been named by Herr Wagner: to *'ascribe value* to things', then he has just as little excuse to call this ascribing *value* to 'the *goods*' themselves, as he would have to speak of *ascribing value* to the 'value' of the things of the external world. But the somersault [*salto mortale*] is made in the expression *'to ascribe value* to the *goods, with respect to* the things of the external world'. Wagner would have been obliged to say: the stamping of certain things of the external world as *'goods'* can also be *called*: *'to ascribe value'* to these things, and this is the Wagnerian *derivation* of the *'concept of value'* pure and simple, or in general. The *content* is not altered through this *alteration* of linguistic expression. It is always only the *labeling* or *fixing in ideas* of the things of the external world which are the means for satisfying human needs; in fact, it is only the *perception and recognition of certain things of the external world as means for satisfying the needs of 'man'* (who as such still suffers in fact from the 'conceptual need').

But Herr Wagner wants to make us or himself believe that he, instead of giving two names to the same content, has rather advanced from the determination 'good' to a *determination* 'value', [which is] developed and distinguished from it, and this happens simply by substituting the word 'goods' for 'things of the external world', *'with respect to'*, a process which is 'obscured' again by substituting for 'the goods', *'with respect to'*, the 'things of the external world'. His own confusion achieves the certain effect of making his reader confused. He could have reversed this pretty 'derivation' as follows: Since man *distinguishes* the things of the external world which are the means for satisfying his needs, the means of satisfaction as such, from the rest of the things of the external world, and *labels* them, *appreciates* them, he ascribes *value to them* or gives them *the attribute 'value'*; this can also be expressed [by saying] that he ascribes to them the attribute *'good'* as a mark of character or considers or assesses them as 'good'. In that way the concept *'good'* is *ascribed* to *'values'*, *'with respect to'*, the things of the external world. And thus the concept '[economic] *good'* in general is 'derived' from the concept 'value'. With all such *derivations*, it is simply a case of *being diverted* from the matter, whose resolution is beyond us.

But Herr Wagner proceeds in the same breath from the 'value' *of goods* to the *'measure'* of this value.

The content remains absolutely the same, were the term value not generally smuggled in. It could have been said: Since man stamps certain things of the external world, which etc., as 'goods', he comes by and by to compare these 'goods' with one another and, corresponding to the hierarchy of his needs, to bring [them] into a certain rank-ordering, i.e. if we want to call it something, *'to measure'* them. Wagner may not speak at all of the development of the *real measure of these goods* here, i.e. of the development of their *measure of quantity*, since this would remind the reader too easily how little is in question here, [i.e.] what is normally understood under *'measure of value'*. [See CAP i. 2.]

(Like Rau, Wagner could not only demonstrate from

'German usage' that the *labeling* of (pointing to) things of the external world, which are the means for satisfying human needs, as *'goods'*, can also be *named*: 'to ascribe value' to these things, but: since the Latin word dignitas = *worth* [Würde], *merit* [Würdigkeit], *rank* [Rang] etc., which, ascribed to things, also means *'value'*; *dignitas* is derived from dignus, and this from dic, *point out*, *show*, *label* [auszeichnen], *indicate* [zeigen]; therefore dignus means *pointed out*; hence also digitus, finger, with which one indicates a thing, points to it; *in Greek*: δείκ-νυμι, δάκ-τυλος (finger); *in Gothic*: *ga-tecta* (*dico*); *in German*: *indicate* [zeigen]; and we could take many more 'derivations' into consideration, that δείκνυμι or δεικνύω (make certain, bring to view, *point out*) has the fundamental stem δέκ (hold out, *take*) in common with δέχομαι.)[19]

Herr Wagner accomplishes such a lot of banality, tautological muddle, quibbling over words, [and] surreptitious manoeuvres in fewer than seven lines.

After this trick, it is no wonder that this obscurantist [*Dunkelmann*] (*vir obscurus*) proceeds with great confidence:

'The much disputed *concept of value*, still *obscured* by many *only apparently profound inquiries*, is elucidated simply' (indeed) (rather 'is complicated'),[20] 'if one, as was done hitherto' (namely by Wagner) 'starts out from need and the *economic nature* of man, and reaches the *concept of* [an economic] *good*, and *to that* concept—*connects the concept of value*' (p. 46).

We have here the *conceptual* economy, whose alleged elucidation by the obscurantist runs to the *'connecting'* ['Anknüpfen'] and, so to speak, to the *'disconnecting'* ['Aufknüpfen', i.e. a hanging].

Further derivation of the concept of value:

Subjective and objective value. Subjectively and in the *most general sense* of *the value of the* [economic] *good* = the *significance*, which

[19] Marx's philological studies included Jacob Grimm's *History of the German Language*, 2 vols., 2nd edn., Leipzig, 1853. (Cf. MO ii. 1861.)

[20] Reading 'verwickelt' for 'verwikkelt' in MEW xix. 367.

'is ascribed *to the good on account . . . of its usefulness . . . not* a property of the thing in itself, even if it [value] has for a pre-supposition the objective usefulness of a thing' (hence [it] has '*objective*' value for a presupposition) '. . . In the *objective* sense we understand under "*value*", "*values*" [and] then also *value-bearing goods*, where (!) good and value, goods and values *become* in essence identical concepts' (pp. 46, 47).

After Wagner has designated what is usually named '*use-value*' as '*value in general*', the '*concept of value*' pure and simple, he cannot fail to recall that 'the derived' (!) 'value' 'is therefore' (well, well!) '*use-value*'. After he has first designated 'use-value' as the 'concept of value' in general, as 'value pure and simple', he reveals that he has only driveled on about 'use-value', hence he has 'derived' it, since for him driveling and deriving are 'in essence' identical thought-operations. But at this point we learn what subjective content there is with the previous 'objective' conceptual confusion of pp. Wagner [i.e. Rau]. In particular, he [Wagner] unveils a secret for us. Rodbertus had written a letter to him, to be read in the *Tübinger Zeitschrift* for 1878, where he, Rodbertus, explains why 'there is only one kind of value', use-value.[21]

'I' (Wagner) 'have endorsed this point of view, whose significance I had already stressed in the first edition.'

On what Rodbertus says, Wagner says:

'This is completely correct, and necessitates an alteration in the customary illogical "division" of "value"[22] into *use-value and exchange-value*, as I had *proposed* it in §35 of the first edition' (p. 48, n. 4),

and this same Wagner places me (p. 49, note) among the

---

[21] Adolph Wagner, 'Einiges von und über Rodbertus-Jagetzow', *Zeitschrift für die gesammte Staatswissenschaft*, xxxiv (Tübingen, 1878), 199–237. (Cf. MEW xix. 582.)

[22] Not in quotes in Wagner (1879), 48 n. 4. (Cf. MEA I. v. 393 n. 3.)

people according to whom 'use-value' is to be completely 'dismissed' 'from science'.

All this is 'driveling'. In the first place [*De prime abord*] I do not start out from 'concepts', hence I do not start out from 'the concept of value', and do not have 'to divide' these in any way. What I start out from is the simplest social form in which the labour-product is presented in contemporary society, and this is the '*commodity*'. I analyse it, and right from the beginning, in the *form in which it appears*. Here I find that it is, on the one hand, in its natural form, a *useful thing*, alias a *use-value*; on the other hand, it is a *bearer of exchange-value*, and from this viewpoint, it is itself 'exchange-value'. Further analysis of the latter shows me that exchange-value is only a '*form* of appearance', the autonomous mode of presentation of the *value* contained in the commodity, and then I move on to the analysis of the latter. Hence this means precisely, p. 36, 2nd edn: 'When at the beginning of the chapter it was said in the traditional way: the commodity is use-value and exchange-value, then this was, strictly speaking, false. The commodity is use-value or a useful object, and "value". It is presented as double what it is, as soon as *its value* possesses a *form of appearance* proper, that of *exchange-value*, *different* from its natural form' etc. [See CAP i. 30–1.] Hence I do not divide *value* into use-value and exchange-value as antitheses into which the abstraction 'value' splits, rather [I divide] the *concrete social form* of the labour-product; '*commodity*' is, on the one hand, use-value, and on the other hand, 'value', not exchange-value, since the mere form of appearance is not its proper *content*.

Secondly: Only an obscurantist, who has not understood a word of *Capital*, can conclude: Because Marx, in a note to the first edition of *Capital*, overthrows all the German professorial twaddle on 'use-value' in general, and refers readers who want to know something about actual use-value to 'commercial guides',[23] —therefore *use-value* does not play any rôle in his

[23] The reference is to Marx's *A Contribution to the Critique of Political Economy* published in 1859 as the first instalment on *Capital*; parts of this work

work. Naturally it does not play the rôle of its opposite number, of 'value', which has nothing in common with it, other than that 'value' appears in the term 'use-value'. He could just as well have said that 'exchange-value' is put aside by me, because it is only the form of appearance of value, but not 'value', since for me the 'value' of a commodity is neither its use-value nor its exchange-value.

If we have to analyse the 'commodity'—the simplest economic concretum—we have to withhold all relationships which have nothing to do with the present object [*Objekt*] of analysis. What is to be said of the commodity so far as it is use-value, I have said in a few lines, but on the other hand, I have emphasized the *characteristic form* in which use-value—the labour-product— appears here; namely: 'A thing[24] can be useful and be the product of human labour, without being a commodity. Who- ever satisfies his own need through his product, does create use-value, but not a commodity. In order to produce a com- modity, *he must not only produce use-value*, but *use-value for others*, *social use-value*' (p. 15). [See CAP i. 7–8.] (This is the root of Rodbertus's *'social use-value'*.) So use-value itself—as the use- value of the 'commodity'—possesses an historically specific character. In primitive community-life [*Gemeinwesen*], in which e.g. the means of life are produced in common and shared out among the communal associates [*Gemeindegenossen*], the common product satisfies the needs of life of each communal associate, of each producer directly; the social character of the product, of the use-value, lies here in *its (common) social character*. [See CAP i. 65 for the contrasting situation in capitalist society.] (Herr Rodbertus, on the other hand, transforms the 'social use-value'

were revised and incorporated into *Capital*, i (1867). Marx has slightly misquoted the term 'commercial advice' ('*Anweisungen zur Warenkunde*') as 'commercial guides' ('*Anleitungen zur Warenkunde*'). (MEW xix. 369, 582; cf. Karl Marx, *Zur Kritik der politischen Ökonomie* (Berlin, 1859), 4 n; CCPE 28.)

[24] The editors of MEW suggest the reading 'thing' for 'product' in the manuscript. (MEW xix. 370.)

of the *commodity* into 'social use-value' pure and simple, hence he talks drivel.)

Thus it would be pure drivel, as issues from the above, 'to connect' with the analysis of the commodity—since it is presented, on the one hand, as use-value or [economic] good, on the other as 'value'—'to connect' on that occasion all kinds of banal reflections on use-values or goods, which do not fall into the realm of the commodity-world, like 'state-goods', 'communal goods' etc., as happens with Wagner and German professors in general, or on the [economic] good 'health' etc. Where the state itself is a capitalist producer, as with the exploitation of mines, forests etc., its product is a 'commodity', and therefore possesses the specific character of any other commodity.

On the other hand, the obscurantist has overlooked [the fact] that my analysis of the commodity does not stop at the dual mode in which the commodity is presented, [but] presses forward, [so] that in the dual nature [*Doppelsein*] of the commodity there is presented the twofold *character* of *labour*, whose product it is: *useful* labour, i.e. the concrete modes [*modi*] of labour, which create use-values, and abstract *labour, labour as the expenditure of labour-power*, no matter in which 'useful' mode it be expended (the later presentation of the production process depends on this); that in the development of the *value-form of the commodity*, in the last instance, of its money-form, hence of *money*, the *value* of commodity is presented in the *use-value* of another, i.e. in the natural form of another commodity; that *surplus value* itself is derived from a 'specific' *use-value of labour-power* which belongs to it exclusively etc. etc., that hence with me use-value plays an important role completely different than [it did] in previous [political] economy, but that, *nota bene*, it only comes into the picture where such consideration [of value, use-value etc.] springs from the analysis of given economic forms, not from helter-skelter quibbling over the concepts or words 'use-value' and 'value'. [See CAP i. 1–155.]

For that reason, the definitions of 'capital' are not connected straight away with the analysis of the commodity, nor even with the discussion of its 'use-value', since it would have to be pure nonsense, so long as we are only at the stage of analysing the elements of the commodity.

But what worries (shocks) Herr Wagner in my presentation is that I do not do him the honour of following the 'tendency' of patriotic German professors [*dem deutsch-vaterländischen Professoral-'Bestreben'*], and of confounding use-value and value. Although German society is far behind the times [*post festum*], it is still, little by little, moving from a feudal, natural economy, or at least from its predominance, towards a capitalist economy; but the professors always stand with one foot in the old muck, which is natural. From the serfs of the landed proprietors they have been transformed into the serfs of the state, in common parlance [*vulgo*], the government. Hence our obscurantist, who has not once noticed that my *analytic* method, which does not start out from *man*, but from the economically-given social period, has nothing in common with the academic German method of connecting concepts ('With words we can in heat debate/With words a system designate');[25] for that reason he says:

'In agreement with *Rodbertus's* and *Schäffle's* point of view, I place the *use-value*-character *of all value* [[at the head]], and emphasize the assessment of use-value to such an extent, *because* the assessment of exchange-value is positively not applicable to many of the most important economic goods' (What is forcing him to these subterfuges? as the servant of the state he feels obliged to confound use-value and value!), '*hence not to the state and its services* or to other economic relations of the community' (p. 49, note).

(This recalls the old chemists before the science of chemistry: because cooking butter, which in ordinary life means butter pure and simple (after the Nordic custom), may have a soft state, they called *chlorides zinc-butter, antimony-butter* etc., buttery humours; they adhered, therefore, in order to talk with

[25] Goethe, *Faust*, I. 1997–8. Mephistopheles is speaking to the Student.

the obscurantist, to the *butter*-character of all chlorides, zinc, [and] antimony (compounds).) The flummery comes to this: because certain goods, especially *the state* (a good!) and its '*services*' (particularly the services of its professors of political economy), are *not* 'commodities', then the opposing characters (which also appear *explicitly* in the *commodity-form* of the labour-product), contained in the 'commodities' themselves, would have to be confounded with one another! Besides, Wagner and consort find it difficult to profess that they gain more if their 'services' are evaluated [*bestimmt*] by their 'use-value', by their material 'content', than if they are evaluated by their '*salary*' (through 'social assessment', as Wagner expresses it), i.e. 'valued' ['*geschätzt*'] by what they are *paid*.

(The one thing that is clearly at the basis of this German idiocy is that linguistically the words: *value* [Wert] or *worth* [Würde] were employed at first for useful things themselves, which existed for a long time just as 'labour-products', before they came to be *commodities*. But that has as much to do with the scientific determination of commodity-'value' as the circumstance that the word *salt* was employed by the ancients at first for cooking salt, and hence even *sugar* etc. figure since Pliny as *kinds of salt* (indeed, all colourless solid bodies soluble in water, and peculiar in taste), so that the chemical category 'salt' includes sugar etc.)

(Since the commodity is purchased by the buyer, not because it has value, but because it is 'use-value' and is used for determinate purposes, it is completely self-evident, 1. that use-values are 'assessed', i.e. their *quality* is investigated (just as their *quantity* is measured, weighed etc. [see CAP i. 2]); 2. that if different sorts of commodities can be substituted for one another in the same useful employment, this or that is given preference etc. etc.)

In Gothic there is only one word for *value* [Wert] and *worth* [Würde]: *vairths*, τιμή (τιμάω—*to assess*, which is to estimate; to determine the *price* or *value*; *to rate, to value* [würdigen] *metaphysically, to assess the value, to hold in esteem, to mark. τιμή—assess-*

ment, hence: the determination of value or price, an estimate, make an assessment. Then: *estimation of value*, also *value*, *price itself* (Herodotus, Plato), αἱ τιμαί—*expenses* in *Demosthenes*. Then: *assessment of value, honour*, regard, honorary post, honorary office etc., *Greek-German Lexikon by Rost.*) [26]

Value, price (Schulze, Glossary) [27] Gothic: *vairths*, adj., ἄξιος, ἱκανός;

Old Norse: verdhr, worthy [*würdig*], verdh, *value*, *price*; *Anglo-Saxon*: verordh, vurdh; English: *worth*, adj. and subst. *value* [Wert] and *worth* [Würde]. [28]

'*Middle High German*: wert, gen. werdes, adj. dignus and in the same way, pfennincwert. [29]

-wert, gen. werdes, value [*Werth*], worth [*Würde*], excellence [*Herrlichkeit*], aestimatio, *commodity of determinate value*, e.g. pfenwert, *pennyworth*.

-werde: *meritum*, aestimatio, *dignitas*, valuable quality'. (*Ziemann, Middle High German Dictionary.*) [30]

Hence *value* and *worth* are completely interrelated, according to etymology and meaning. What hides the matter is the *inorganic* (false) *mode of inflection* of value [*Wert*] which became current in New High German: *Werth, Werthes*, instead of *Werdes*, for the High German *d* corresponds to the Gothic *th*, not *th = t*, and this is also the case in Middle High German (wert, gen. werdes, the same). According to the Middle High German rule the

---

[26] Valentin Christian Friedrich Rost, *Deutsch-Griechisches Wörterbuch*. The 10th edition was published in Göttingen in 1874. (Cf. MEW xix. 595, 645.)

[27] Ernst Schulze, *Gothisches Glossar*, Magdeburg, [1848]. (Cf. MEW xix. 595.)

[28] Marx discusses the meaning of the term 'value' in *Theorien über den Mehrwert*, iii (4th edn.; Stuttgart, 1921), 355 n. (Cf. MEA I. v. 397 n. 2.) This note is omitted in MEW xxvi(3) and TSV iii.

[29] Pfennigwert in MEA I. v. 397.

[30] Adolf Ziemann, *Mittelhochdeutsches Wörterbuch zum Handegebrauch*, Quedlinburg, 1838. (Cf. MEW xix. 597, 650.) See also Wagner (1879), 46.

d at the end of the word would have to become t, hence wert instead of werd, but genit[ive] werdes.

But this has just as much, and just as little, to do with the economic category 'value' as with the *chemical value of the chemical elements* (atomicity) or with the chemical equivalents or equivalent values (compound weights of the chemical elements).

Furthermore, we notice that even in the linguistic relationship—if from the original identity of *worth* [Würde] and *value* [Wert] it follows, as from the nature of the thing, that this word is applied to things, [to] labour-products in their natural form— it was later directly transferred, unaltered, to *prices*, i.e. to value in its developed value-form—i.e. exchange-value, which has as little to do with the matter as [the fact] that the same word was employed extensively for worth in general, for honorary office etc. Hence there is no linguistic distinction here between use-value and value.

We come now to the obscurantist's [own] authority, to *Rodbertus* (whose essay is to be seen in the *Tübinger Zeitschrift*). What the obscurantist cites from Rodbertus is the following:

In the *text, p. 48*:

'There is only *one type of value*, and that is use-value. This is either *individual* use-value or *social* use-value. The first stands opposed to the individual and to his needs, apart from considerations of social organization.'

(This is sheer nonsense (see *Capital*, p. 171), where it is said: that the *labour-process* as purposeful activity for the manufacture of use-values etc. '*is equally common*' 'to all its' (human life's) '*social forms*' and '*is independent of any of them*'. [See CAP i. 163-4.] In the first place, the word 'use-value' does not stand opposed to the individual, rather *concrete use-values* [do so], and *which of these* 'stand opposed' to him (with these men everything 'stands'; everything is 'standing'), depends wholly on the level of the social process of production, hence corresponds to 'a social organization'. But if Rodbertus wants to state only the triviality that use-value, which actually confronts the individual as an object of use, confronts him as an individual use-value for him, then this is a trivial tautology or false, since for an individual, the need for a professorial title, or the title of privy councillor, or for a decoration, not to speak of such things as rice, maize, or corn, or not to mention meat (which does not confront the Hindu as the means of nourishment), is only possible in some quite definite 'social organization'.)

'The second is the *use-value* possessed by a *social* organism, consisting of many individual organisms (respective individuals)' (p. 48, text). [Wagner is quoting Rodbertus.]

What fine German! Does it deal here with the 'use-value' of the 'social organism', or with a use-value found in the possession of a 'social organism' (as e.g. land in primitive community-life), or with the determinate 'social' form of use-value in a *social organism*, as e.g. where commodity-production is dominating, the use-value which a producer offers must be 'use-value for others', and in that sense, 'social use-value'? We want nothing to do with such windbaggery.

Hence to another proposition by Wagner's Faust [i.e. Rodbertus]:[31]

'Exchange-value is only the historical covering and appendage of social use-value from a determinate historical period. Since one is opposing to use-value *an* exchange-value *as a logical antithesis*, one puts a logical concept in logical opposition to an historical concept, which is not logical procedure' (p. 48, note 4). 'That is', as Wagner exults [*jubelt ibidem* Wagnerus], 'that is completely correct!'

Who is the 'one' who perpetrates this? Certainly Rodbertus

[31] The allusion is to Goethe's *Faust*, where the character Wagner serves as a foil to the hero; Marx suggests that Adolph Wagner is Rodbertus's pedantic assistant.

has me in mind, since he has written a 'great fat manuscript' against *Capital*, according to R. Meyer, his servant [*famulus*].[32] Who places in logical antithesis? Herr Rodbertus, for whom 'use-value' and 'exchange-value' are by nature two mere 'concepts'. In fact in every price-list every single sort of commodity goes through this illogical process of distinguishing itself from the others as a *good*, a *use-value*, as cotton, yarn, iron, corn etc., of presenting an '[economic] good' [as] qualitatively different in every respect [*toto coelo*] from the others, but at the same time presenting its *price* as qualitatively the same, [i.e.] presenting a quantitatively different thing *of the same essence*. It presents itself in its natural form for him who uses it, and in the thoroughly different *value-form*, 'common' to it with all other commodities, as *exchange-value*. We are dealing here with a '*logical*' antithesis only in the works of Rodbertus and German schoolmaster-professors allied to him, who start out from the 'concept' value, not from the 'social thing', the 'commodity', and let this concept divide (double) itself all by itself, and then argue about which of the two fantasies is the real Jacob!

But what lies in the murky background of these florid phrases is simply the immortal discovery that in all circumstances man must eat, drink etc. (one cannot go further all at once: to clothe himself, or to have a knife and fork, or bed and lodging, since this is not the case *under all circumstances*); in short, that he finds in all circumstances external things ready in nature for the satisfaction of his needs, and must take possession of them or must prepare them from what is found in nature; in this his actual conduct he always relates himself practically [*faktisch*] to certain external things as 'use-values', i.e. he always deals with them as objects for his use; hence use-value is, according to Rodbertus, a 'logical' concept; therefore, since man must also breathe, 'breath' is a 'logical' concept,

---

[32] Rudolph Hermann Meyer (1839–99); political economist; biographer of Rodbertus; author of *Political Bosses and Corruption in Germany*, Leipzig, 1877. (Cf. MEW xix. 641; TP no. 5, p. 65.) In *Faust*, II, Famulus is servant to Faust.

but certainly not a 'physiological' concept. Rodbertus's complete vapidity comes forth, however, in his antithesis of 'logical' and 'historical' concepts! He understands 'value' (the economic value, in contrast to the use-value of the commodity) only in its form of appearance, in *exchange-value*, and because this only arises where at least some part of the labour-products, the objects of use, function as '*commodities*'—however, this does not happen at the beginning, but only in a certain period of social development, hence at a determinate level of historical development,—then *exchange-value* is a 'historical' concept. If Rodbertus—I will say further below why he has not seen it— had analysed the exchange-value of commodities further—for this exists simply where the *commodity* comes in the plural, [where there are] different sorts of commodities—, then he [would have] found 'value' beneath this form of appearance. If he had inquired further into value, then he would have found that here the thing, the 'use-value', serves as the mere *objectification* of human labour, as the *expenditure of equal human labour-power*, and hence that this content is presented as an *objective* character of the *thing*, as [[a character]] which pertains *to it* materially, although this objectivity does *not* appear in its natural form (but [this is] what makes a special *value-form* necessary). [See CAP i. 41–55.] Hence he would have found that the 'value' of a commodity only expresses in a historically developed form, what exists in all other historical forms of society as well, even if *in another form, namely, the social character of labour*, so far as it exists as the *expenditure of 'social' labour-power*. If 'the value' of the commodity is only a determinate historical form of something which exists in all forms of society, then so is the 'social use-value', as he characterizes the 'use-value' of the commodity. Herr Rodbertus takes Ricardo's measure of the quantity of value; but just as little as Ricardo has he grasped or explored the substance [*Substanz*] of value itself; e.g. [he does not explore] the '*mutual*' ['gemeinsame'] character of the [[labour-process]] in primitive community-life as the community-organism [*Gemeinorganismus*] of labour-powers allied to one another and hence that ['mutual' character] of *their labour*, i.e. the expenditure of those powers.

At this point further discussion of Wagner's twaddle is superfluous.

Measure of the quantity of value. Herr Wagner has included me here, but finds to his regret that I have *'eliminated'* the *'labour of capital formation'* (p. 58, n. 7).

'In commerce regulated through social organs, the determination of *assessed values*, with respect to *assessed prices*, must proceed under the consideration of this *moment of cost*' (so he calls the quantum of labour expended etc. in production), 'as also happened in principle in earlier assessment by authority and assessment through trade, and would happen again with a possible *new system of assessment*' (he means socialist!). 'However, in free commerce the *costs* are *not* the *exclusive* basis for determining exchange-values and prices nor could they be in a *conceivable social condition*. For independent of costs, there would always be fluctuations of use-*value* and demand, whose *influence on exchange-value and prices* (contract-prices, like assessed prices)[33] then modifies the *influence of costs* and must modify' etc. (pp. 58, 59). 'For the' (especially this!) 'penetrating correction of the socialist teaching on value . . . we are indebted to *Schäffle* (!), who says, *Social Body*, III, p. 278: No kind of social influence on demands and productions can avoid the fact that *all demands* stay qualitatively and quantitatively each in balance with productions. But if that is so, then the *social quotients of cost-value cannot at the same time* function *proportionally as social quotients of use-value*' (p. 59, n. 9).[34]

That this only amounts to the triviality of the rising and falling of *market-prices* over or under the value [of a commodity] and to the presupposition that his [Marx's] theory of value, developed[35] for *bourgeois* society, *prevails* in the 'Marxian social state'—this is attested by Wagner's words:

[33] Wagner's parentheses.

[34] Marx has made minor errors in copying this passage: *Bedürfuis* for *Bedarfs*, *Bestimmungsgrund* for *Bestimmgrund*, *sozialen* for *gesellschaftlichen*, *eintreten* for *stattfinden*. (Wagner (1879), 58–9; MEW xix. 376; cf. MEA I. v. 401 nn. 2, 3; TP no. 5, p. 65.)

[35] Reading 'entwickelte' for 'entwikkelte' in MEW xix. 376.

'They' (the prices) 'will from time to time more or less diverge' (from costs), 'will rise with the goods whose use-value has become greater, fall with those whose use-value has become less. *Only in the long run* could costs be made continuously applicable as the deciding regulator' etc. (p. 59).

Law. One passage suffices for the fantasy of the obscurantist on the economically creative influence of *law*, although he patters on and on about that inherently absurd viewpoint:

'The individual economic system has at its head, as the organ of technical and economic activity . . ., a *person* as the legal and economic subject. Again it is not a purely economic phenomenon [*Erscheinung*], but it is, at the same time, dependent on the form of *law*. For this determines who counts as a person, and who can stand at the head of an economic system' etc. (p. 65).

Communication and *transportation* (pp. 75–76) *p. 80* (note).

From *p. 82*: where the '*exchange* [Wechsel] *in the (natural) components of the mass of goods*'[36] (of an enterprise, alias with Wagner [it is] christened '*exchange of goods*', for Schäffle's '*social exchange of material*'—at least a case of that is clarified; I have employed the word, however, for the 'natural' process of production as the material exchange [*Stoffwechsel*] between man and nature) [i.e. this term] is *borrowed* from me, where the material exchange appears at first in the analysis of C-M-C [commodity-money-commodity], and the interruptions [*Interruptionen*] of the formal exchange are later designated as interruptions of the material exchange. [See CAP i. 78–88.]

Moreover, what Herr Wagner says on the '*inner exchange*' of the goods found in a branch of production (as he says, in an 'individual economic system'), partly in respect of their

---

[36] Wagner writes: 'The operation of the economic system leads necessarily to a continuous *exchange*, analogous in fact to the natural material exchange *in the (natural) components* of the mass of goods which are at the disposal of the economic system at a given time.' (Wagner (1879), 82; cf. MEA I. v. 402 n. 1.)

'use-value', partly in respect of their 'value', I discuss with the
analysis of the first phase of C-M-C, namely C-M, the example
of the linen-weaver (*Capital*, pp. 85, 86/87), where this is the
conclusion: 'Hence our commodity-possessors discover that the
same division of labour, which makes them into independent,
private producers, [also] makes the social process of production
and their relations in that process independent of them themselves, [and] that the independence of persons from one another
is completed in a system of all-round material dependence'
(*Capital*, p. 87). [See CAP i. 76–83.]

Contracts for the commercial acquisition of goods. Here the
obscurantist gets mine and his upside down. With him there is,
first, the law, and then commerce; in reality it's the other way
round: at first there is *commerce*, and then a *legal order* develops
out of it. In the analysis of the circulation of commodities I
have demonstrated that in a developed trade the exchangers
recognize each other tacitly as equal persons and owners of the
goods to be exchanged respectively by them; they *do* this while
they offer their goods to one another and agree to trade with
one another. This *practical* [faktische] relation, arising through
and in exchange itself, only later attains a *legal form* in contracts
etc.; but this form produces neither its content, the exchange,
nor the relationship, existing in it, of persons to one another,
but vice versa. On the contrary with Wagner:

'*This acquisition*' (of goods through commerce) 'necessarily presupposes a determinate *legal order*, on the *basis of which*' (!) 'commerce
is carried out' etc. (p. 84).[37]

Credit. Instead of giving the development of money as the
means of payment, Wagner makes the process of circulation, so far
as it takes place in the form that the two equivalents are not

---

[37] Wagner continues: 'To begin with, we must recognize here a *property-
right* of the economic system in the goods produced by it, and in
connection with or as a consequence of it, an economic right . . . the
right of contract.' (Wagner (1879), 84; cf. MEA I. v. 402 n. 3.)

opposed simultaneously in C-M [commodity-money], directly into the '*practice of credit*' (p. 85 et seq.), whereby there is 'connected' [the fact] that this is frequently combined with 'interest'-payment; [this] also serves to establish the 'giving of trust' and hence 'trust' [itself] as a basis of 'credit'.

On the legal understanding of 'assets' of [Georg Friedrich] *Puchta*[38] etc., whereby *debts* also belong there as *negative constituents* (p. 86, n. 8).

Credit is '*consumptive credit*' or 'productive credit' (p. 86). The former is dominating in the lower level of culture; the latter,[39] in the 'higher'.

On the *causes of indebtedness* (causes of pauperism: fluctuations in the harvest, army service, competition of slaves) in ancient Rome (Jhering, 3rd *edn.*, p. 234, II, 2. *Spirit of the Roman State*.)[40]

According to Herr Wagner 'consumptive credit' rules in the 'lower level' [of culture] among the 'lower, servile' classes and the 'higher, prodigal' classes. In fact: in England, [and] America, '*consumptive credit*' *is generally dominating with the formation of the deposit-bank system*!

'In particular, *productive credit* . . . is proved to be an economic factor of the national economy adhering to *free competition*, [and] based *on private property in real estate and on movable capital*. It is connected with the *possession* of assets, not with the asset as a purely economic category', hence it is only an 'historico-*legal category*' (!) (p. 87).

---

[38] Georg Friedrich Puchta (1798–1846); jurist; author of *Lectures on present-day Roman Law*, 2 vols., 6th edn., Leipzig, 1873; contributor to Rudolph von Jhering's *Cases in Civil Law*, Leipzig, 1847. (Cf. MEW xix. 644; TP no. 5, p. 65.)

[39] The editors of MEW xix suggest the readings 'former' and 'latter' for 'latter' and 'former' in the manuscript. (MEW xix. 378.)

[40] Rudolph von Jhering. *Geist des römischen Rechts auf den verschiedenen Stufen seiner Entwicklung*, Leipzig, 1852–78. (Cf. MEW xix. 592, 636.) Marx has copied the reference from Wagner (1879), 87, n. 10; cf. MEA I. v. 403 n. 2.

Dependence of the individual economic system and of assets on the effects of the external world, especially on the influence of conjuncture[41] [Konjunktur] *in the national economy.*

1. *Alterations in use-value*: improved in some cases through the *course of time*, as a condition of certain natural processes (*wine, cigars, violins* etc.).

'*Worsened* in the great *majority* [of cases] . . ., [use-values are] resolved into their material constituents, *accidents* of all kinds'. The '*alteration*' of exchange-value in the same direction, '*raising*' or '*lowering in value*', corresponds [to this] (pp. 96, 97). *See the leasing of houses* in Berlin (p. 97, n. 2).[42]

2. *Altered human knowledge of the properties of goods*; hence '*increased assets*' in the *positive case*. (*Use of hard coal for the smelting of iron* in England about *1620*, as the clearing of forests already threatened the continuation of iron works; chemical discoveries, as that of iodine (use of iodized sources of salt). Phosphorus as a means of fertilizing. Anthracite as fuel. Material for gas lighting, for photographs. Discovery of dyes and pharmaceuticals. Guttapercha, india rubber. Vegetable ivory (from Phytelephas macrocarpa).[43] Creosote. Paraffin-wax candles. Use of *asphalt*, of *pine-needles* (pine-needle wool),[44] of gas in blast furnaces, hard coal tar for the preparation of aniline, woollen rags, sawdust etc. etc.) In the *negative case*, the *diminution*

---

[41] '. . . a particular state of affairs, *esp.* of a critical nature'. (OED *s.v.* Conjuncture 2.)

[42] Wagner writes: 'There is, in modern big-city *rent contracts*, a characteristic example of the economic and legal *fiction* of the equality of the parties at the conclusion of the contract, e.g. in Berlin, where this is usual: "The tenant bears the damages to the dwelling, and particularly to the windows, incurred through hail, storm, and other unavoidable natural events." ' (Wagner (1879), 97, n. 2; cf. MEA I. v. 403 n. 4.)

[43] '. . . the hard albumen of the nut or seed of a South American palm, *Phytelephas macrocarpa* . . . used for ornamental work, buttons, etc.' (OED *s.v.* Ivory 2.)

[44] A wool-like fiber extracted (since 1840)from pine and spruce needles, used for textiles and padded furniture. (GDW *s.v.* Waldwolle 2.)

of *usefulness and hence of value* (as with the discovery of trichina in pork, poisons in colourings, plants etc.) (pp. 97, 98). Discoveries of *mineral products* in the earth, of new useful properties in its products, discovery of new employment for them increases the *assets of the owners of landed property* (p. 98).

3. *Conjuncture.*

Influence *of all* the external 'conditions', which 'essentially co-determine' 'the *provision of goods for commerce*, their *demand and supply*' . . . hence their '*exchange-value*', also that '*of the single finished good*'; [this is] 'wholly or primarily independent' of the 'economic subject', 'with respect to the owner' (p. 98). *Conjuncture becomes* the '*decisive factor*' in the '*system of free competition*' (p. 99). The one [person]—'by means of the *principle of private property*'—gains by 'what he has not *earned*', and thus the other suffers a '*forfeiture*', '*economically undeserved losses*'.

On *speculation* (n. 10, p. 101). *Price of housing* (p. 102, n. 11). *The coal and iron industry* (p. 102, n. 12). *Numerous alterations in technology* reduce the values of industrial products, as of instruments of production (pp. 102, 103).

With the 'national economy *advancing* in population and well-being there *prevail* . . . *favourable prospects*, even if there are also occasional temporary and local setbacks and fluctuations in *landed property, especially in cities* (great cities)' (p. 102).

'So conjuncture effects gains, particularly for the *landed* proprietor' (p. 103). 'These, like most other *gains in value from conjuncture* . . . [are] only *purely speculative gains*', to which correspond '*speculative losses*' (p. 103).

Ditto on the 'corn trade' (p. 103, n. 15).

Thus it must 'obviously be recognized: . . . the economic condition of the individual or family' is '*in essence*, too, a *product of conjuncture*', and this 'necessarily detracts from the meaning of *personal economic responsibility*' (pp. [[104,]] 105).

Hence the '*present organization* of the national economy and the *legal basis*' (!), 'hence private property in . . . land and capital' etc., 'is' 'an *arrangement*, mainly *unalterable*', so after a lot of waffle, there is no means 'for combatting . . . *the causes*' ([and] the evil conditions arising therefrom, as ever, stagnation of the market, crises, sacking workers, reduction of wages etc.) 'hence *not* [a fight against] the evil itself', while Herr Wagner intends to combat the 'symptoms', the 'consequences of the evil', since he hits 'speculative *gains*' with 'taxes', [and] the 'economically undeserved' '*losses*', the product of conjuncture, with a 'rational . . . *system of insurance*' (p. 105).

This, says the obscurantist, is the result, if one takes the present mode of production with its 'legal basis' to be 'unalterable'; his investigation, however, which goes deeper than socialism, will go to the heart of the 'thing itself'. We shall see eh? [*Nous verrons, wie?*]

The individual, principal moments which form the conjuncture.

1. *Fluctuations in the harvest yield of the principal means of nourishment* under the *influence of the weather* and political relations, like disturbances of cultivation through war. Producers and consumers influenced thereby (p. 106). (On *grain dealers*: *Tooke, History of Prices*; for *Greece*: *Böckh, Public Economy of the Athenians,* I. 1. §15;[45] for *Rome*: *Jhering, Spirit,* p. 238. *Increased mortality of the lower orders* nowadays with each *small* rise in prices, '*certainly a proof of how little the average wage* for the mass of the working class *exceeds the amount absolutely necessary* for life' (p. 106, n. 19).) *Improvements in the means of communication* ('at the same time', it is called in n. 20, 'the most important presupposition of a speculative corn trade which equalizes prices'), *altered methods of agriculture* ('*rotation of crops*', by means 'of the cultivation of *different* products, which are differentially increased or decreased through different weather conditions'); hence the *smaller variations in the price of grain within a shorter space of time* compared 'with the middle ages and antiquity'. But the fluctuations now are still very large. (See note 22, p. 107; the facts are there.)

---

[45] Thomas Tooke (with William Newmarch), *History of Prices . . . from 1793 to the present Time,* 6 vols., London, 1838–57.

August Böckh, *Die Staatshaushaltung der Athener,* 3 vols., 2nd edn., Berlin, 1851. (Cf. MEW xix. 596, 648, 588, 629.)

2. *Alterations in technology. New methods of production.* Bessemer steel instead of iron etc. p. 107 (and note 23). *Introduction of machines in place of manual labour.*

3. Alterations in the means of communication and transport, which influence the *geographical* [räumliche] movement of men and goods: In that particular way . . . the *value of the land* and of articles of a *lower specific value* [are] affected; whole branches of production [are] pressed into a difficult transition to other methods of management (p. 107). (On that, n. 24 ibid. *Rise in the value of land in the vicinity of good communications*, on account of the better sale of the products produced here; *facilitation of increased population* in cities, hence the *enormous rise in the value of land in cities* and of *value* in the vicinity of such places. *Facilitated export* from *regions with hitherto cheap prices for grain* and for other agricultural and forest raw materials, [and] for mineral products, into regions with higher prices; hence the straitened economic condition of all elements of the population with fixed incomes in the first regions, against protection of the producers and particularly of the landed proprietors there. For the contrary effect, the facilitated *supply* (*import*!) of grain and of other material of a lower specific value. Protected consumers, disadvantaged producers in the country where it is delivered; necessity to transfer to other productions, as in England, from growing corn to producing meat in the 1840s, on account of the competition of cheap East European corn in Germany. Difficult conditions for (present-day) *German farmers* on account *of the climate*, then [also] on account of the *recent steep rise in wages* which they cannot slap onto products as easily as industrialists etc.)

4. *Alterations in taste!* *Fashions* etc., often quickly carried out in a short time.

5. *Political alterations* in national and international commerce (war, revolution etc.); *trust and mistrust* thereby [become] *ever more important* with the growing division of labour, improvement of international commerce etc., effects of the credit factor, terrible dimensions of modern warfare etc. (p. 108).

P

6. *Changes in agrarian, industrial, and commercial politics.* (Example: reform of the British corn laws.)

7. Alterations in the *geographical distribution* and in the *total economic condition of the whole population,* like the emigration from the country into the cities (pp. 108, 109).

8. *Alterations in the social and economic condition of the individual strata of the population,* as through the granting of freedom [for labourers] to combine etc. (p. 109). (The French 5,000,000,000[46] n. 29 ibid.)

Costs in the individual enterprise. Under 'value'-producing 'labour', into which all costs resolve, 'labour' must particularly be taken in the correct *broad* sense, in which it 'comprises *all* that is necessary to human activity consciously directed towards securing a return', particularly also 'the *mental labour* of the director, and the activity through which capital is formed and employed', 'hence' the '*capital gain*' repaying this activity belongs to the 'constitutive elements of cost'. 'This point of view is in contradiction to the socialist theory of value and costs and the critique of capital' (p. 111).

The obscurantist falsely attributes to me [the view] that 'the *surplus value* produced by the labourers *alone* was left to the capitalist employers in an *improper way*' (n. 3, p. 114). Well, I say the direct opposite; namely, that commodity-production is necessarily, at a certain point, turned into 'capitalist' commodity-production, and that according to the *law of value* governing it, 'surplus value' is properly due to the capitalist, and not to the labourer. Instead of yielding to such sophistry [*Sophistik*, i.e. the 'law of value' governing capitalist production], the character of the obscurantist as a *Kathedersozialist* [academic socialist, or 'socialist of the chair'] is proved by the following banality, that the

'unconditional enemies of the socialists' 'overlook the numerous cases of *exploitative relations* in which the nett profit is not divided

---

[46] Reparations (in francs) paid by France to Germany after the Franco-Prussian War of 1870–1. (Cf. MEW xix. 582.)

rightly (!), the employers' *costs of production* for *a single enterprise* are diminished to the disadvantage of the workers (also, of the loan capitalists) and to the advantage of those who provide work' (loc. cit.)

National income of England and France (p. 120, χ–φ).
The gross annual product of a nation:

1. Totality of the goods *newly* produced in a year. *Domestic raw materials* to be set down in entirety, according to their value; the *objects derived from such and from foreign material* (in order to avoid the double accounting of raw materials) [to be set down] for the *amount of the increase in value achieved by factory work*; the *raw materials* and *semi-manufactured*[47] [goods] sold and *transported* in *trade*, [to be set down] for the amount of the increase in value effected thereby.

2. *Import of money and commodities from abroad*, from the title to the income [received] from *secured claims* of the home country, from *extending credit*, or by the *capital investments* of citizens resident in foreign countries.

3. The *carrying of freight* by the *domestic shipping business* in *external trade and mutual commerce*, paid for in real terms by means of the importation of foreign goods.

4. *Cash or commodities* from abroad *imported as remittances for resident foreigners*.

5. *Importation of uncompensated gifts*, as with *continuing tribute* from a foreign land to the home country, *continuing immigration, and hence regular* [import of the] *assets of immigrants*.

6. *A surplus of value from the import of money and commodities, resulting from international trade*,[48] (but then to be deducted, 1. *export[s]* to foreign countries).

---

[47] Marx has written 'semi-manufactured' [*Halbfabrikate*] for 'manufactured' [*Fabrikate*]. (Wagner (1879), 121 n. 3; MEW xix. 382; cf. MEA I. v. 407 n. 1.)

[48] Ryazanov comments that Marx has mistakenly written 'inland' for 'international'. (Wagner (1879), 122; cf. MEW xix. 382; MEA I. v. 407 n. 2.)

7. *Amount of value* [received] *from the utilization of useful assets* (as of dwelling houses etc.) (pp. 121, 122).

To be deducted for the *nett product* and other things, the 'export of goods as payment for the *carrying of freight by foreign ships*' (p. 123). (The matter is not so simple: The *price of production (domestic)* + *freightage* = *selling price*. If the home country exports its own commodities in its own ships, then the foreign countries pay the costs of freight, if the market price prevailing there etc.)

'Regular payments to *foreign subjects abroad*, to be reckoned [in Wagner's text: named] as part of continuing tribute' (bribery, as from the Persians to the Greeks, *salaries of foreign scholars* under Louis XIV, Peter's pence)[49] (p. 123, n. 9).

Why not the *subsidies* which the German princes regularly derive from France and England?

See the naïve sorts of *divisions for the income of private persons*, which consist of 'state and clerical services'[50] (p. 125, n. 14).

Individual and national assessment of value.

In his *Researches into the mathematical Principles of the Theory of Wealth*, 1838,[51] Cournot calls the *destruction of a part of a stock of commodities*, in order to sell the rest more dearly, 'a true creation of wealth in the commercial sense of the word' (p. 127, n. 3).

Compare the decline of *stocks* for consumption by private individuals, or *as Wagner calls it, their 'use-capital'*, in our cultural period, especially in *Berlin*, p. 128, n. 5, p. 129, nn. 8 and 10; for

---

[49] Annual contribution from Catholics to the Papacy; originally a silver penny from each family on the feastday of St. Peter. (Cf. MEW xix. 582; TP no. 5, p. 65.)

[50] Wagner writes: '. . . services of the church and state are put down as parts of the incomes of private persons . . . [this] appears in one respect as a consequence of the subsumption of services under economic goods.' (Wagner (1879), 125 n. 14; cf. MEA I. v. 408 n. 1; MEA gives the reference to Wagner's note incorrectly.)

[51] Augustin Cournot, *Recherches sur les principes mathématiques de la théorie des richesses*, Paris, 1838. (Cf. MEW xix. 588, 631.)

that, [there is] too little money or proper *working capital in the business of production* itself, p. 130, and on the very same page, n. 11.

Relatively greater significance of foreign trade nowadays, p. 131, n. 13, p. 132, n. 3.[52]

[52] Note 13 continues onto p. 132; the reference is to point 3 of the note. (Cf. MEA I. v. 408 n. 4.)

Notes on Manuscripts, Texts and other English Translations

Marx's *Introduction* (1857) to the *Grundrisse*

The manuscript (together with the rest of the manuscripts published as the *Grundrisse*) is held by the Marxism-Leninism Institute in Moscow. (MO ii. 173–4.)

A German text was first published in Kautsky (1903). Another version, corrected against Marx's manuscript, was published in the first volume of the original two-volume edition of the *Grundrisse* (Moscow, 1939–41), and reprinted in GR 5–31. The first edition of the *Grundrisse* is rare in the West; the British Museum has two copies of volume i, one printed in Moscow (shelfmarked Ac. 9654. c/32) and the other copyrighted in Amsterdam (shelfmarked 8208. g. 5), but it has none of volume ii. The German text was published again in 1961 in MEW xiii. 615–42, with minor changes and possibly some editorial polishing. I have preferred the version given in the *Grundrisse*.

Other English translations appear in:

Karl Marx, *A Contribution to the Critique of Political Economy*, trans. N. I. Stone (2nd edn.; New York and London, 1904), 265–312.

David Horowitz (ed.), *Marx and Modern Economics* (London, 1968), 21–48.

Karl Marx and Frederick Engels, *German Ideology*, Part One, ed. C. J. Arthur (London, 1970), 124–51. The translator is not named.

CCPE 188–217. The text was translated by S. W. Ryazanskaya.

McLellan (1971a), 16–46.

Karl Marx, *Grundrisse*, trans. Martin Nicolaus (Harmondsworth, 1973), 83–111.

The versions published in the volumes edited by Horowitz and McLellan were based on the translation by Stone. The versions in CCPE and in the volume edited by Arthur are very similar.

Marx's *Notes* (1879-80) *on Adolph Wagner*

The manuscript is preserved in the International Institute for Social History, Amsterdam. (MO ii. 1532.) Marx's *Notes* were preceded by a list of fifty-four book-titles compiled from Wagner's bibliography, but these are omitted from the published versions. The dating of the manuscript, and of the large notebook from which it came, is uncertain. The editors of MEW xix state that the manuscript was written in the second half of 1879 to November 1880, and was contained in Marx's excerpt-notebook for 1879–81. (MEW xix. 581.) Rubel dates the manuscript as 1880, and says that the notebook contained extracts made during the years 1881–2. (Rubel (1956), 196; MO ii. 1531–2.) Ryazanov gives the corresponding dates 1881 and 1880–1. (MEA I. v. 377, 380.) And in CHRR 380 both the manuscript and the notebook are dated ca. 1880.

The first complete publication of the text was in a Russian translation edited by Ryazanov and published in 1930 in MEA I. v. 380–408. (This version is overlooked in Rubel (1956), 196; cf. CHRR 380.) The complete German text was first published in 1962 in MEW xix. 355–83.

Other English translations appear in:

[Issued by] British and Irish Communist Organisation, *Karl Marx on Value*, trans. Angela Clifford (Belfast, 1971), 7–34.

TP no. 5, pp. 40–65. The translator is not identified.

Further Reading

Marx's *Introduction* (1857) to the *Grundrisse*

T. B. Bottomore and Maximilien Rubel, intro. *Karl Marx, Selected Writings in Sociology and Social Philosophy* (1956, repr. Harmondsworth, 1969), 32–5.

Short analysis of the text, particularly part (4).

Klaus Hartmann, *Die Marxsche Theorie* ([West] Berlin, 1970), 239–51.

Brief analysis of the text as an important step in the development of Marx's critique of political economy.

Georg Lukács, *History and Class Consciousness*, trans. Rodney Livingstone (London, 1971), 1–26, and *passim*.

First published in 1923. Lukács cites this text in connection with his argument that '. . . orthodoxy [in Marxism] refers exclusively to *method*.'

Mario Dal Pra, *La dialettica in Marx* (2nd edn.; Bari, 1972), 283–325.

Discussion of the text with particular reference to Engels's views on method and to Marx's work in the *Poverty of Philosophy*.

Rubel (1968), pp. xci–xciv; see also MO i. 233–4.

Short summary of the text and its relation to Marx's plans for a published work on political economy.

Walter Tuchscheerer, *Bevor 'Das Kapital' entstand* ([East] Berlin, 1968), 331–9.

Summary of the text.

Galvano della Volpe, 'Methodologische Fragen in Karl Marx' Schriften von 1843 bis 1859', *Deutsche Zeitschrift für Philosophie*, vi ([East] Berlin, 1958), 777–804.

Contains (on pp. 792–803) a discussion of the text in connection with Marx's conception of science.

Jindřich Zelený, *Die Wissenschaftslogik bei Marx und 'Das Kapital'* (Frankfurt, 1969), 51–66, and *passim*.

Marx's text figures in the author's discussion of 'The Problem of the Starting Point', and 'The Relation of the Method of theoretical Presentation to actual History'.

Marx's *Notes* (1879-80) *on Adolph Wagner*

[Issued by] British and Irish Communist Organisation, intro. *Karl Marx on Value* (Belfast, 1971), 1–4.

Discussion of Wagner's views.

Athar Hussain, 'Marx's Notes on Adolph Wagner: An Introduction', TP no. 5, pp. 18–34.

An Althusserian reading of the text.

Rubel (1968), p. cxxi; see also MO ii. 1531–2.

Places the text in the context of Marx's career.

D. Ryazanov, intro. 'Kriticheskie zamechaniya o knige Adol'fa Vagnera', MEA I. v. 377–9.

Discussion of German and Russian socialism and political economy of the 1870s and 80s.

Zelený, *Die Wissenschaftslogik*, 290–1.

The author links the *Notes* (1879–80) with the *Introduction* (1857) to the *Grundrisse*.

Index